P9-DGT-320

# Methods that Matter

# Methods that Matter

## Six Structures for Best Practice Classrooms

### Harvey Daniels and Marilyn Bizar
National-Louis University

Stenhouse Publishers
York, Maine

Stenhouse Publishers, 431 York Street, York, Maine 03909
www.stenhouse.com

Library of Congress Cataloging-in-Publication Data

Daniels, Harvey, 1947–
Methods that matter : six structures for best practice classrooms
/ Harvey Daniels and Marilyn Bizar.
p.   cm.
Includes bibliographical references (p. 251).
ISBN 1-57110-082-2 (alk. paper)
1. Teaching.   2. Interdisciplinary approach in education.
3. Group work in education.   4. Educational tests and measurements.
I. Bizar, Marilyn.   II. Title.
LB1027.D24   1998
371.102—dc21      97-47516
CIP

Interior design by Joyce C. Weston

Cover collage by students of Linda Voss at Washington Irving School and
Eleanor Nayvelt at Clinton School, both in Chicago, in collaboration with
artist Cynthia Weiss

Cover photograph by Bob Tanner

Insert photographs by: page 1 Aiko Boyce; pages 2 and 3 Bob Tanner; pages
4 and 5 Rachel Bleckman; page 6 Pete Leki; page 7 Diane Reckless, Chicago
Nature Conservancy; page 8 Shelley Rosenstein-Freeman (top) and Kathy
Daniels (bottom)

Typeset by Technologies 'N Typography

Manufactured in the United States of America on acid-free paper
03 02 01 00         10 9 8 7 6

# Contents

# 7. Reflective Assessment   202

# Acknowledgments

THIS BOOK HAS been a long time coming, and it has had more than the usual number of mentors, collaborators, helpers, partners, coaches, and contributors.

Our first and loudest thanks go to the two dozen teachers who contributed ideas, stories, and articles to this book. Whatever credibility and usefulness this volume has owes largely to the thoughtful, frank, and practical accounts of classroom instruction these professionals have shared.

The idea of writing about Best Practices in education goes back to 1989, when we wrote a proposal to the Joyce Foundation in Chicago. We wanted to publish a newspaper for Chicago teachers that would focus steadily on instructional methods in the classroom. In those early days of Chicago school reform, we were concerned that amid the hubbub of restructuring the system's governance and finances, people might get distracted from the ultimate aim of school reform: enhancing the interaction between kids and teachers, every day. Joyce said yes, beginning an eight-year, twelve-issue run of the *Best Practice* newspaper. In 1993, the North Central Regional Educational Laboratory (NCREL) stepped in as our publisher, distributing the newspaper to its eight-state region and putting our text on the Internet.

The newspaper and its related projects are based at National-Louis University in Chicago, where the two of us serve in the Department of Interdisciplinary Studies. Our graduate program enrolls mainly midcareer elementary and secondary teachers seeking master's degrees, who meet in an intensive, school-based, cohort program focused on improving instruction across the curriculum. In addition to being our students, colleagues, and friends, many of our program graduates and adjunct faculty have also contributed to this book.

Lately, the two of us have been working in a new branch of the university, the Center for City Schools. The Center serves as an umbrella for a dozen interrelated, foundation-funded projects that support teachers and parents in Chicago schools. In addition to the Joyce Foundation and NCREL, this work has been supported by the DeWitt Wallace–Readers Digest Fund, the Chicago Annenberg Challenge, the Polk Bros. Foundation, the Lloyd A. Fry Foundation, the Chicago Tribune Foundation, the J.C. Penney Foundation, the Prince Charitable Trust, the Oppenheimer Family Fund, the Quest Center of the Chicago Teachers Union, and the McDougal Family Foundation.

One of our Center's most ambitious and character-building projects has been helping start a new, small Chicago public (not private, not charter) high school on the near west side of the city. In 1995, with lead teachers Kathy and Tom Daniels, we were scouring the city for a neighborhood where residents wouldn't oppose the establishment of a new high school. In 1996 we had 132 freshmen in our newly rehabbed building across from Michael Jordan's United Center, and were still unpacking boxes and tinkering with the schedule. Today, we have 260 freshmen and sophomores, we just got on the Internet at last, we're still tinkering with the schedule, and we're already running out of space. Threaded through this book are stories about the amazing students and dedicated faculty who are pathfinding every day at 2040 West Adams, trying to bring to life the ideals of our ambitious name: Best Practice High School.

No university professors can pursue all these disparate, off-campus projects without a highly supportive dean, and we have the prime example in Linda Tafel. As Dean of the National College of Education, Linda has enthusiastically supported our efforts over the past five years, encouraging us to carry on our college's 110-year commitment to urban education. Linda says that our college's founder, Elizabeth Harrison, who started the nation's first professional training school for kindergarten teachers in 1886, would approve of what we're up to.

Perhaps the greatest joy in our work comes from the fellowship we enjoy among the Center's team of full-time teacher-consultants, Barbara Morris, Pat Bearden, Pete Leki, Toni Murff, Marianne Flanagan, Yolanda Simmons, Lynnette Emmons, Bobbi Stuart, and Julie Flynn. We have borrowed all these amazing people from different branches of the Chicago Public Schools (classrooms, parent councils, computer labs) and watched with delight as they have entered hundreds of colleagues' classrooms, sharing their expertise with tact, energy, and concern.

Arnold Aprill, Executive Director of the Chicago Arts Partnerships in Education (CAPE), has showed us our future, repeatedly pointing out the deep parallels between reading, writing, and the arts. After working with Arnie and the wonderful CAPE artist corps for three years, we finally got it. Today, our own work is arts-infused, and so is this book, thanks to Arnold's vision of the arts as a lever for school renewal.

Jim Vopat, director of the Milwaukee Writing Project and founder of the Parent Project, is an old friend entangled with us in countless ways. We've worked to create a Chicago-Milwaukee connection for parents and teachers, exchanged models of staff development, and taught together at the Walloon Institute in Petoskey, Michigan. More important, we always draw insight from Jim's fresh and openhearted ideas about children and childhood. Drawing on his disparate experiences as a curator of children's art exhibits, a Senior Fulbright Scholar in Sri Lanka, and a graceful writer, Jim has a readiness to be delighted by kids that never fails to inspire us.

Steve Zemelman, Director of the Center for City Schools is our partner, alter ego, budget guru, and precious friend. In varying combinations over twenty years, the three of us have coauthored books, conducted research, bragged about our children, published articles, taught workshops, carpooled all over Chicago, led summer institutes, helped start a new high school, celebrated too many birthdays, and written dozens of grant proposals—and somehow, we're better friends than ever.

The faculty and students of Washington Irving School in Chicago, led by their amazing principal, Madeleine Maraldi, have been especially important to our growth—and our morale—over the past decade. They have showed how to do school reform right, putting kids first and adhering to the principles and methods of Best Practice, sometimes in the face of fierce pressures to the contrary. They've been rewarded, after years of effort, with accomplished graduates, elevated test scores, and national recognition. They deserve every accolade.

For the past few summers, most of the people mentioned above and many of this volume's contributors have been gathering at the Walloon Institute. There, in an energizing northwoods atmosphere, we spend a week with other teachers, parents, and principals from around the country, all of whom are trying to bring Best Practice teaching and learning to life in their schools. We don't know whether it's the provocative speakers, the respite from back-home pressures, the late-night dormitory debates, or the lumberjack buffets, but we always come back from Walloon smarter, stronger, and more committed than ever to progressive principles. Our thanks go to the thirty-member staff who make Walloon possible each summer, and so does our invitation to interested readers to join us up north next summer—we'll be there.

*Methods that Matter* was one of the more complicated manuscripts we have ever worked on, with drafts, artwork, photos, references, and correspondence swapping back and forth among more than forty people.

Somehow, Clarke Schneider kept track of all the people and kept communication flowing, while Allison VanDuse massaged the articles from Apple to IBM, from authors to readers, and from editor to publisher. Throughout the life of the *Best Practice* newspaper, our designer and production consultant has been Carol Jones of JonesHouse, who masterminded our evolution from a thin, quick-yellowing newsprint rag to an attractive and graphically interesting publication. Our lead photographer has been Bob Tanner, a filmmaker-turned-teacher, whose affection for children and eye for the teachable moment have infused so many pictures in the newspaper and in this book. For other photos in this volume, we are grateful to the many article authors who provided pictures to accompany their words.

When the idea for this project first took shape, we knew immediately that it had to be a Stenhouse book. Just as we anticipated, Philippa Stratton has gone far beyond the call of editorial duty in helping this book live up to our dreams for it. She was a thorough and insightful reader of the text, sat patiently at Marilyn's dining room table helping us sift through the promising tangle of ingredients, provided daily telephonic hand-holding, and patiently accommodated countless last-minute authorial U-turns.

To whatever extent this book seems orderly and coherent, credit goes to our peerless consulting reader Brenda Power. Not only did she review our draft closely and speedily; she saw in the manuscript a pattern of organization that not only solved some problems, but also crystallized the authors' intentions.

One of the best ways to learn about education is to have some children and then watch what happens. Harvey's children, Marny and Nick, have provided quite a demonstration over their nineteen and thirteen years. Travelling through schools that embody the best of Best Practice, they have grown into two creative, passionate, independent, and completely different young people. Elaine Daniels, in addition to mothering these now-large children, teaches, advises, and supervises student teachers, and always manages to be Harvey's friendliest and most insightful reader.

Marilyn would like to thank her husband Michael Koch for his support, his pride, and for always making her laugh. His unique brand of craziness helps to make life and work doable. The many young adults in her life—Josh, Michael, Stacy, Jeffrey, Liza, Dina, Laurie, and Mark—continue the ongoing task of teaching her to talk less and listen more. For all of this, she is grateful.

# CHAPTER 1

# Best Practice: From Principles to Programs

IN RECENT YEARS, the term "Best Practice" has entered the everyday vocabulary of school teachers, administrators, board members, policy makers, education reporters, and even everyday citizens. This venerable phrase, borrowed from the seemingly more revered professions of medicine and law, seems to confer a bit of certitude upon the unruly doings we call public education. Now, school district mission statements and curriculum guides trumpet their institutional allegiance to "Best Practice." Blue-ribbon committees bestow golden apples on teachers who manifest "Best Practice." Conference programs glibly promise their attendees templates for "Best Practice" classrooms. Accreditation teams search out "Best Practices" at site visits. Aspiring politicians pledge to bring "Best Practices" to the schools of their districts, should they be elected. The Chicago Public Schools, where we have conducted most of our own staff development and research work, now maintains a separate department with the mission of supporting "Best Practices." And we knew for sure that the catchphrase had deeply rooted itself in today's educational jargon when one teacher recently took us aside to darkly confide that a certain colleague down the hall "wasn't really Best Practice."

The one common feature of all these utterances is that hardly anyone who uses the term "Best Practice" defines what it *means*. It's simply what you are supposed to say, a phrase that vaguely substitutes for "good," "with-it," "mainstream." "Best Practice" has become a generic, ceremonial seal of approval, a fuzzy pledge of okayness, a genuflection to whatever everyone else is doing—or claims to be doing. Sometimes it seems as though "Best Practice" is about to take the place of the term "quality education"—a blessing that of course everyone wants for their children, but that has absolutely no shared definition.

We think the term "Best Practice" does mean something, something very concrete and particular, and something well worth defending. It is not at all vague. Genuine Best Practice embraces certain educational ideas and activities, while clearly ruling others out. It has a deep basis in research, in the study of child development and learning, in the history and philosophy of American education. Best Practice, under other older names, has a long and distinguished pedigree and is manifested through a limited and distinctive set of classroom practices.

It may be a bit hypocritical for the two of us to complain about the fadification of Best Practice. Indeed, if the term falls a bit too easily from the tongues of Americans these days, we ourselves may deserve some of the blame. Since 1990, we have edited a regional newspaper titled *Best Practice,* distributed by the North Central Regional Educational Laboratory and carrying stories of teachers working to implement new standards of instruction in their classrooms. In 1993, Harvey, along with colleagues Steven Zemelman and Arthur Hyde, published a book called *Best Practice: New Standards for Teaching and Learning in America's Schools.* In that volume, we summarized the recommendations of the many standards projects then emerging from professional associations, research centers, and curriculum groups around the country.

In both the book and the newspaper, we have constantly pointed out the many underlying similarities and the unspoken consensus among all these standards projects. In spite of their diverse subject specialties and discipline loyalties, groups as disparate as the National Council of Teachers of Mathematics and the Center for the Study of Reading have all been saying the same basic things about teaching and learning. In their various reports, all these organizations have called for classrooms that are:

- student-centered
- experiential
- reflective
- authentic
- holistic
- social
- collaborative
- democratic
- cognitive
- developmental
- constructivist
- challenging

Since these diverse groups affirmed these shared principles, it was not surprising that their official recommendations looked so much alike. Most of the standards documents mandated similar shifts in the ways classrooms were organized and run. They called for a rebalancing of the ingredients of schooling—students, time, space, materials, experiences, and assistance. Some of the key shifts suggested included:

## Less

whole-class-directed instruction, e.g., lecturing

student passivity: sitting, listening, receiving and absorbing information

prizing and rewarding of silence in the classroom

classroom time devoted to fill-in-the-blank worksheets, dittos, workbooks, and other "seatwork"

student time spent reading textbooks and basal readers

attempt by teachers to thinly "cover" large amounts of material in every subject area

rote memorization of facts and details

stress on competition and grades in school

tracking or leveling students into "ability groups"

use of pull-out special programs

use of and reliance on standardized tests

## More

experiential, inductive, hands-on learning

active learning in the classroom, with all the attendant noise and movement of students doing, talking, and collaborating

emphasis on higher-order thinking; learning a field's key concepts and principles

deep study of fewer topics, so that students internalize the field's way of inquiry

time devoted to reading whole, original, real books and nonfiction materials

responsibility transferred to students for their work: goal setting, record keeping, monitoring, evaluation

choice for students; picking their own books, writing topics, team partners, research projects

enacting and modeling of the principles of democracy in school

attention to varying cognitive and affective styles of individual students

cooperative, collaborative activity; developing the classroom as an interdependent community

heterogeneously grouped classrooms where individual needs are met through individualized activities, not segregation of bodies

> delivery of special help to students in regular classrooms
>
> varied and cooperative roles for teachers, parents, and administrators
>
> reliance on teachers' descriptive evaluation of student growth, including qualitative/anecdotal observations (Zemelman, Daniels, and Hyde 1993)

In specific reports, these general directions were backed up with dozens, sometimes hundreds, of specific recommendations concerning different bodies of content and grade levels. But behind the details lay a consistent and surprising commitment to the shared, underlying principles. The National Council of Teachers of Mathematics led the way, describing math as a special kind of thinking instead of a body of content, calling for the integration of writing and art into math, and arguing for the importance of estimation and real-world problem solving. The National Science Teachers Association forswore the powerful tradition of "curriculum coverage," arguing instead that students should delve more deeply into a smaller number of topics. Though highly politicized and subject to right-wing attack, even the social studies standards called for students to *do* history, not merely absorb the official ingredients of "cultural literacy."

However bold they seemed, all these principles and recommendations were nothing particularly new. As one of our longtime teacher-reformer friends sighed when we put this list of principles on an overhead projector at a recent workshop, "Well, duuhhhh!" At least some educators have been calling for American schooling to be more experiential, reflective, and democratic throughout the whole history of this country and back through the ages. John Dewey would have recognized and embraced these principles (though he might have asked someone to explain "constructivism" to him), as would other educators from America's enduring progressive tradition.

So, yes, we admit it: Best Practice is just another name for progressive education. It is a contemporary term that points to the same basic set of overlapping beliefs and practices that has been struggling for acceptance in American schools for generations. And once again, progressive education is in danger, not just of being cast out by its critics, but of being corrupted by its newfound friends. Every day, the ideals of Best Practice are being misunderstood, watered down, debased, co-opted, and sometimes sold back to educators in false and empty guises. So it is time once again to explain and defend these ideas before they are washed away by the next wave of shallow and uncomprehending "reform."

# From Prescriptions to Pedagogy

So it turns out that there is a firm definition of Best Practice after all. We have a set of clear and interlocking principles, some relative valuings of different classroom activities, and, within particular subject areas, scores of authoritative recommendations guided by these ideas and values. Still, for an individual teacher, whose day-to-day job is to translate educational philosophy into classroom reality, all these abstractions and more/less charts may be too vague to help you teach your solar system unit. And the welter of well-meant micro-suggestions from the NCTM and twenty-seven other educational groups may be a little overwhelming. How is a teacher who, like any other human being, probably can't change more than a few elements of their professional behavior at once, supposed to bring life to such complex ideals? How can a teacher grow toward, enact, embody, and live out the meaning of Best Practice in a real, workaday classroom?

Our main contribution to this puzzle is the insight that there are six basic structures that help to create Best Practice classrooms.

- Integrative Units
- Small Group Activities
- Representing-to-Learn
- Classroom Workshop
- Authentic Experiences
- Reflective Assessment

If teachers can manage and master these six fundamental ways of organizing instruction, they will automatically be enacting the ancient principles of progressive education, heeding the recommendations of national curriculum groups, and embodying the spirit of school reform. In the chapters to come, we will explain each of these structures in detail, showing the history and development of each, acknowledging the teachers and authors who developed strong and replicable versions of them. And most important, we'll share several reports about each structure, written by teachers who have implemented them in real, diverse classrooms around the country.

These six structures or patterns are applicable to all grade levels and subject areas, from early childhood through college. They are the building blocks of instruction that allow teachers to organize the ingredients of schooling: students, time, space, materials, experiences, and assistance. We sometimes call these structures the *fundamental, recurrent activities*. By this we mean that once teachers have mastered their management and students have internalized their norms, these six structures become the palette from which teachers and kids together can paint rich, vibrant cycles of learning during which these key activities alternate, strand, interweave, and are cycled through the curriculum for days, weeks, or years.

These activities are processes, not bodies of knowledge. They are broad generic strategies. Or, to use the most unpopular possible term, they are *teaching methods.* Today, teaching methods are often scoffed at by school critics like E. D. Hirsch (1996) as irrelevant education-school fluff. But the fact is that the way we teach school subjects is tremendously important to whether and how much students learn. These six structures work. They are validated by decades of practitioner reports, documented in educational literature and research, and richly supported by the principles of group dynamics, the field of study that describes the ways groups of people can be organized to maximize their efforts. To be concerned with pedagogy is not, as Hirsch accuses, to be "anti-knowledge" or "anti-fact." On the contrary, giving serious attention to the structures and processes of learning reflects a deep respect for the importance of facts and knowledge. We don't want to raise yet another generation of Americans who laugh proudly that they "forgot everything they taught me in school." We experiment seriously with methodology because we want students to embrace, internalize, and recall far more of the curriculum than has traditionally been the case.

Though they are process-oriented and adaptable to all disciplines, these structures are also highly *rigorous,* specific, and tightly organized. They require considerable teacher skill to implement properly. Far from being "loosey-goosey" or "touchy-feely" (it's interesting to note how often progressive practices are demeaned by cutesey epithets), these structures demand more management from teachers and more discipline among students than traditional presentational methods. They require both teachers and students to play a much wider range of roles throughout the school day, to shift smoothly among them, and to manage and monitor their own work across many dimensions. In short: It's not just "sit 'n git" anymore.

These six structures are *recurrent.* They are meant to be used over and over, phasing in and out of the schedule throughout a school year, and from year to year as teachers orchestrate a healthful balance of activities for their students. Before they can be put into the rotation, of course, every structure requires that teachers invest time in preparing students. But once they are oriented, students can operate within and use the structure throughout a year and throughout their school lives, with periodic refreshers and updates.

These six structures are *overlapping*. Authentic experiences will be at the core of any well-designed integrative unit or small group work. Representing-to-learn happens across all the other structures as students plan inquiries, keep notes, record findings, initiate and answer correspondence, and share their learnings. Reflective assessment is also stranded through all the other structures, as evaluation becomes an integral part of instruction. The teacher-student conferences held during a workshop session will be both a form of assessment and a part of instruction, while the peer conferences that are a regular feature of such workshops are an important kind of collaborative small group. Indeed, most broad classroom projects will embody many of these structures at once. For the purposes of this book, we have needed to separate the six structures, highlighting their individual ingredients and features. But back in any real classroom, teachers will reassemble them into unique hybrids and seamless combinations.

These structures are also *conceptually asymmetrical*. That is, they aren't quite apples and apples. There are valuable representing-to-learn activities that take no more than a few minutes of class time, while a typical integrative unit will probably occupy whole days or weeks. Some structures, like reading and writing workshops, have clear-cut, codified pedagogies already in print, while others, like centers, have a much sparser professional literature littered with misleading corruptions. Some of the structures are clearly stepwise pedagogies, while others, most notably authentic experiences, aren't methods at all, but rather types (or even locations) of experience. We have tried to probe and resolve these discrepancies, but every time we attempt to delete one element or combine it with another, something urgently important is lost. We appear to need all six ingredients in order to describe the Best Practice paradigm.

Sadly, as these activities have increasingly become recognized, adopted, and applied across the country, they have also been opened to more misunderstanding and misapplication. At worst, the methods become platitudes, undergoing the same degenerative process that afflicts the term *Best Practice* itself. *Classroom workshop* offers a cautionary example. In the early 1980s, this highly structured method of literacy instruction was described by such authors as Donald Graves (1983), Lucy Calkins (1986), and Nancie Atwell (1987). They outlined a very complex, but nontraditional, approach to developing children's reading and writing—a holistic, developmental process featuring student choice of books and writing topics, strong teacher modeling, extended student practice, guided peer feedback, and a portfolio assessment system.

Within a few years' time, however, the term *workshop* had drifted away from the careful and narrow definition of its inventors, until by the late

1990s almost any activity involving student reading or writing, including methods totally contradictory to the original model, were being blithely labeled *workshop*. Some of this deterioration was caused by textbook publishers who appropriated and willfully corrupted the term, but the rest owes to teachers' characteristic failure to respect and protect our own professional culture.

Which is to say that, in order to work properly, the six structures must be implemented roughly the way they were designed. While adapting and personalizing are necessary elements of good teaching, a reasonable degree of adherence to the original model is also required. Assigning writing activities that mostly involve copying or regurgitating correct answers, conducting conferences where students have no voice, designing collaborative projects that are really just competitive memorization games, or implementing integrative units in which students have no interest—these are not Best Practices, whatever they are named.

# Implicit Factors

Within all six of these classroom structures, and across them as a set, several important values are threaded. On the surface, these structures are simply mechanisms, delivery systems that allow students to learn important curricular content and academic skills. But at a deeper level, they also work to develop the kind of rich and supportive psychological climate that young learners need and deserve. Among the vital ingredients of this climate are choice, responsibility, expression, and community.

## Choice

Student ownership and initiation of learning have always been tenets of progressive education. In recent years, William Glasser (1986) and Alfie Kohn (1995) have again detailed a critique that is as familiar as it is irrefutable. The thirteen years of submission and passivity customarily provided to young people by American schools is an exceedingly poor preparation for resourceful, self-initiating problem solvers, not to mention free and critical citizens. Indeed, the bland but unrelenting authoritarianism of American schools discourages and alienates the majority of children, as it channels them toward long-abolished assembly-line jobs and a mentality to match. If we really want to raise the kind of young people we claim to treasure, we have to start inviting them, from preschool onward, to make meaningful decisions and choices, living with all the consequences that choice entails.

Each of the six key activities inherently gives students a real voice and some meaningful choices. In *workshop,* students choose, from an approved range of options, what to write, read, or investigate. As a part of *reflective assessment,* teachers help students write and talk about their learning, set academic goals, reflect on their progress, review their own work and records. As they *represent* their learning through writing or art, students are often invited to decide for themselves what mode, style, genre, or medium of expression will best leverage their thinking.

## Responsibility

The other side of the coin of choice is *responsibility.* If we are to restructure big parts of the school day for students to make decisions about their learning, select and explore alternatives and pursue some of their own interests and goals, then we have to hold them accountable for finishing the jobs they start, monitoring their own performance, submitting their learnings to public exhibition, critically appraising their own work or artifacts, and making even better choices the next time, as their understanding of the process of inquiry grows.

These six key structures invite just such responsibility. In the *workshop,* students have regular conferences with the teacher to review progress, assess work samples, and set goals. In well-structured *integrative units* or *small group* investigations, students must select topics, find resources, identify targets, build schedules, make contributions to the wider group, create required tangible products, and regularly report to the teacher as they proceed. In *reflective assessment,* we ask students to set academic goals, save their work in folders, track and discuss their progress, keep their own records, and join with the teacher in creating reports for parents and other interested audiences.

## Expression

In her remarkable 1969 book, *Young Lives at Stake,* the English educator Charity James passionately reminded teachers of a simple fact about human beings: people need to make stuff. It comes with our genes. We are driven to shape and decorate and act upon our environment, whether that means painting the walls of our caves, grinding grain into flour, spinning stories around the fire, forging tools, or creating performances with our violins. Expression, in all of its manifold forms, is a key to learning and thinking. And yet, more than ever today, the expressive arts are being marginalized in public education, systematically pushed out of school schedules, curriculum, and budgets. In spite of their manifest capacity to captivate children and ignite the curriculum, the arts have become a bystander in the current school reform movement.

▲ Harvey: My two children have had an extraordinary education at the Baker Demonstration School at National-Louis University. For years I have tried to explain to workshops of curious teachers what makes Baker different and special. Although the school is equipped with all the usual progressive declarations and pedigrees, something beyond the letter of the official mission statement always seemed to be going on. Finally, after we'd had children in the school for almost ten years, it dawned on my wife (who later explained it to me) that, along with all the other things that Baker teachers so consciously and carefully do, there is also a deep, abiding focus on children's *expression*.

Though Baker is not officially an arts-centered school, the teachers are attuned and committed to nurturing children's expression in every possible medium: writing, singing, storytelling, painting, hypercard, dance, dialogue journaling, drama, poetry, fashion design, conversation, or photography. You can always pick out a Baker student because they are much more likely than "normal" kids to suddenly burst into song, dance, writing, or to drag you over to the computer to run their stack. They expect you to pay attention and take them seriously. And you always know a Baker teacher, because when a kid starts to express, they drop everything and attend. They stop and they listen and they smile and you can see their wheels start to turn as they think, "Wow. This is interesting. I wonder where this came from. How can I sustain this? Where does it fit in? What might be this kid's next step?"

How powerful and formative to have your early, tentative expressions met with this kind of fascinated and respectful response from the adults at your school—not just from doting parents at home. It implies that you are a part of the human conversation and are expected to have something unique and worthwhile to contribute. It invites you to express more, to attend to other's expressions, to learn how grown-ups shape and hone and improve their own expressions. It affirms that your personal search through the different media and art forms is part of a serious lifelong quest to know more and communicate better. All children deserve to meet this kind of response in school, to have their expressions cherished. ▲

Thus, as you look into the structure of the six key activities featured here, you see that each one carries many opportunities for students to find a wide range of *expression* for their ideas and feelings. Amid all these activities, kids make real stuff—artworks, writing, stories, performances, exhibitions, posters, research reports, semester goals, book reviews, sculptures, and bar graphs. And they don't just create these products in solitude for their own satisfaction, but for traffic with real audiences of peers, teachers, families, and communities—people with whom these products and performances can be shared and discussed.

## Community

Traditional schooling, with its silent and solitary seatwork, tracking and ability grouping, and competitive grading, is highly individualistic. In its most toxic forms, education becomes a zero-sum game that pits students against each other. Classmates become enemies. The implicit motto is I cannot win unless others lose. In this setting, the idea of classroom community is anathema; indeed, if students come together at all as a group, they are more likely to coalesce against a teacher than to join with him as a community of learners.

On the other hand, the six structures we focus on here are social and cooperative by nature. As part of their inherent design, they contribute to building community. They invite the expression of the individual, yet they also offer ways for students to connect, to team, to collaborate. These structures tend to create a group esprit, the sense that there is a commonality of interest and purpose, that a classroom of students is *in this thing together.* Looked at in terms of group dynamics theory, these activities invite students to participate in the development of classroom expectations and norms, to develop widely dispersed friendship patterns, to shoulder some leadership and responsibility, to communicate with others through a broad array of communication channels, and to negotiate and resolve conflicts.

## Time Sharing in Best Practice Schools

How much of the time do we actually use these best practice methods? All day, every day? Once a week, for an hour? What's the balance? In genuinely progressive schools and classrooms, these six featured activities constitute *the majority of the school day, week, or year*—more than half (and maybe more like three-fourths) of the time kids spend in school. After all, these structures allow students rich exploration and active practice in subject areas, in a context of teacher guidance and peer interaction, with plenty of coaching and feedback.

Still, the big six structures are not the only activities that need to occur during a school day, year, or in a student's career. Obviously, there are some ingredients on the old "less" list that still have merit and value. There remains a significant place for some traditional, teacher-directed, presentational activities. For example, reading good literature aloud to children is one teacher "performance" that should never be curtailed because kids of all ages should have opportunities to hear the sounds of literature. And hey, a little lecturing is OK, in brief and rememberable bursts, especially for older kids. A whole class can sometimes read the same book together, and be guided by the teacher in interpreting the text. Memorizing a few dates, state capitals, poems, or math facts might not be such a bad idea. And teachers should definitely make sure that primary children know the sounds that letters make, so that they can decode and comprehend text. These traditional school activities aren't evil—they've just been vastly overemphasized, and need to be put back into reasonable balance with all the other ways of spending children's precious school time.

The problem has been that these old teacher-centered activities have gobbled up whole days—whole years—so that kids never got a chance to digest, consolidate, and most importantly *use* the ideas that teachers presented. Kids don't get enough practice moving concepts from the pale and passive world of something that was mentioned into the robust world of personal application. After all, every contemporary learning theory—behaviorist, cognitive, information processing—has one common feature in its paradigm of learning: for human beings to assimilate information they must somehow *act on it.*

But acting on information takes time and support, and that's exactly where the six key structures come in. They help to rebalance the school schedule, providing large, well-structured periods of time during which students can act upon the ideas and information that teachers have presented in their now more proportionate fraction of the school day. The Best Practice structures help us create a new mix of presentation, demonstration, practice, application, coaching, and reflection that is far more likely to help students remember what teachers say, understand ideas that are discussed, grasp concepts that are introduced, master skills that are modeled, care about the process and value their place in it.

Still, we must be careful not to let the old teacher-centered fox back into the henhouse. Ancient pedagogical habits die hard, and teachers probably wouldn't have originally chosen their vocation if they didn't crave the spotlight on some deep psychological level. The hunger to "really teach something" has probably derailed more student-centered innovations than administrative cowardice and textbook company co-option combined.

Luckily, there are ways to strike and defend a balance. Indeed, many of the Best Practice structures can be infused with small doses of traditional, teacher-directed activities. A leading example of this blending is mini-lessons in reading-writing workshops, an idea now well-developed in the professional literature (see Calkins 1990; Avery 1993; Harwayne 1992; Atwell 1987) whereby the teacher designs short, pointed, and well-timed presentations and embeds them in the context of a long chunk of student practice time. This kind of teacher-directed lesson offers the greatest possibility that the information will actually transfer into the work of students, since it may be applied and practiced promptly.

There's one other category of time expenditure in school that's separate, not exactly a method or a structure, but rather a diffuse pursuit using many structures: community building and maintenance. Even though, as we've argued, the six Best Practice structures do tend to nourish relationships and groups, some of this work often needs to occur separately. Depending on the age of the students and the goals of the teacher, such community building may involve periodic and structured class meetings, acquaintance-building activities, conflict resolution or mediation programs, advisory periods, and the like. Some systemic reform efforts, like the Comer Project, make individual and group relationships an especially significant part of the school calendar. At the high school we recently helped to start in Chicago, the faculty gives big chunks of time to special group-building activities early in the year, commits two and one-half hours per week all year to an advisory period, and runs an active peer mediation program to deal with problems that arise. Happily there has been a recent burst of research and writing on the topic of community building in the classroom, with especially valuable contributions from Kathy Short (Short and Burke 1991), Ralph Peterson (1992), and Judith Ferrara (1996).

## The Schoolship: A Floating Classroom

▲ Harvey: Last summer my daughter and I took a half-day cruise on the *Inland Seas,* an 80-foot schooner that sails Lake Michigan with the mission of educating passengers about the complex and fragile ecology of the Great Lakes. From mid-April through October, the boat sails with two shiploads a day, mostly middle school students and their teachers, with occasional charters for teacher-educators and environmental groups. Marny and I boarded the schoolship at Harbor Springs on a drizzly July morning with thirty other passengers and were a bit surprised when Captain Tom Kelly began the cruise by asking us to form into groups of five or six and to assign ourselves a nautical name. Hooking up with a fun-loving retired couple and another gentleman, we dubbed our team the Keelhaulers.

Next, the crew handed us a learning log in which, they explained, we would be recording our experiences, findings, and impressions of the trip. Before boarding, we were given a safety briefing and invited to sign the official ship's manifest. And then we cast off—the Keelhaulers, the Sharks, the Pirates, the Barracudas, and the Landlubbers—along with the ship's energetic crew of naturalists and sailors. For the next three and a half hours, we studied Lake Michigan in a dozen hands-on ways. We worked, we tested, we sampled, we experimented, we observed, we recorded, we discussed, we questioned, we laughed a lot, and we even sang—sea chanteys, of course.

For the first hour, we anchored just off shore and alternated between whole-group and team activities. Our onboard limnologist (lake scientist) Mark Mitchell demonstrated how to take a variety of weather readings, including wind direction and velocity, cloud types and coverages, air temperature, barometric pressure, and wave height, which we recorded in our logs and compared with other groups. Mark then used a thermometer on a measured string to locate the thermocline, a shifting spot deep in the water where the temperature drops off suddenly, and where fish tend to congregate. That day, the water temperature was 67 degrees at the surface, 60 degrees at thirty feet, and dropped to 49 degrees at forty feet.

Next, each team was given the equipment to test water transparency two ways: with the traditional black-and-white secchi disc, which is lowered into the water on a measured rope; and (even more fun) by dropping colored peanut M&M's into the water (really) and timing the interval until they disappeared. According to the Keelhaulers' group data chart, our red M&M disappeared fastest, within twenty-two seconds, while the green one windmilled visibly through the depths for thirty-seven seconds. This dramatized for us the way water splits the spectrum of light, causing the different colored candies to remain visible for different lengths of time as they sink. (Yes, fish eat leftover M&M's. Presumably the milk chocolate melts in their mouth, not on their fins.)

Next, we tested water samples for temperature, pH, and dissolved oxygen, which led us to an intense discussion about acid rain. Some of us were worried that we could lose our beloved Michigan lakes to this chemical peril. We learned that the fine limestone marl on the bottom of many midwestern lakes protects them, by trapping the acidity that has killed off some rocky-bottomed lakes in New England. Finally, deploying the same kind of equipment used by marine researchers, we collected samples of the water from the bottom to the surface, a scoop of bottom sediment, and an assortment of fish from the trawling net which was dragged behind the ship as we motored for a few minutes.

Then it was time to turn off the engine and put up the sails, all of which was accomplished by the greenhorn crew, under the command of sailmaster Remy Champt. Mainsail, foresail, staysail, and jib up and filled in twenty knots apparent wind. The ship seemed to leap toward the far shore, and Captain Kelly called for five minutes of quiet time, so people could focus on the sensory experience of sailing. We all welcomed this order. Each person found a spot on deck, sat and breathed deep, drinking in the wind, the spray, and the view of hills above the bay. In the creak of the hull, the flap of the sails, and the splash of the bow wave, you could suddenly feel a kinship with the sailors of old, the explorers of these lakes. It was a sweet moment.

For the next hour and a quarter, our teams rotated through five learning stations set up around the ship, using the samples we had collected to study different aspects of lake ecology. At one station, we worked with the sediment sample in which we found everything from midge fly larvae, to side-swimming minishrimp called amphipods, to wood chips dumped by logging operations of one hundred years ago. At a second station, we studied the fish that had been collected and temporarily placed in tanks. We reviewed the physiology of fish, using charts to determine the species we had caught: brook stickleback, johnny darter, spottail shiner, mottled sculpin, crayfish, and clumps of zebra mussels. Climbing down the gangway into the cabin, we came to the plankton station, where under the microscope our water sample came startlingly alive. As a person who has lived on fresh water lakes his whole life, I was stunned. I thought that plankton was for the ocean. But there they were: our Lake Michigan water was teeming with countless creepy magnified crablike critters. Of course! What did I ever think the little fish ate?

Next we moved to the navigation station where we identified our position on a chart, talked about shipping routes, studied paths taken by immigrating species (like the zebra mussels currently invading Lake Michigan), and learned about watershed boundaries. We looked at all the different equipment used to guide the boat, from the traditional compass to the latest global positioning system (GPS) receiver. Finally we reached the seamanship station, where each person got a chance to steer the boat and chat with the captain. He explained the principles by which the ship captures the wind's power and turns it into motion, showing how the different lines control the sails. Some of us immediately noticed the large digital speedometer conspicuously mounted above the cabin, and a jolly rivalry broke out among the unreconstructed competitors among us. Who could drive the boat fastest when their turn at the wheel came? "Jeff!" I heard myself shouting from the helm to a friend on board, "You only had it going 8.76—but now we're over 8.9!"

Now we are sailing back to port, the crew leading us in more chanteys. Our minds are awhirl with information; we feel connected to the water and the wind; we understand in our bones so much about how the ecosystem called a lake works. Above all, we are simply amazed, dazzled by the miraculous complexity and interrelatedness of the lake's ingredients. As we fill out our evaluation forms at the dock, we can't find enough superlatives to thank the crew for this marvelous experience. The trip is too short; the lake we thought we knew all our lives will never be the same. We want to go right back out there. ▲

Sounds like an exhilarating and powerful learning experience, doesn't it? Did you also notice that the *Inland Seas* crew was using all six structures in our formula for exemplary teaching and learning? That's what dawned on Marny and me as we drove back home from the dock. Wow, we laughed, we just took a cruise on the S.S. *Best Practice!*

The whole voyage constituted an ambitious *integrative unit* on the ecology of the Great Lakes. We spent much of the morning in collaborative *small groups,* working through five carefully designed learning centers. We were constantly *representing-to-learn,* as we kept logs of our findings, reactions, and questions. The whole ship took a *workshop* approach, where masters of each "trade" (limnology, navigation, seamanship) demonstrated their craft and then apprenticed us to them, immediately allowing us beginners to try the whole thing—raising the anchor, reading the secchi disc—with careful guidance and coaching. We used several forms of *reflective assessment,* recording findings, comparing them to those of other groups, trying to resolve discrepancies, and speculating on what might have caused them. We reflected on our own learning in our logs, and at the end of the voyage we wrote an evaluation of the program and the instructors—an assessment which the ship's crew uses to revise and plan future programs.

The overarching uniqueness of the schoolship, of course, was the *authentic experience* it provided. We spent the whole day working with real stuff—sails, water, air, bottom sediment, fish, plant life, and countless scientific tools. When you looked at your own water sample on the microscope's video monitor and saw the screen fill with wriggling, tentacle-studded phyto- and zooplankton, it was *really* real. When you took your turn guiding the huge wheel of that forty-one-ton boat, feeling the power of the steel-hulled ship striding over three-foot waves, it was real—real fun.

When I later phoned Captain Tom Kelly to compliment him on his shipboard pedagogy and its unwitting adherence to Best Practice principles, he just laughed. "We're just trying to teach the stuff so the kids remember it," he said. But, as Captain Kelly went on to explain, "The ship's program has been very carefully thought out. We believe that people can learn more about ecology by doing rather than reading or hearing someone talk about it. Comprehension and retention are so much greater." Tom also knows how different the *Inland Seas* feels to kids from their regular classroom. "The experience kids have aboard our schoolship is like a mountain on the plain of their everyday school experience."

Reading about the schoolship as an exemplar of Best Practice education, the reader might be tempted to rejoin: "Well, glad you had a nice sail, but we can't very well take America's fifty million schoolchildren out on an ecology boat every day, now can we?" Well, yes and no. Of course the *Inland Seas* offers an extraordinary, rare, and costly form of learning, but every kid should take a few trips like this, whatever it costs. We should make no apology for funding these kind of paradigm-busting, mind-expanding, life-changing out-of-school experiences (let's even say it—adventures) for children. The people who work in outdoor education have long been arguing, and often proving, that such programs can have profound effects on children, whose imagination, self-esteem, and even career ambitions can be permanently fired by a single day in the real world. As Gary Nabhan and Stephen Trimble have written in *The Geography of Childhood* (1995), all young people need "wild places" to grow by, lakes or woods where they can make their individual connection to the natural world, grounding their sense of belonging on the planet.

We would argue that it is not only wild places that children need, but all kinds of authentic places. Every setting is a chance to reinvent yourself and see what happens when you act upon your surroundings. That's one reason why at our new Best Practice High School, all students spend one half-day per week in internships all over Chicago, where they serve, work, learn, observe, and grow—probably the most important three hours of their week.

Still, no matter how passionate our call for adding more real-world, schoolship-type experiences to every child's curriculum, American students will continue to spend most of their time "at sea" in public schools. But our classrooms needn't be barren shores. If the crew of the *Inland Seas* can implement the six key structures of Best Practice teaching out on the water, then so can those of us back on land. We can arrange time, space, and materials to create powerful, transformative voyages of learning—where every kid takes a turn at the wheel. We can give students voice, choice, responsibility, expression, and connection in their school lives.

We possess the tools and structures to make it happen; we just have to put them to work. That's what this book is about.

# The Design of This Book

Each of the next six chapters gives a detailed and practical picture of one Best Practice structure. We start each section with a descriptive essay, outlining the method, tracing its history and roots, acknowledging its pioneers, and listing the structure's vital features. Next, hear several teachers, representing different grade levels and school communities, tell how they adopted the basic model, adapted it to their students, and made it their own.

There are two types of teacher stories in each chapter. The first, which we call Variations, are narratives, stories that show you a classroom and its inhabitants engaged in the structure, usually over a length of time. In the second, titled Step by Step, teachers take you behind the scenes of their practice, explaining how they got started, planned their innovations, equipped their classrooms, trained their students, managed their activities, solved problems, sustained their energy when things got tough, and found colleagues for sharing and support.

Though these contributors cover the range from kindergarten through college, we think that each of their stories has value for all teachers, not only for people who happen to teach at the same grade level. Because the six Best Practice methods are truly generic, meaning that they really do work across subjects and up through the grades, vital tips or translatable stories about management, organization, materials, scheduling, evaluation, or record keeping can come from colleagues at any grade level.

Many of the stories are detailed enough that other teachers can use them as the basis for their own classroom experiments. But no one here is bragging or trying to make it sound easy. Nobody thinks they have perfected themselves as teachers. Indeed, many of this book's contributors describe themselves as being "in process," "on the road," "part way there," or even "taking baby steps." All of these teacher-authors know firsthand that change is hard, and many have written about their frustrations as well as their triumphs. For most of us who teach, change comes in small, hard-earned increments, not in one sudden, dramatic transformation.

Taken together, these sets of descriptions and stories provide a basic understanding of the six Best Practice classroom structures, but they probably won't answer every question that a teacher contemplating a full-scale classroom implementation might raise. We think this book occupies a kind of middle level in the pyramid of resources about any one of these activities. For example, many books and standards reports endorse the workshop model, but without explaining it. In this book, we explain the basic structure of workshop and offer four stories of teacher variations. Readers who want even more detail about workshop can turn to whole books that focus closely on this single structure. That's one reason we provide reading suggestions at the end of each chapter.

As you read along, you'll also notice that these teacher stories aren't just about strategies and practices, but also about theories and ideas: the articles mention whole language, integrated curriculum, process writing, reader response, and other large concepts about schooling. That's because teaching is idea-driven work; teachers who are in charge of their own professional growth want to know where innovative strategies come from, how activities can be translated up and down the grades, and what research supports them. Teachers want to know how their own daily experiences and experiments fit in with those of colleagues around the country; they are eager to become part of the wider professional conversation that constantly bounces between the concrete and the conceptual. Teachers want activities that will work with real kids on Monday, but they also want to understand why things work, so they can answer their own questions and make their own choices down the line.

The other recurrent feature of these articles is that they are all rooted in teachers helping other teachers grow, whether in official peer-led workshops, by passing along classroom materials, through casual faculty lounge dialogue, or by sharing professional articles like these. Just as we are rediscovering the power of peer tutoring—of kids teaching kids—so too are we rediscovering the professional energy that is unleashed when teachers teach teachers.

For too long, teaching has been an isolating profession where colleagues work just a few steps apart but feel miles away. Today, educational reform is starting to break down the cellular organization of schools, bringing groups of teachers together to plan, share, reflect, and perhaps to build, at last, the kind of professional community which teaching has never quite enjoyed.

We hope this book can be part of that endeavor. So join us, as we teach each other, about the meaning of Best Practice, about the structures of teaching, about the methods that really matter.

# CHAPTER 2
# Integrative Units

**W**HEN DOZENS OF different educational organizations began developing curriculum standards documents over the past decade, they dutifully stayed inside the traditional subject field boundaries. The National Council of Teachers of Mathematics talked about good teaching and learning in mathematics only, the Center for the Study of Reading kept to issues of literacy, the American Association for the Advancement of Science limited itself to recommendations about biology, chemistry, and physics, and so forth. Each group talked about Best Practice in terms of the instructional methods, structures, and strategies to be increased or decreased within its own discipline. At one level, there's nothing to apologize for in this. All American educators have inherited a professional world in which knowledge is generated and reported within certain long-established fields. Indeed, these national curriculum organizations themselves are built on the traditional subject-matter separations.

Yet we increasingly realize that the separate-subject approach too often leaves students with a disconnected view of knowledge and fails to reflect the way that real people attack real problems in the real world. In school, knowledge and learning are typically compartmentalized, offering no view of how it all comes together to reveal the big picture. But what's the sense of separating mathematics from science when one is such a powerful set of tools for solving problems in the other? Why separate reading from writing, history from art, literature from science, or, for that matter, natural language from mathematics? Life is holistic. The real world presents us, both kids and adults, with complex events that aren't divided into neat subject areas or forty-minute periods. Real living requires us to draw on many domains of knowledge, multiple strategies of thinking, and diverse ways of knowing.

In response to the lure of coherence, creative teachers are crossing the old subject boundaries, translating models from one field into another, importing promising ideas from other subjects, designing cross-curricular investigations, and developing rich thematic units that involve students in long-term, deep, sophisticated inquiry. Teachers are venturing into these exciting new territories because they are convinced that there is a better way to teach and learn. They believe that students can learn subject matter—even mandated content and "basic" skills—in the midst of complex, holistic, integrated experiences, and not just through separate and sequential lessons. These teachers are supported by several growing models—whole language, problem-based learning, interdisciplinary studies, the middle school movement—each of which has curriculum integration as a key ingredient of its vision.

But this doesn't mean that traditional subject fields are disrespected and abandoned as the curriculum becomes more integrated. On the contrary, as our colleague James Beane (1995) points out, the disciplines of knowledge are the "useful and necessary ally" of curriculum integration. In Beane's view, curriculum should come out of problems, issues and concerns that are posed by life, with the disciplines of knowledge being called upon to support student investigation and study. As Beane puts it:

> Notice that, in order to define curriculum integration, there must be reference to knowledge. How could there not be? If we are to broaden and deepen understandings about ourselves and our world, we must come to know "stuff" and to do that we must be skilled in ways of knowing and understanding. As it turns out, the disciplines of knowledge include much (but not all) of what we know about ourselves and our world and about ways of making and communicating meaning. Thus authentic curriculum integration, involving as it does the search for self and social meaning, must take the disciplines of knowledge seriously—though again, more is involved than just the correlation of knowledge from various disciplines. (100)

If students experience well-designed curriculum integration, they will need to enter, draw upon, operate within, and become knowledgeable about many discipline fields.

▲ Marilyn: Last summer, I was able to observe curriculum integration close-up at an innovative summer institute for Chicago students and teachers supported by the DeWitt Wallace–Reader's Digest Fund. The project, called "Students at the Center," is a collaboration of professional development organizations from four disciplines—the Chicago Algebra Project, the Chicago Metro History Education Center, the Chicago Arts Partnerships in Education, and the

Illinois Writing Project. The idea is to help middle grade teachers move toward student-centered, constructivist pedagogy, embodied in integrative curriculum units. The summer institute, involving 240 sixth through eighth graders at Caesar Chavez School and forty teachers from twelve Chicago schools, was a laboratory of curriculum integration. The teachers worked with consultants from the different professional development organizations to design thematic units, teaching young people together each morning. Then the teachers and consultants gathered each afternoon to debrief, troubleshoot, and replan upcoming days of instruction.

In one memorable classroom, the teachers and kids were working with the consultants to integrate reading, writing, and the arts. The students had been reading a novel by Gary Paulsen called *Sisters,* about two teenage girls growing up in very different circumstances, one amid privilege and the other facing great challenges. The consultant in residence, artist Cynthia Weiss, was there to help the kids and teachers tap the connection between the visual arts and reading and writing. Cynthia explained to the students that they were going to use portraiture to help them express their feelings about the book and better understand what they had read.

She began by asking what a portrait was, accepting a wide range of student responses. Then Cynthia broadened the students' definitions a bit, explaining that portraits can come in various forms, and that they would shortly be doing portraits of the two young women in the book. Students brainstormed ways that the characters could be represented by their faces, their homes, their feelings, their families, or by specific events and experiences. Cynthia passed out black construction paper and brightly colored chalks and invited the students to draw on the paper just to get comfortable with the medium. Next she showed pages from several picture books to provide examples of how other artists had revealed aspects of characters in their illustrations. When the students were ready, Cynthia gave out new pieces of black paper and invited them to divide the paper in half and open up their minds to what they wanted to say about the two young women.

The results were immediate. Students jumped right in and began creating portraits, many talking quietly to each other as they put chalk to paper. As I walked through the room watching and listening, it was obvious that this art experience was fun and energizing. But were the portraits really helping the kids to dig deeper into the meaning of the novel? I went around to the students, who were seated at tables of four, and asked them to talk about their portraits and about the book. In each group I approached, the students were eager to explain their drawings and talk about the sections of the book that had moved them to do their art. One girl told me that doing the portrait had helped her to think about the two young women, and how close her own experiences were to that of one of the characters. She said that she knew that she would have to work hard to avoid similar pitfalls in her own life. I left the classroom feeling that this small experiment with curriculum integration, bringing together the tools of art and literacy, allowed students to act upon their thinking in an especially powerful and energized way. ▲

# Forms of Integration from Primary Grades to High School

Curriculum integration can take many different shapes at different grade levels. Primary teachers have long practiced integration by building units around themes such as the solar system, insects, or grandparents. In such classrooms, students might read about grandparents, interview their own grandparents, study family photos and artifacts, trace immigration patterns on world and U. S. maps, bring grandparents in as classroom "experts," and write and draw in response to all these experiences. Many intermediate grade teachers integrate literature and history by having students read novels that connect to the social studies topics being studied: westward expansion, the Civil War, the Industrial Revolution. Reading *Little House on the Prairie* or *Sign of the Beaver* can bring a texture to the study of the pioneer experience that few textbooks can provide, and can help ignite curiosity that leads students to explore textbooks, primary sources, and other historical records. The integration of literature and history is one way to show students that learning is connected and that history is composed of multiple stories about real people, stories that can be found in a variety of sources.

Some of the most sophisticated integration work comes out of the middle school movement, which makes integration the centerpiece of curriculum and supports it with block scheduling and teacher teaming. While in some middle schools, interdisciplinary instruction is mainly harnessed to teacher-chosen themes that retain the separate identities of each subject, Beane (1991) has developed a variation he calls "integrative," in which the curriculum is designed around real concerns students have about themselves and their world. This form of integration begins with a complex series of brainstorming and listing activities designed to gather students' questions and issues. From these lists of topics, units of the curriculum are collaboratively developed by teachers and students. Teachers can "back-map" from students' genuine questions to many of the mandated ingredients in district or state curriculum guides. If young people say they want to study diseases (as they often do) teachers can plug in plenty of biology, math, and history, along with reading, writing, researching, and representing.

Curriculum integration often seems harder to achieve at the secondary level, where subject-area boundaries are guarded by bell schedules, departmentalization, course requirements, and state mandates. At Best Practice High School in Chicago, teachers are making forays across these borders. Some days, BPHS looks a lot like regular high school, with students studying physics, art, or algebra separately. During other days and weeks, students are engaged in complex interdisciplinary studies that blend all the city- and state-mandated subjects into broad negotiated, thematic, integrated units. From our earliest planning meetings, the whole faculty agreed that time sharing was OK; that integrated instruction could alternate with more traditional forms of teaching. Students can enjoy a cycle of integration, two or three weeks during which all kinds of thinking are intertwined, with teachers serving not as subject specialists but more as inquiry coaches. Then, everyone can shift back to a few weeks of traditional organization and scheduling.

When we opened BPHS in 1996 with 140 freshmen, our first integrated unit was called "Here We Are." Since all of us were coming from the four corners of Chicago to a neighborhood and a building that few of us knew well, it seemed natural to investigate this particular place—a place in the city, in the history of Chicago, in the migration of different peoples, in the transformation of the prairie. After a neighborhood walking tour and some reading of local history, teachers helped students brainstorm possible areas of investigation about this special corner of Chicago. The kids eventually identified eight inquiry topics, including the architecture of the building, the ethnic history of the neighborhood, and the achievements of the past graduates of the school. The students each selected their favorite topic and, over parts of the next couple of months, worked with one teacher who had volunteered to coordinate that particular study. In order to achieve this, we had to create a variable class schedule, with teachers dropping their discipline-specific lessons for a day here and a week there so that we could regroup by topics. Toward the end of the project, we set up exhibitions, performances, and publications through which students shared the results of their inquiries. Community residents, school alumni, and other students provided us with real audiences and feedback.

Our first integrated unit had some highlights. Kids had to take responsibility for their own work, and teachers got the opportunity to coach them as researchers, thinkers, and communicators. The students needed to gather information, sift and winnow it, and somehow make it their own. Everyone learned some urban and social history. Many kids made good use of computers in recording and displaying their findings, and art was infused through many of the projects. Still, both teachers and kids thought the unit dragged on too long, losing energy as curriculum integration alternated with separate-subject work over weeks and weeks. Another problem was that students' interest wasn't deeply engaged in this topic from the start. "Here We Are" had been the teachers' idea—a logical idea, to be sure. But the problem was, the kids didn't really care enough about this old building or its neighborhood to sustain weeks of investigation. Ooops.

For our next cycle of integration, we wanted to try a more modest and limited project that would offer kids real ownership while still "covering" some required subject-matter material. Three teachers—of geography, English, and art—got together and quickly discovered some integratable interests. In geography, students needed to learn about the major land forms (mountains, deserts, plateaus, rivers, harbors) and their impact on human development. In art, students were scheduled to study several computer graphic and illustration programs, as well as to continue their yearlong exploration of artistic media. In English, the curriculum guide called for more practice of reading and writing in nonfiction genres.

Aiko, Peter, and Kathy created a two-week unit culminating in a "Design Your Own Island Nation" project (see page 8 of the color insert), which required every student to: (1) create and map a plausible country containing a variety of landforms and posit patterns of economic and human development that were congruent with those geophysical attributes; (2) represent some aspect of the country in an appropriate art form (drawing, HyperCard, sculpture, fabric art); and (3) write an extended piece about the country in an appropriate nonfiction genre (a constitution, a set of laws, a historical record). Raquel Torres, whose country featured a snowcapped mountain area, figured that a ski resort would be a key economic development, so she selected a stockholders' annual report as her nonfiction genre (see Figure 2.1).

Raquel's report orchestrates a good deal of subject-matter knowledge as well as process skills. She's learned about integrating geophysical forms and economic principles; computing, charting, and graphing statistics; composing and editing within a highly structured nonfiction genre; and using computer desktop publishing, illustration, and text programs to enhance a product. Though not all the students' efforts were quite as

**1 9 9 7**

# ANNUAL

*R   E   P   O   R   T*

## Message To Our Stockholders

We are pleased to report that Shifter Valley Ski Resort, Inc. achieved adequate earnings for the financial year ending October 30. Net income increased to $1,786,000, as compared to $1,071,600 last year.

Shifter Valley's improvement was a result of increased attendance and lower expenses as a percentage of sales. In winter 1996, over 15 million people took to the slopes in Shifter Valley. Earnings also increased by encouraging additional customer spending at the recently completed lodges, restaurants, and pro shops located near the ski area.

In conclusion, we remain optimistic about Shifter Valley's future growth opportunities as we continue to expand. We have acquired adjacent property, which will enable us to double the number of ski runs by this winter. By making our increased size the centerpiece of our marketing, we hope to increase attendance even further.

Thank you for your continued confidence and support as we work diligently to enhance this resort. With your support, we hope to exceed our recent phenomenal growth in the next financial year.

*Raquel Torres*
Chief Executive Officer
*December 15, 1997*

*Shifter Valley Ski Resort, Inc.*

**Figure 2.1** Raquel Torres' imaginary island nation of "New Einel" featured a profitable ski resort.

polished as Raquel's, the island nation unit generated a feeling of energy and ownership. Kids stitched needlepoint topographical maps of their countries, designed and sewed national flags, and wrote extended histories —at least one of which mysteriously involved members of the Beatles at every key juncture. This project, a brief and modest spurt of integration, evoked kids' sense of playfulness and exploration as well as their commitment to create something valuable. For the faculty, this was an important step ahead of the "Here We Are" unit, probably because it was smaller and certainly because we had learned a lot from our first attempt.

*Table 1: Statement of Income*

| | fiscal Year | | |
| | 1995 | 1996 | 1997 |
|---|---|---|---|
| Net sales | $7,352,100 | $9,802,800 | $16,338,000 |
| Cost of goods sold | 4,382,550 | 5,843,400 | 9,739,000 |
| Gross profit | 2,668,650 | 3,858,200 | 6,597,000 |
| General and administrative expenses | 1,496,700 | 1,997,600 | 3,326,000 |
| Operating income | 1,471,950 | 1,962,600 | 3,271,000 |
| Interest expense | 85,050 | 113,400 | 189,000 |
| Provision for income taxes | 582,300 | 776,400 | 1,294,000 |
| Net income | $803,700 | $1,071,600 | $1,786,000 |
| Net income per common share | 0.13 | 0.17 | 0.29 |
| Weighted average shares outstanding | 2,717,550 | 3,623,400 | 6,039,000 |

## Summary of Results

The financial year ending October 31 was the most successful in the history of Shifter Valley Ski Resort, Inc. As shown in Table 1 above, the end of year results for Net Sales ($16.4 million), Gross Profit ($6.6 million), and Net Income ($1.8 million) were AVSRI records.

Exceptional snowfall boosted attendance, particularly during the holiday season. More important, however, was the return on substantial investments in facilities (eg. skating rinks, lodges) and intra-resort transport (lifts, gondola). Together, these make Shifter Valley New Einal's finest.

Particularly impressive is the year to year growth. Sales jumped by over 60% versus last year, and more than doubled over FY 1995. Gross profits increased by 69% over last year, while net income growth reached nearly 75%.

Despite sluggish regional economic growth, AVSRI performance excelled based on two principal factors.

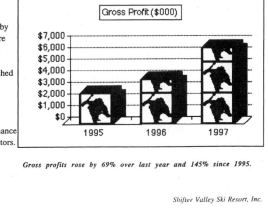

Gross Profit ($000)

*Gross profits rose by 69% over last year and 145% since 1995.*

*December 15, 1997*

*Shifter Valley Ski Resort, Inc.*

**Figure 2.1** (continued)

At the end of that first year at BPHS, we set aside a few days to plan with students what the sophomore curriculum might look like. Following Barbara Brodhagen's and James Beane's model, students worked with facilitators in small groups to identify concerns they had about themselves and their world. Though the student body at BPHS is a very heterogeneous mix of city kids, their "self" concerns are not much different from those of young teenagers anywhere: facing issues of identity, trying to envision the future, getting into college, choosing careers, getting married and having families, dealing with peer pressure (gangs), coping with

### Negotiating Curriculum
### BPHS Model

The goal of this process is to develop several student-chosen themes that can become curriculum units to be investigated. The students identify questions and concerns about themselves and about the world. These questions and concerns eventually lead to themes.

**Step 1.**  The facilitator explains to the group of students that we are interested in their questions because we want to build a curriculum around subjects of interest to them.

**Step 2.**  Students are seated at tables and are asked to take about five minutes to individually jot down questions and concerns they have about themselves. The facilitator may model some questions such as "Will I go to college?" and "What will my job be when I grow up?"

**Step 3.**  In groups of four or five, students are asked to share their "self" questions and concerns for about fifteen to twenty minutes to find topics they have in common. The students are looking for those questions that are most common. The facilitators go around the room helping students to arrive at a consensus. In some cases, the facilitators help students see that different questions are about the same issue. For example, "Will I have kids" and "Will I get married" are questions about family.

**Step 4.**  The group appoints a recorder to list their common concerns on pieces of chart paper, which are hung around the room.

**Step 5.**  The students circulate through the room for about five minutes looking at the lists.

**Step 6.**  The spokesperson from each group shares their chart with the whole class.

**Step 7.**  The facilitator helps the students to combine common concerns into a more comprehensive one. For example, if one group asks if a cure for cancer will be found, and another group wonders whether there will be a cure for AIDS, the facilitator helps them find a more inclusive question, such as, "Will we ever find cures for all the deadly diseases?"

These steps are followed a second time to find students' concerns about the world. Out of these two sets of student concerns come the themes or issues to be investigated throughout the year.

**Figure 2.2** The BPHS model for establishing curriculum units followed these seven steps.

pressure to take drugs, staying healthy, getting along with others. When students looked out at the world, they found themselves wondering about racism (would people of different races ever learn to get along?), immigration, violence, pollution and the environment, war, and the effects of technology on the future. The BPHS model for establishing curriculum units followed the seven steps in Figure 2.2.

When we teachers looked carefully at the lists of student concerns spread around the room on chart paper, we realized that they addressed themes that could guide huge chunks of the sophomore curriculum. So, certain separate-subject teaching will be sharing time with several integrated units, block-scheduled and spread across the year. In these studies on cultures, "isms," family history, the environment, and violence, teachers will abandon the boundaries of their disciplines and work with groups of students to generate inquiry, allowing the students' questions and concerns to lead the way. The products of these inquiries will be varied; from reports and presentations to videotapes and art exhibits. Students will work together with teachers to develop rubrics for what makes an effective demonstration of knowledge and competence in the different types of projects. We trust that students' participation in planning these units from the ground up will enhance their engagement and achievement over the year.

# Crossing Boundaries Requires Teachers to Change Roles

The separate-subject tradition is strong and durable, and crossing curriculum boundaries is not just tinkering with the curriculum. At Best Practice High School, our first-year forays into integration were clumsy, and neither students nor teachers were completely comfortable with letting go of their traditional views of how schools work. The most important lessons we learned were that this kind of learning requires big blocks of concentrated time, and that both teachers and students need to change their roles. Students can no longer be viewed as cognitive living rooms into which the furniture of knowledge is moved and arranged, and teachers cannot invariably act as subject-matter experts. Sometimes, teachers need to be generalists, becoming learners alongside their students. In classrooms where students are helping to plan and negotiate the curriculum, teachers need to ask their own authentic questions right along with the students and pursue ideas that are new to them, just like everyone else.

Teachers who are learning in their own classrooms are very often working at the edge of their comfort zones in areas where they have not gone before. But by taking this risk they contribute something rare and vital: direct modeling of how a resourceful and curious adult thinks—how she encounters and deals with new information. Too often in school, teachers simply relay ideas which they themselves long ago encountered and digested. Now, with negotiated and integrated curriculum, teachers are in on the exploration too. These teachers are showing kids how to think and are exemplifying the principles that learning never ends, that even teachers have room to grow, and that students have knowledge to be shared and valued.

At Addison Trails High School, Katy Smith, with her partners Ralph Feese and Robert Hartwig, work with high school students on a yearlong curriculum that integrates English, social studies, and science. In their class, students help decide not only what they are going to learn but also how they are going to learn it and how they will demonstrate their learning. These role changes were not always comfortable. According to Katy, "At times our role did seem to have shifted from 'disseminator of information' to 'collator of note cards.' More than once we questioned whether we were on the right track, and there were times when we inwardly agreed with the student who said that 'it would be a lot easier if you two just taught and we just obeyed and learned!' Easier, probably. Better? We thought not" (1993, 37).

In this chapter several teachers talk about doing curriculum integration. We begin with three rich Variations. Katy writes about how her suburban high school gradually developed a three-subject interdisciplinary program, making sure students not only engage more and care more, but also meet state objectives and conquer standardized tests. Katy's inspiration for guiding this transformative process was the work of Jim Beane, who helped her to see the power and the promise in student negotiation. In the next piece, Steve Zemelman gives a glimpse of curriculum integration with and for young children. Steve tells about the collaboration among eight kindergarten teachers who designed a "hands-on" experience with the moon. Just as Katy does with her suburban high school students, these inner-city elementary teachers involved their students in deciding what questions should be addressed in the curriculum.

Our third Variation comes from Linda Voss, Eleanor Nayvelt, Donna Mandel, and Cynthia Weiss—two teachers and two artists—who developed an ambitious yearlong, cross-school, arts-intensive, multicultural curriculum with African American, Hispanic, and Russian immigrant children. Their sophisticated project demonstrates the possibilities that can occur when teachers and artists collaborate. You will read about ways that children can challenge their own preconceptions about other ethnic groups and make important personal connections through the arts. In this story, we are reminded why art is one of the key avenues into the minds and the hearts of students and teachers.

In the section that we call Step by Step, Judy Johnstone and Suzy Ruder show that it is OK to start small with curriculum integration, to begin with "limited partnerships" combining two subjects instead of seven, and lasting a day or two, not months or years. Judy and Suzy tell about "Interdisciplinary Field Trips," which helped convince both teachers and students of the importance of curriculum integration. Especially in the change-resistant world of secondary schools, such incremental steps may be the most promising path to innovation. Judy and Suzy looked at the daunting challenge of integrating their high school curriculum and came up with a simple answer: let's do it one day at a time, literally.

# Further Reading

Beane, James. 1993. *A Middle School Curriculum: From Rhetoric to Reality*. Columbus, OH: National Middle School Association.

———. 1997. *Curriculum Integration: Designing the Core of Democratic Education*. New York: Teachers College Press.

Boomer, Garth, Nancy Lester, Cynthia Onore, and Jon Cook. 1992. *Negotiating the Curriculum*. London: Falmer Press.

Davies, Ann, Colleen Politano, and Caren Cameron. 1993. *Making Themes Work*. Winnipeg: Peguis.

Five, Cora Lee, and Marie Dionisio. 1995. *Bridging the Gap: Integrating Curriculum in Upper Elementary and Middle Schools*. Portsmouth, NH: Heinemann.

Lindquist, Tarry. 1995. *Seeing the Whole Through Social Studies*. Portsmouth, NH: Heinemann.

Manning, Maryann, Gary Manning, and Roberta Long. 1994. *Theme Immersion: Inquiry-Based Curriculum in Elementary and Middle Schools*. Portsmouth, NH: Heinemann.

Messick, Rosemary, and Karen Reynolds. 1992. *Middle Level Curriculum in Action*. White Plains, NY: Longman.

Short, Kathy G., Jean Schroeder, Julie Laird, Gloria Kauffman, Margaret J. Ferguson, and Kathleen Marie Crawford. 1996. *Learning Together Through Inquiry: From Columbus to Integrated Curriculum*. York, ME: Stenhouse.

Springer, Mark. 1994. *Watershed: A Successful Voyage into Integrative Learning*. Columbus, OH: National Middle School Association.

Steffey, Stephanie, and Wendy J. Hood. 1994. *If This Is Social Studies, Why Isn't It Boring?* York, ME: Stenhouse.

Stevenson, Chris, and Judy Carr. 1993. *Integrated Studies in the Middle Grades: Dancing Through Walls*. New York: Teachers College Press.

Tchudi, Steven, and Stephen Lafer. 1996. *The Interdisciplinary Teacher's Handbook: Integrated Teaching Across the Curriculum*. Portsmouth, NH: Boyton/Cook.

Vars, Gordon. 1993. *Interdisciplinary Teaching in the Middle Grades: Why and How*. Columbus, OH: National Middle School Association.

# Variations

## Grains of Sand, Negotiation, and Interdisciplinary Study

KATY SMITH

In November of 1991, I attended a very irritating presentation. Please understand: the presentation was not intended to be irritating. In fact, nationally noted curriculum expert James Beane had come to share with us his insights into building student self-esteem. Beane did not give a prepared talk; rather, he hung butcher paper around the room, invited us to write our questions and suggestions, and then tailored his remarks to the needs we had expressed. I was impressed by his flexibility and interested in his negative comments about packaged self-esteem programs, classroom management, and the like. Then, toward the end of his talk, he slipped in the irritating part, the way an ocean current slips a grain of sand into an oyster shell.

Beane said that the one thing that makes the greatest impact on students' self-esteem is involving them in planning their own curriculum. He went on to describe a middle school project he had been involved in. In this program, students were allowed to generate the topics for that year's studies. The students' questions were serious ones, their work sounded dynamic, and I was irritated. How, in the state of Illinois, with IGAPs and ACTs, PSATs and CRTs looming over every curriculum decision, could I, as a classroom teacher, relinquish control to students? On the other hand, if I truly wanted to build student self-esteem and to practice the democracy I had been teaching about, how could I not consider getting my students more involved? I had always allowed for student choice in free reading materials, had given options on writing assignments and test questions, had allowed for some discussion of classroom rules—but negotiate the curriculum? I was too unsettled even to ask articulate questions at the end of the evening. But that grain of sand had found its way in, and I could not stop thinking about what had been said.

At the time I heard Beane's presentation, I had recently begun my fourth year of team teaching American Studies, an interdisciplinary program that integrates American Literature and U. S. history, taught at the eleventh-grade level in my school. Throughout our experience as a team, my partner, Ralph Feese, and I had enjoyed many ups and suffered through some downs. We had continually searched for ways to improve the quality of our course, to make it "work" better, both for the students and for us. During our four years together we had learned a great deal about each other's subjects, which enabled us to look at the curriculum through a more interdisciplinary lens. The lines delineating our traditional subject areas had blurred more and more as we moved from parallel teaching to a truer model of team teaching, and we enjoyed our shared knowledge and responsibility. I went to school the day after Beane's talk and shared my reactions with Ralph.

Ralph's response was similar to mine: How could we possibly do something like negotiate curriculum, given the systemic factors that were part of our school day? However, a grain of sand must have penetrated Ralph's shell as one had mine, for we found ourselves continuing to discuss the concept of negotiating curriculum frequently and intensely. We remembered that in the past our students had been most difficult to deal with when they felt powerless to effect change in the classroom, and that the more we had entrenched ourselves in decisions, the more they had resisted. We acknowledged that although we were sharing knowledge and responsibility between us, for the most part we had been leaving the students out of the loop. We laughed ruefully that while we had been teaching about the ideals and processes of democracy, we certainly had not been living them in our classroom.

By February of that year, we had done enough research and preparation and felt confident in our rationale to test-run a negotiated unit with our students. We took the time to think through the key concepts that needed to be taught and tried to envision the range of possibilities that the students could suggest. We talked to each other a lot and decided that we were ready and willing to trust our students' ideas. We chose our annual immigration unit for our trial, using a modification of the K-W-L process to begin. We asked the students to list what they Knew (or thought they knew) about immigration as well as what they Wanted to know. On the "L" list, we asked them to indicate how they thought they could Learn what they wanted to know. We were impressed to find that they asked the same types of questions we ourselves had generated for past classes; they had ideas and resources for learning that went beyond what we had ever done before. As the unit progressed, their work showed understanding of the concepts that had always been part of our curriculum; their discussions showed high levels of involvement and thinking. We felt good about the quality of their work, and the students indicated that they felt invested in their learning because they had generated the unit syllabus. In fact, their final course evaluations revealed that this unit had been the most memorable one of the year for them. Ralph and I agreed that we had found a methodology that corresponded to our philosophical ideals, and we worked toward being ready to negotiate the curriculum for the whole course the following year.

We began the next year by involving our students in the development of a Class Constitution before moving into the course content. We then started the immigration unit—our test-run of the previous year—feeling confident that the content would fall into place while we focused on teaching the process. Our hopes were realized when the students produced a unit syllabus that rivaled any we or our colleagues ever produced and then went to work enthusiastically to find the answers to the questions they had asked. We used the negotiating process throughout the year to develop the course of study, and while it was sometimes exhausting, it was more often exhilarating. In fact, we published an article in *Educational Leadership* (Smith 1993) about this class and its special year.

For the following school year, Ralph and I were joined by a third team member, biology teacher Rob Hartwig, to pilot a program for freshmen. We were charged with the challenge of integrating the study of world cultures, language arts, and biological science. We began that year in a similar fashion, by developing a Class Constitution. In an ideal world, we would have gone on to utilize Beane's model in its pure form, having our students develop the themes to study throughout the year. In the world of state and local tests, we chose the themes ourselves, based on the existent curriculum; however, the negotiating model was and is still in practice in much of our unit development. Over the past four years, our Freshman Studies Program has grown from our original group—sixty students with one team of three teachers—to nearly two hundred students with three teams of three teachers.

One constant as the program has expanded has been the commitment to student voice and choice, and each team has adopted and adapted the negotiating model.

For example, early each year, Rob, Ralph, and I begin a unit on Africa.

Included on the syllabus over the years have been such student-generated questions as "How are knowledge and culture passed along through the oral tradition?" "What are schools like in Africa?" "What technology do they have?" "What are the main food sources?" "Why are some African countries [and other countries] called 'Third World?' Is there such thing as a 'Second World' country?" "What was Apartheid and how did it develop?" Some of their questions seem very sophisticated while others are less so, but in order to find the answers to them, students have to learn information from each of the traditional content areas and then integrate that information. Each year, they have "covered the content" of the biomes found in Africa; examined geography and cultural development; read many types of literature, including fables, proverbs, and autobiographies—with a great deal of vested interest, since the material provides answers to their own questions.

It takes time for a grain of sand to become a pearl, and it is extremely rare for any pearl to be without rough spots, bumps, and irregularities. One of the biggest rough spots we encounter is the students' initial disbelief that we teachers are really interested in and responsive to their questions, but this problem dissipates over time. Another bump we have encountered is the concern that essential content will be shortchanged and the students will be unprepared for standardized tests and future course work. A recent analysis of the performance of our first two groups of Freshman Studies students on state and local assessments, ACT tests, and their subsequent English, science, and social studies courses shows that these students outscored peers who took "traditional" classes; the process of learning to ask questions and to negotiate seems to have helped them master any content that they have needed.

In a presentation to our board of education, one of our students said, "Learning this way helps me link facts and information together. It's like a chain: if I am having trouble remembering something, I can usually remember something else that links to it." Rough spots, bumps and all, we believe that negotiating the curriculum with our students has paid off. Time and effort have transformed James Beane's ideas from an irritating grain of sand into something lustrous and often wonderful.

# The Moon Unit: Steps Toward Integrated Learning

STEVEN ZEMELMAN

How do teachers create opportunities for experiential, hands-on learning, particularly when they're working with primary-age children who need lots of guidance as they do things? The kindergarten teachers at Disney Magnet School in Chicago asked if I would help create such an activity, and we agreed to design and run the unit together. Disney is a big school, with eight kindergarten teachers, so two willing risk takers, Audrey Laufman and Liz Ostman, volunteered to work with me as a planning committee.

The teachers had already chosen a topic: the moon. They wanted to see what could be done with science, and weren't entirely happy with the existing curriculum. Looking back, we would have done better to consult the children on this, but we're still learning what it means to integrate subjects in a meaningful way. Fortunately, just as this request came up, I was reading a lively manuscript for the National Council of Teachers of English called *Empowering Ourselves to Inquire: Preservice Teacher Education as a Collaborative Enterprise* by Wayne Serebrin (1998). It described a yearlong effort with a class of prospective primary-grade teachers to help them view teaching as a constructive response to kids' needs rather than as a mechanized routine. A high point was the creation of "playscapes" for the children in their student-teaching classrooms—settings that worked with children's real questions and invited learning through play. I recommended the manuscript for publication and borrowed the approach immediately!

Taking Serebrin's lead, I first went to the children. Audrey gathered her energetic troop on the floor one morning and I asked, "Do you ever wonder about the moon? Do you have questions about it, or wish you understood more about it?" The kids responded immediately—not with questions, but with answers. Kindergartners are wonderfully confident human beings, not yet beaten down by the judgments of schools. They told me plenty, and when anyone did have a question, someone else supplied an answer. But adults are persistent. We explained to the kids about asking questions. We cheated and turned some of their statements into questions. And of course not everyone was so sure about the assertions some kids made. Here's what emerged:

How does an eclipse work?
Are there people or aliens living on the moon?
Why are there little circles on the moon?
Why does the moon follow you when you're riding in a car? (Try explaining that one!)
The moon looks little, but it's really big—why?
How does the moon change from a little slice to a half to a whole?
Why is the moon a cold-looking color?

How do astronauts get to the moon?

Why do astronauts put American flags on the moon?

How do astronauts carry things on their back? And what's in those packs?

Is there a car on the moon?

Now the challenge: what activities could address some of these questions and involve active play at the same time? The following letter, sent to the rest of the kindergarten teachers, describes what we ultimately planned for the children:

Dear Friends:

Audrey Laufman, Liz Ostman, and I have planned a special integrated-learning science project on the moon for kindergarten children, which will be available to your classes during the week of May 1–5. Learning will be centered in a moon playscape, to be located in the first floor commons area, featuring centers for exploring concepts and information connected with the moon. The activities are based on actual questions Audrey's children have asked. These stations and their learning areas within the fields of science, math, language arts, and physical development are as follows:

1. Astronaut backpacks. Children select and pack objects in backpacks and weigh the packs to ensure the total is within five pounds. They mark their selections on a graph to compare preferences for items chosen, and then write, draw, or dictate reasons for these selections. Learning areas: problem solving, measuring, graphing, and speaking or writing to explain ideas.

2. Lunar vehicles. Children make model vehicles using wood, pipe cleaners, and glue, and record on a graph the size wheels they choose for navigating lunar terrain. The vehicles can be taken home. Learning areas: problem solving, small-motor coordination, and graphing.

3. Moon-phase box. The children take turns looking into a large, darkened box and moving a styrofoam ball to various positions to see how light from a hole in the box forms crescent, half-circle, and whole-circle shapes like those seen on the moon. They draw what they observed and write or dictate explanations about why the shape changes and how this might relate to the moon. Learning areas: observing, drawing inferences, and speaking or writing to explain ideas.

4. Clay moonscapes. Children make models of moon surface fea-

tures, based on photographs of the lunar landscape that are displayed on a bulletin board. The clay is then returned to its holder for others to use. Learning areas: observing and small-motor coordination.

5. Appearance of differing size. In pairs, children look through a tube to observe a large ball at different distances to see how distance affects the appearance of size. One child observes while the other carries the ball, standing at various spots marked on the floor. They then trade places so each gets to observe. They draw, write, and/or dictate explanations of what they observed and how it might relate to the moon. Learning areas: observing, drawing inferences, and speaking or writing to explain ideas.

There will be brief tape-recorded instructions at each activity to guide the children. Please feel free to organize your kids' visit(s) to the moon playscape as you see fit. You may wish to explain the basic steps in the centers at the start of your children's visit. We'll have construction paper, crayons, and other materials at each station for children to record their observations and ideas; and you can choose one or two stations to monitor, or move about to help children with the tasks, take dictation, guide them as they mark on the charts, etc. I will be available at various times throughout the week to help out as well.

# How Did It Go?

We learned a tremendous amount as we ran the playscape over an exhausting but fascinating four days. First, the nitty-gritty: kindergarten kids need an older guide at each station if they are to get the most out of it. The taped instructions were a clever idea, but got lost in the shuffle. To solve this we drafted and trained a very willing group of sixth graders. The older kids saved the day, had fun, and learned about younger children, but they unfortunately also acted like overly efficient border guards, stamping passports and moving children along briskly (see Figure 2.3). This shows the training school actually provides for students!

A handy trick also helped bring order to the near chaos. After the first round of confusion, I found Liz Ostman on the floor marking out a large square with colored tape next to each play station. This allowed teachers and sixth graders to send kids who had finished one activity on to the next in a clear and positive way. It provided just enough order so the project could proceed.

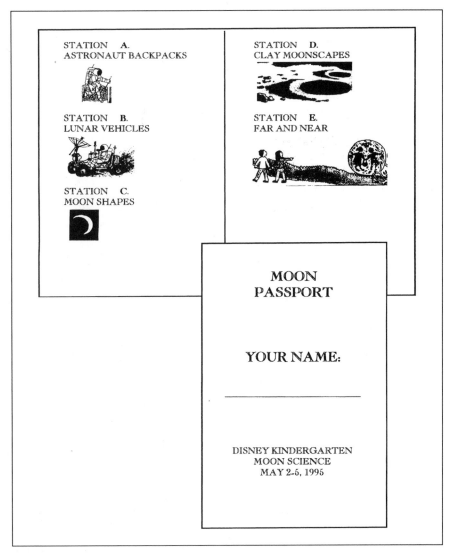

**Figure 2.3** Moon passports were stamped as students entered each of five stations.

As for the activities, some proved better than others. Observing a ball through a tube actually did the best job of answering one of the questions on the kids' list. Everyone could see that up close the ball filled the whole viewing space, and as it moved farther away it appeared to shrink. This didn't capture imaginations too strongly, however. The moon phase box was popular because children could crawl inside, where it was dark. However, sometimes the sixth graders rushed them through, so they hadn't fully grasped what might be learned. The lunar vehicles were the greatest hit. We ultimately used chunks of pink styrofoam, styrofoam cups for radio antennae, coffee cup lids for wheels, and pipe cleaners as axles (solving a big worry about kids extracting nails to jab each other on the bus). The result was tables full of pink and white little fluffs of cloud. The kids got some good small-motor exercise and lessons in patient handiwork out of this, although not much science.

Still, everyone had a grand time. However, finally, what was needed was a fuller involvement of the children both before and after their actual visit to the moonscape. According to Jim Beane's levels of curriculum integration, we were somewhere between "fusing subjects" and "student-concern-centered curriculum." We weren't yet fully engaging student choice or achieving sufficient depth to call our effort an "integrated" one. Of course, some of the teachers conducted additional activities on their own. But next year, we'll expand the unit to help each group ask questions and connect the questions with the activities. We'll provide lots of picture books and information for kids to look over and have read to them, offer choices of follow-up activities and nighttime observations, and debrief afterward to discover what they learned. The core event, playing at the moonscape, is just a beginning. And—oh, yes—we're really going to train those sixth graders in open-ended discussion and teaching techniques, and then put them to work setting up the whole thing!

Here is a more detailed list of the moon centers, with their goals, outcomes, descriptions, and assessments and the name of the teacher who masterminded each one.

## Station A—Astronaut Backpacks (Liz Ostman)

- Goal: To have children select and graph their own preferences from a table of space materials.
- Outcome: Children will write, draw, or dictate reasons for their preferences and answer questions about the graph.
- Description: Children select and pack objects in backpacks and then weigh them with scientific scales to check that the contents are under five pounds. Objects can range from food to supplies to games. Create graphs based on the supplies to show students' preferences. Ask students to state why they chose each item as it is graphed.
- Assessment: Verbal questioning by a teacher or parent.
- Suggestions: Backpacks should be big. Have parents or teachers help with the center. Use a scale with large numbers.

## Station B—Lunar Vehicles (Elizabeth Segiel)

- Goal: To have children be able to identify the correct size of wheels for the lunar vehicle that they will drive on the moon.

- Outcome: Students will be able to correctly identify and pick the correct size wheel on their moon vehicle.
- Description: Prepare two different sizes of wheels for the students to select. Prepare a vehicle base for each student to use to assemble their vehicle. Ask students which size wheel they would select for their moon vehicle and ask why they would choose that particular wheel size. Have students put on their selected wheels to their moon vehicle and glue a styrofoam cup somewhere on the top. Students should put their names on the vehicles and graph the size of wheel they choose to use on their vehicle.
- Assessment: Verbal questioning by a teacher or parent. Ask the students why they chose the specific wheel size and why.
- Suggestions: Students should be versed in the moon's surface and talk about the appropriate shapes for a rocky, cratered, hard surface. Parents or teachers must be at this center.

## Station C—Moon Shapes (Carrissa Mazzeffi)

- Goal: To have children identify the different phases of the moon.
- Outcome: Students will identify the different phases of the moon (full, half, and crescent) after a sitting in the box.
- Description: Create a large box for children to sit in and move around in one at a time. Paint the interior of the box black. Cut a circular hole at the top of the box. Provide a styrofoam ball for the child to use when enclosed in the box. When a child sits in the box, tell her to first hold the ball high, next at shoulder level, and then close to the bottom of the floor. Tell the child to always focus her attention at the top of the ball. After she has left the box have her draw on a piece of paper what she viewed in the box.
- Assessment: A child should be able to draw three distinct phases of the moon upon exiting the box (full, half, crescent).
- Suggestions: Students should be versed in the moon's phases before participating in this center. The outside of the box should be painted with fluorescent paint and stars could be attached to the interior. A large box is preferable. A teacher or parent must manage this center.

## Station D—Clay Moonscapes (Audrey Laufman)

- Goal: To have children know about the surface of the moon.
- Outcome: Students will understand there are craters on the moon and the moon goes through different phases.
- Description: Children should hear stories and see pictures about the moon. Previous to this activity, they were given a particular page for

homework that guided them through observing the moon. Clay is set up on a table and children are instructed to form different phases of the moon with craters and rocks on it.

- Assessment: Each child is asked to form a moon with craters and rocks and to show it to a parent or teacher.
- Suggestions: This type of unit takes a lot of work and preparation. Instead of using parent volunteers, we use upper grade children and work around their schedules. We also need a bigger budget—$60 is not enough for 180 students.

## Station E—Far and Near (Joyce Campbell)

- Goal: To have children know about the concepts of near and far in relation to the moon.
- Outcome: Students will understand the difference between far and near in relation to the Earth and moon.
- Description: Six pieces of tape should be placed on the rug. Hanging in the background should be a diagram of what the students are supposed to do in the center. A person should instruct the students that they are going to partake in an activity to learn about *far* and *near*. A Nerf ball and a paper towel tube is needed for the activity. One student should hold the ball and the other student should hold the tube against his eye. As the student with the ball moves, the other student should be asked to describe what is happening to the ball. Both students should take turns doing this, and at the end of the activity they should be instructed to draw what they viewed.
- Assessment: A child is asked to draw what she/he saw when looking through the tube.
- Suggestions: This center requires either a parent or teacher to aid the students. Also, preparation for the students is needed before they participate in the activity or they will be lost.

## Station F—Astronaut Puppets (Linda Wishney)

- Goal: Giving children an opportunity to have fun doing a culminating activity while improving their small-motor skills and developing their vocabulary.
- Outcome: To understand that the moon is part of our universe and that astronauts in rocket ships have visited the moon.
- Description: For this activity, you will need paper bags, glue, crayons, and scissors. Children will color, cut, and paste an astronaut face and body. The face is placed on the part of the bag that folds down on the bottom. The body is pasted on the top of the bag. Children will hold

their bags up and tell about something they learned while on the moonscape.

- Assessment: Children will state three things about the moonscape.
- Suggestions/Culminating Activity: For this activity, you will need crayons, scissors, glue, and craft sticks. Have the children choose one of the pictures that have been included. They will cut them out and glue a craft stick to the bottom. They may hold up their puppets and tell about something they learned about the moon.

# Immigration and Family History Through the Arts: A Story in Many Voices

LINDA VOSS, ELEANOR NAYVELT, CYNTHIA WEISS, AND DONNA MANDEL

Linda: It is mid-March. Darkness has fallen outside my classroom window. This is my last parent-teacher-student conference of the day. From my chair I watch with great emotion as Brandi and her mother move, dipping, swaying, and twirling in perfect sync, two graceful birds joyfully trying out their wings on the first spring breezes; sharing how Brandi had brought school home, teaching her mother and the members of her church to story dance—or, as they called it, "worship dance."

My teaching path has led me from schools in Chicago's Humboldt Park, with a Latino and African American population, to an international school on a Caribbean island, to a Lincoln Park school integrated by thirds—African American, Latino, and white. In each of these diverse settings, I have felt challenged to create community where children separated themselves by ethnic difference. One step was for me to live by the adage that "children do as we do." By sharing with them my own diverse friendships and family (African American father, German mother, Panamanian uncle, German Turkish cousins) I showed my classes that not everyone sees difference as a cause for division.

Then I came to Washington Irving three years ago. We are an inner-city school on the West side of Chicago, about half African American and half Latino, with a few white and Asian children. I soon learned that many of my students viewed whites as people who either have no problems, or are all racists and are all the same. We also had rifts in the classroom between the Latino and the African American children. Of course these conflicts are found schoolwide and throughout the community at large.

I know African Americans and Latinos who are so overwhelmed by perceived differences between themselves and white Americans, whom they haven't been exposed to until adulthood, that they limit themselves professionally to avoid working with whites. I wanted my students to begin meeting and getting along with people from outside of their own community before they too became isolated and fearful.

Meanwhile, my old friend and colleague Eleanor Nayvelt was teaching third grade across town at Clinton School, where she worked with recent Russian immigrant children in a special bilingual program. Because we were both concerned about our students' ethnic separateness and lack of contact with other groups, we wanted to find a way to work together. Years before, when we had been students at the University of Illinois, Eleanor and I had developed an interdisciplinary curriculum we called the "Chicago-Leningrad Connection," which was designed to help young America and Russian children learn about each other's culture, history, and arts.

Now, we realized there was a chance to bring that "dream" curriculum to life. We agreed that an arts-integrated, multicultural, cross-school project would be our aim, with language arts playing a strong role. In this way, we could develop children's critical thinking through a project-based curriculum, complexly interwoven with opportunities for them to interpret their world and express themselves through different art forms. As Charles Fowler says in his book *Strong Arts, Strong Schools: The Promising Potential and Shortsighted Disregard of the Arts in American Schooling* (1996), "The subject matter of the arts is as broad as life itself, and therefore the arts easily relate to aspects of almost everything else that is taught . . . They tell us about people: how they thought and felt and what they valued. They help us define ourselves, as well as other people and other times" (48).

In our interdisciplinary history unit, we wanted to include forms of communication that weren't dependent on verbal ability or English competence, so that children whose strengths lie in other areas would have chances to develop their intelligences. The arts seemed the ideal, nonthreatening vehicle to bring students together, and help us all examine ourselves and each other. We planned an engaging but rigorous study that would offer all the children opportunities to assimilate information from different sources and to create a rounded picture of their world. We hoped that by using the arts to develop pride in their own ethnic contributions, our students would become more tolerant, empathetic human beings who would learn to go beyond stereotypes.

**Eleanor:** I started teaching at Clinton School immediately after graduation. It was important for me to teach the "Russian children." I made it my personal goal to help them in the assimilation process, to ease the culture and language shock. From my own experience I know that this shock is not easily overcome. I came to Chicago at the age of thirteen from the former Soviet Union and studied at a small, private Jewish day school, where no bilingual program or ESL was offered. While I remember my experiences there fondly in many ways, my transition into the "American System" was rather painful, although eventually successful. At first I really wanted to belong and would do anything to sit at the same lunch table with my American classmates. But I was different and not readily accepted. I wore dresses while they all wore jeans. I ate different foods and was not familiar with the current soap operas. I decided to use my pride in my culture as a defense mechanism, as a shield. I decided to remain Russian, and I gave up trying to belong.

With this personal history, one of my goals was to support the pride that the Russian children have in their culture, and use it as a positive vehicle in their assimilation. In contrast to using cultural identity as a shield, I wanted my students to bring their pride to the table with other children in this country, as equals, as a means for growth and mutual respect. I wanted them to enter into relationships with other children based upon their own strong sense of identity. I wanted my Russian students to add a flavor to the American pie and bring home other flavors for their families to taste. I dreamed that they could become both self-respecting and tolerant, and not grow up to partake in the racism that exists here.

**Linda and Eleanor:** In the fall of 1996, we began to assemble the resources and plan the specific activities of our extended collaboration. We got mini-grants from the Oppenheimer Family Fund and the DeWitt Wallace–Reader's Digest Chicago Students at the Center project to cover the costs of art supplies, buses for field trips, and the services of artist Cynthia Weiss, history consultant Roger Passman, and dancer Donna Mandel.

The relationship between our two classes officially began when our students wrote letters to each other, which we used to pair them off. (This is why, throughout the year, the Irving students continued to refer to the project as "our Russian pen pals.") After the exchange of correspondence, we gathered in person for the first time, joining in a "getting to know you" activity with artist Cynthia Weiss. On the appointed day, the Irving students arrived at Clinton School, and found Eleanor's class sitting upstairs in the library. The twenty-eight Clinton students were all seated with empty chairs beside them, which were systematically filled by the twenty-five Irving students. The atmosphere was charged with the discomfort and excitement of the children as they looked at each other for the first time. Cynthia welcomed the children, explaining that in a few minutes they would be making portraits of each other.

**Cynthia:** First I had the children get the feel of the possibilities of the chalks they would use by having them look carefully at their own skin tones and practice blending colors to create the ranges of dark and light browns that prevailed in one class to the paler tones more prevalent in the other. Then they blended the color of their partner's skin. Next I quickly demonstrated drawing a portrait using a child as a model. Now the children were confronted with the difficult task of looking each other in the face. While children worked on these drawings, conversation was flowing.

From the bright-colored chalks on black paper emerged representations of the faces in the room (see pages 2–3 of the color insert). Each student wrote their own name and the name of their partner on their art work. The portraits read; "Brandi, by Vitaly" and "Vitaly, by Brandi." The portrait process gave them a safe structure during their first meeting, to observe each other, first with curiosity and then with respect. Following a lively discussion of the work and the activity, we broke for a meal that included ethnic foods: Russian pastries, chips with salsa, Spanish and Southern rice, guacamole, and chocolate cake. Despite having to go down four floors for the bathroom, some shyness, a couple of small arguments amongst the boys, and a sense of herding cattle as we moved fifty-three children around, it was a good beginning.

Once our students had become acquainted with their "pals," we arranged a number of field trips to help them share new experiences together outside of the classroom. Our first trip was to the Museum of Contemporary Art to see its special retrospective exhibit of Chicago artists. The Clinton and Irving students were partnered with their pen pals as a docent led us to the first piece in the show. There we were, adults and children, standing before a huge color photograph of the back of someone's head. Against a neutral background, the sleek, blond, pageboy haircut left the image with an ambiguous gender.

The docent said to Eldorado, "If I were to ask you what you are, you would say you are [pause] a boy, right?" she prompted.

Then she turned to his partner, Natalia, and asked her, "If I were to ask you what you are, you would say, 'I am . . .'"

"A girl, " Natalia responded to the pattern presented.

"But I don't understand why you say this," Dima cried emphatically. "If someone asked me, I would say I am a human being!"

His intuition about image, and about the artists' intentions, certainly surpassed the docent's explanation. As we walked through the exhibit, Dima continued, despite his limited English, to express other insights. I whispered to Linda, "it's amazing how hard he struggles with the language to find the right words for his thoughts." Linda responded, "Well, my students are going through that same struggle themselves." Then we looked at each other and thought the same thought, "Aren't we all?" It is a continual search to pin down our ideas and make them clear to the world, whether in our own language or in a new one we are acquiring.

Our tour moved on to the Black Light room, a re-creation of an artist's exhibit from the 1970s. The kids ran through the room laughing in delight to see their white shirts and shoelaces glow in the dark. We admired the way some children's brown skin became velvety black, and how all the children's white teeth shone like the Cheshire Cat's. Eugene, a Russian boy, was wearing grey from head to toe. Unclear on the workings of a black light, he tugged on my sleeve and said, "Miss, please, why am I not changing?" We found a small white tag on the back of his shirt and showed it to him. He ripped it out to see it better. He held on to this glowing white square like it was a talisman containing the magic of the museum. Linda, Eleanor, and I were delighted by how fresh this contemporary, conceptual art became, seen through the eyes of the children.

**Linda and Eleanor:** We also took our groups to an innovative dance performance in the Cultural Center, where the dancers involved the children. One of the dancers was from the Ukraine and spoke alternately in Russian and English. The Russian kids squealed with delight as he swooped around the dance floor, with Virgillia laughing on his back, a bird in flight, an airplane, telling the story of his journey to the United States. The dance performance directly tied into our plan to have children write stories about their families' migrations to Chicago, eventually choosing one story from each culture to represent in dance. At Clinton School, this project would fit into the required third-grade study of Chicago history, while at Irving the activity would satisfy fourth-grade Illinois history mandates.

**Linda:** To help discover their own immigration stories, students needed to use family members as primary sources. One memorable source was Brandi's great-aunt, a member of the African American Genealogical Society, who came in freezing weather to tell us about seven generations of her family tree and history. After I modeled asking questions, helping to translate her responses to the students, they pursued their own questions. Even my most difficult students quietly listened until it came time to ask questions, and then joined enthusiastically in the conversation. By the time she left we all had a pretty good understanding of how different life in rural Mississippi in the early 1900s was from the way we live today in Chicago.

**Linda and Eleanor:** By delving into their family stories, the children build a foundation for examining history and seeing themselves as part of it. Brandi now knows that World War II presented opportunities for African Americans to migrate from Mississippi to Chicago, just as her great-aunt moved here in 1944 to work in a munitions factory. Yelena understands that her family is a part of the continuing exodus of Russian Jews from the Soviet Union in a climate of renewed nationalism, anti-Semitism, and economic decay. James now knows that his relatives are among many Chinese immigrants drawn to work in America's health care professions. Armando realizes that his story, like that of many other Mexicans in the class, is that the United States offers his parents work opportunities that are lacking in Mexico. To collect these stories, we developed questions that all of the children used to interview the oldest available member of their family. This is much like the authentic work historians do when they use primary sources like interviews, journals, letters, and newspaper accounts to piece together a picture of what happened in the past.

**Eleanor:** You could not hear a sound or a movement. All of the children were listening with great intensity. I saw the whole gamut of emotions on the faces of my third graders: sorrow, fear, empathy, understanding, sadness, and joy. We were listening to a tape recording of Dima's grandfather, interviewed by his grandson. He told about experiences, worries, and concerns similar to those of most of the other families that have immigrated from the former Soviet Union. Dima asked careful questions, and if the answer did not immediately make sense, he probed until his grandfather's responses became clear. We were all moved. Perhaps for the first time, the children had the opportunity to hear the emotional side of why their families made the fateful decision to immigrate. Admiring his skillful and sensitive questioning, I could not help but wonder if Dima might become a reporter someday.

**Cynthia:** I visited the children again, this time to help them study the art of Marc Chagall, Romare Bearden, and Frida Kahlo. The children viewed these Russian, African American, and Mexican artists as exciting, different, but equally valuable models on which to base their own work. The students spent a long time looking at and discussing slides of paintings by Marc Chagall. Chagall's nostalgic paintings of his Russian hometown, outside of Vitebsk, were filled with his memories of roosters and moons, dancers and fiddlers on the roof. Some of the Russian children had lived near Vitebsk themselves, and all of them knew firsthand about a longing for things left behind.

But it was the Irving School children, African American, Mexican American, and Chinese, who seemed the most intrigued by Chagall's dreamlike imagery. They filled their drawing papers with upside-down houses and floating figures, to represent their own early childhood stories. Chagall's icons, tied to a specific time and place, provided a universal language that all the students could embrace. These images were pieced together in several panels where shapes and colors overlapped and images blended together to tell stories of who we were as a group.

The students then studied the work of Romare Bearden, an African American painter who was active in the Harlem Renaissance, and read *The Block,* a collection of poems by Langston Hughes. Each student made a collage of their own home with photographs and patterned paper. They could choose to show either their Chicago home or a past home in another city. Donald, a wonderful artist in Linda's class, suggested that we take the individual collages and make a "composite" block of our own. Rather than have the adults create the composition, we asked the children to decide how to put the block together. This task, like a choreographer's in dance, involved higher-order thinking skills. The students had to create an overall design that connected the parts in a meaningful way. They had a heated discussion about their options and took a vote. We had two groups of students composing the work; both groups decided to put the Atlantic Ocean in the center of the composition to show the water that the Russian children had crossed to come to America.

One of the groups also created a place in their design for Chicago homes, and their families' earlier homes in places like Mexico and Mississippi, with a collage train track connecting the bottom and top of the picture. The students brought their personal experiences and the knowledge of their families' histories to their discussion on spatial relationships.

As they composed the collage, they acknowledged each other's immigration and migration stories. The beautiful finished work represented the realities of the students' lives. Finally, the children examined the Mexican artist Frida Kahlo, particularly her series of self-portraits. In this style the children created self-portraits with oil pastels, weaving things of personal importance into the backgrounds and borders. During discussions of this work students seemed to demonstrate a deepening understanding of self and community.

**Linda:** A parent, Brenda Kneedly, invited my class to participate in an African American History Month poetry performance at Cook County Hospital where she works. Brenda is a poet herself and came to recite some of her poems at a schoolwide poetry recital. Both classes wrote poems topical to our project. Alongside the poetry and artwork, our classes met with Donna Mandel, a choreographer and dance consultant, whose Fluid Measure Performance Company creates performances that tell personal stories through dance, theater, visual arts, and music.

**Donna:** First, I introduced children to the choreographic tools of shape, levels in space, and energy or dynamic quality in dance. While one group did their artwork in a classroom, the other met with me to choreograph dances of selected family histories in a performance space. To begin, I led the students in the creation of movements to represent words. Each story was divided into three parts and small groups of children from both classes were assigned a piece of the story to choreograph. Once they were done, I had them create a choreographic score by drawing pictures and symbols that would remind them of the chosen movements. Their movements were put to music from the culture represented by the piece. This melding of movement with music was difficult but helped to flesh out its identity. I infused traditional moves from dances in the same culture to smooth transitions. The kicking of feet from a Russian troika signaled the beginning and ending of Yelena's story. Floating butterflylike, "claim movements" from a Chinese "Animal Frolic" framed James' family's immigration story. Brandi's migration story included a very cool slide and a group twirl; a variation on a lindy hop move framed its beginning and end. Following this lead, the children also included movements that they had learned elsewhere. A "strike-a-pose" move from "Vogue" was woven into Armando's immigration story. Alternate meetings at both schools provided opportunities to finish the artwork and rehearse the dance pieces.

**Linda and Eleanor:** At Irving, our project culminated in a major show with dances, poetry, and the discussion of our artwork, which appeared on a backdrop behind the stage. At Clinton, kids presented dances coupled with slides of their artwork in an "International Festival." At the end of the year, students at both schools received a copy of the book with their poems, artwork, and family stories. As the project came to a close, we felt it was important to celebrate and spend some social time together. So we went on a picnic to a lakeside park, where we viewed mosaic benches that depict events from Chicago history, created by our own partner Cynthia Weiss and other artists. Afterward we ate and played together. At first each class started their own games, then slowly children from the other class joined in until there was no division, just groups of joyful children playing soccer, Frisbee, ball, Red Rover, and a Russian game similar to Duck, Duck, Goose called Hide the Handkerchief.

We felt that this project was a success both academically and socially. As Charles Fowler says:

> Because the arts often express a sense of community and ethnicity, they are one of the main ways in which humans define who they are. Because the arts convey the spirit of the people who create them, they can help young people acquire inter- and intracultural understanding. The arts are not just multicultural, they are transcultural, inviting cross-cultural communication and understanding and teaching openness toward those who are different from us. (1996, 52)

This transcultural connection was one of the highlights for us. All the children learned about the contributions of each other's ethnic groups to our collective interpretation of the world. They reveled in the invitation to understand and express themselves in a range of styles. As they worked together, each contributing a piece, an understanding, a skill, an experience, or an idea to a work of art, they grew to see their own and each other's value.

In this unit, we managed to briefly bypass the ethnic segregation that decades of court decisions and mandates have not been able to resolve in Chicago. We are not saying that this limited exposure was a solution, but we do believe that all cross-group experiences are precious and worthwhile. The modeling of teachers is also important. As schoolteachers, our friendship—as a Russian immigrant, a German-speaking African American, and a diverse group of working artists—showed our students that relationships can transcend ethnic differences when they are based on the informed self-respect and openness to difference. The contributions of everyone who collaborated on this project demonstrated what could happen when people—different, diverse, various, and disparate people—work together.

# Step by Step
## Breaking Down Department Walls with Interdisciplinary Field Trips

JUDY JOHNSTONE AND SUZY RUDER

> Today was very cool and exciting. At first when I heard that we were supposed to have fun and learn at the same time, I laughed, but this is one of the most funnest field trips. It actually ranks up there with the Great America field trip. I learned how things Changed.

The student who wrote this "Bus Ticket" was commenting on his day taking what we call an "Interdisciplinary Field Trip." Such comments were just what the planning team of teachers were hoping for after our special day of exploring the topic of Change. Student and faculty learners had discussed personal life changes, visited a stone quarry searching for fossils, climbed a moraine to view glacial transformations, and experienced a Native American powwow. This experience was the most recent of three similar interdisciplinary days designed by a team of Orland Park's District 230 teachers.

The model for interdisciplinary field trips originated during a 1991 staff development program. Realizing that many structural elements of high schools conspire against curriculum reform and integration, we hit on the idea of "reforming" our high school one day at a time. We designed some demonstrations of integrated curriculum for kids and teachers, starting with an "in-school field trip" on changing roles in the family. On three occasions, groups of fifty kids and ten volunteer teachers went off to a closed library for four hours of intensive investigation, reading, writing, and talk—as fellow learners on a first-name basis. Everyone enjoyed a surprisingly powerful, intimate, and energizing learning experience.

Out of the "in-school field trips" came the idea for designing interdisciplinary field trips across the year so that students and teachers could get a taste of learning rooted in the common concerns of teachers and students, and crossing subject boundaries. The delighted teacher-participants urged their assistant superintendent, Tim Brown, to support the design of such field trips, both in and out of the building. Thus our collaboration began spontaneously, out of teacher interest and enthusiasm. Immediately, the district team, including faculty from English, math, science, social studies, art, home economics, and special services began planning for the following academic year. The trips were designed so that participants from all ages and abilities could experience real success. The key activities were designed to be collaborative and to encourage reading, writing, listening, speaking, and problem solving as well as to include all the disciplines of the team planners. As the interdisciplinary team developed the plan, it made every effort to create a balance among departments as well as to create a community of learners.

Because of wide-ranging interests and levels of expertise, the faculty had major difficulty arriving at a theme. After long, winding discussions of the subject areas represented, two themes eventually emerged: Technology and Choices, and Changes. In 1992–93, the Technology and Choices trip was conducted on five separate occasions, joined by the Changes trips in the spring and fall of 1993. Usually sixty to eighty students and ten to twelve teachers participated in each event.

As each field trip day unfolded, participants were encouraged to get to know new people so that the traditional cluster of friends could be momentarily expanded and teacher-participants could be accepted as part of the community of learners. In the Technology and Choices experience, students and teachers grappled with the very real problems of genetic engineering and the choices it presents for them personally as they look toward future life and family planning. During a lively discussion of the abortion issue, participants expressed opposing views. Later students commented that it was encouraging to have their opinions respected equally with those of teachers.

In Changes, students left the building to visit local sites where change was as omnipresent in the geologic formations and historical features as it was in their own personal lives. One faculty member commented: "Not only did I learn some geological and paleontological facts, but teaching about science and the environment should be done this way, that is, by touching, seeing, and becoming involved. Students were extremely well behaved and interacted well with other students and teachers."

Following the field trips, the learners were asked to demonstrate their newfound understanding of the day's topic. For instance, in Changes, some students chose to create a fossil for the future using clay, others

**Figure 2.4** High school students share their findings from a field trip on "change."

wrote lyrics for songs demonstrating their understanding of the formation of Moraine Valley, and others wrote narratives and poetry about personal change. The enthusiasm crescendoed in the valley as all shared their learning. Students created, shared, and celebrated in a newly established community of learners.

All the learners in this community expressed enthusiasm for this experience in the evaluations collected at the end of each field trip. Students commented:

- Today I learned about things I never knew had so much history. It was all right here in front of my nose. I realized that it is hard to organize this type of experience, but not only was it educational but it was eye-opening. It gave me a chance to learn in a natural way.
- If man would take the time to look around at his changing world maybe he would appreciate it more. During this trip, I saw a lot of changes—the way I thought about the planet . . . If I can change and you can change, everybody can change. F = Fun/have more of it!

- People were nicer. I learned easier. We were in a very relaxed setting. I loved learning about the area.

Faculty stated:

- I learned that many students are much more motivated to learn when given a variety of options . . . I had a great time working on songs with students for our culminating experience! I taught poetry in minutes—rhyme scheme and meter. We manipulated language—it was fun!
- The trip was well planned. It was obvious that a great deal of time and effort was put forth toward organizing the lesson. I especially like to see everyone getting along so well, and there seemed to be something for everyone—both the artistic and the analytical were satisfied.
- I saw both individuals and groups examining things. I heard students and teachers asking all sorts of questions. I saw people take leadership roles while others were more passive independent learners. I saw kids thinking, writing, singing, talking—they were all learning.

Weeks later, as one student was preparing her portfolio for her English class, the subject of the Changes field trip surfaced as the student reflected upon her growth as a learner:

Change was the main idea of my interdisciplinary field trip. It was a way of teaching a combination of subjects such as science, English, and history. It was a fun way of learning. It was weird to find out about Orland Park millions of years ago. We dug for fossils at the quarry . . . we learned about Moraine Valley and how it got its name. We also learned about Indian poetry and writing. At the end of each site, we would record the weather, time, and the description of the site. This helped us keep a record of what we learned. The best part of all was the activity at the end of our field trip. It was neat that we got to choose the activity of our interest. From clay work to writing it was all an excellent way of learning. I wrote a narrative about a change that has occurred to me. We shared our pieces in my group and it was nice to hear the changes that occurred.

Is the day-long interdisciplinary field trip an end in itself? Not really. It is a small beginning, a catalyst for rethinking the way curriculum is delivered, an attempt to break down the walls that traditionally divide content-area teachers and prevent us from seeing obvious connections.

At the end of the academic year, the staff took a few moments to reflect on these experiences:

- I now see a larger opportunity to do cross-disciplinary curriculum. I started to do "period" field trips and "got my class back!" with these experiences.
- I "railroaded" some of my science colleagues into our last workshop on Changes—now they're caught.
- Is there some way to make this more permanent? Can we go back to allow kids some choices to explore on their own: meet again, make choices, and possibly get credit?
- The experiences we shared were terrific! The planning and authentic assessment were wonderful practice. Kids like and learn better in a warm, well-structured atmosphere.
- I was impressed with the richness that our diversity brings to curriculum and planning. I also was amazed at how well everyone worked together!

The future isn't defined for us. We are defining it for ourselves. We are teachers taking charge. Best of all, we are building a community of learners with our students. Who can ask for anything more? We must and will.

# CHAPTER 3
# Small Group Activities

THE PROGRESSIVE branch of today's school reform movement has always been guided and inspired by the work of John Dewey, who argued that schools could create community and support democracy. He emphasized the social aspects of learning and viewed schools as places where students could practice democracy and have opportunities to work together to identify and solve problems. He envisioned schools where students would bring democracy to life by making choices and working collaboratively to develop and carry out projects (Dewey [1938] 1963). Dewey emphasized the process as well as the content of education and believed that students would learn a great deal both about themselves and about the world by learning to work collaboratively with others.

It seems that much of the world is finally catching on to Dewey's ideas. In businesses and factories, workers who once toiled alone have been reorganized into teams, task forces, and "quality circles." Across the country, corporations are working to "flatten" their organizations, offering more input, participation, decision making, and ownership to once-silenced workers. Businesses are spinning off autonomous "boutique" micro-companies, where, freed from the hierarchical constraints of corporate culture as usual, small creative groups "think outside the box." While these nascent forms of capitalistic cooperation are obviously aimed more at the maximization of profit than at the perfecting of democracy, they also underscore one pragmatic and unromantic conclusion: small-group collaboration works.

Many American schools, on the other hand, still cling to the factory model of organization, with each "worker" harnessed to a solitary spot on the assembly line of education—a desk bolted to the floor. Students continue to do much of their work alone; indeed, consulting with others, in many school circumstances, is still considered to be cheating and can be severely punished. In many classrooms, learning is often limited to the memorization and practice of those ingredients called "the basic skills." Well, we guess if memorization is the goal, then asking others for help may indeed be cheating. But we set an abysmally low standard of education when we reduce reading, writing, math—even thinking itself—to "skills" used mainly to memorize and regurgitate facts.

The predominance of competition in America classrooms obviously reflects our school system's distasteful role as a socioeconomic screening mechanism, apportioning rewards and chances to selected students on questionable pretexts. There are some complex and ugly issues here that individual classroom teachers are unlikely to conquer or transform. But we can clearly see that putting kids in constant individual opposition is archaic and impractical. While there may be some benefits to matching yourself occasionally *against* others, individual conquest is not the only life skill. Indeed, the world keeps telling us that young people need much more experience working *with* groups of partners. Students already get plenty of dog-eat-dog contention in school; now they need more chances to work in small teams with common purposes—just like adults do every day, in their offices, law firms, gas stations, departments, insurance agencies, grocery stores, city councils, and ad agencies.

We think collaboration is here to stay in American business and in education. Working with others is not a passing fad that will soon be out of favor. Many adults, when asked to identify their most meaningful learning experiences in school, warmly remember working with friends to address difficult problems that would have been hard to solve on their own.

 **Marilyn:** As I look back over my very traditional education in the Chicago Public Schools, the only content that stands out in my mind are the few topics we were allowed to attack in groups. In eighth-grade math, which had very few highlights for me, we were put in groups of three, given an income, expenses, and income tax forms, and told to figure our taxes. Possibly, this experience is memorable because these kinds of semi-authentic activities were a rare burst of sunlight in my rather dreary schooling; here, we were asked to do something real and to work with others to accomplish it. This group activity enabled me to learn and understand this material deeply, to learn from and teach my classmates.

In order to understand the tax forms, compute the necessary figures, and complete the paperwork, we were forced to talk constantly to each other, clarifying concepts, asking questions, reviewing the directions, checking our reasoning, challenging each other's ideas. We had to externalize our thinking, get it out on the table. We had to explicitly talk through ideas that, if we were working alone, probably would have remained internal and implicit—and possibly, sloppy or unconsidered. Many heads really are better than one, and so is plenty of discussion better than solitary assumptions. To this day, I am the one person in my family who understands and figures out the taxes. This collaborative learning experience was one that actually prepared me for a life task and has been valuable to me throughout my life. ▲

When typical American grown-ups are asked to reach back into their past and think of something that they learned easily, in or out of school, they usually recall some kind of social-collaborative learning—a knitting circle, a basketball team, a book discussion group, a tennis club. They think of groups where they worked and practiced, where there was always someone to be coached by, where others were at different levels of proficiency, where diversity was an advantage rather than a liability, and where learners were cooperating rather than competing.

Adult citizens and business leaders aren't the only ones to recognize the value of cooperative activity. The recent educational standards reports issued by many of the subject-matter organizations have underscored the need for teamwork and cooperation in school. Most of these documents agree that the preoccupation with teaching isolated skills and information should be replaced with a concern for the child's thinking; the intellectual process and the particular ideas, conceptions, and meaning in the issues and materials addressed. Thinking is best taught when students wrestle with issues and problems that come out of and connect the disciplines. Reading, writing, and mathematics are tools that students use in order to fully experience the "thinking curriculum."

Since the thinking curriculum requires active participation in the learning process, teachers who value student thinking structure their classrooms to give students time to think, problems that are worthy of thinking about, and other students with whom to think (Hyde and Bizar 1989). Collaboration is the mainstay of these classrooms, where projects are often substituted for workbooks and worksheets and where questions and inquiry—rather than textbooks and rote learning—become the guideposts of learning.

More and more of what we might call "thinking schools" are popping up every day. In *Schools that Work* (1993), George Wood describes a number of the most promising schools and classrooms around the country—our most exciting, stimulating, and rigorous learning communities. According to Wood, these classrooms are easy to spot, and we all recognize them the moment we step inside. The walls are generally filled with varied examples of student art work and writing. Books and materials are everywhere, and students are working (often noisily) around the room. And one nearly universal feature is their frequent use of collaborative, task-oriented student groups, placing them at the heart of the learning process, not at the periphery.

In the schools that Wood singles out, "it's hard to find a room with desks lined up in straight rows, presided over by a lectern and a chalkboard full of notes. Instead, desks, or just as likely tables, are arranged in small groups throughout the room. There is a delightful sense of purposeful clutter to these classrooms and schools. They are places to do things in, not places to sit and watch" (xiii). Upon entering one of these classrooms, it is often hard to spot the teacher, who is usually working with one or another of the small groups, and children welcome visitors and are eager to guide them on a tour of the interesting projects in which students are engaged. The classrooms are decentralized and student-centered, which is to say that students' work, very often organized in the form of pairs and teams, partnerships and task forces, is the center of attention.

## Models of Collaboration

There are many structures for implementing cooperative, student-as-partners work in elementary and secondary schools. Some have been around American classrooms for ages, though used sparingly, while others have been devised only in the last few years. David and Roger Johnson have been the modern pioneers in this effort, offering particularly helpful structures, variations, rationales, and research findings. Whatever the vintage or source, however, all effective models of collaborative work have one thing in common: solid procedures for keeping groups productive. If a teacher is going to turn kids loose in several simultaneously-meeting groups, he by definition can not be managing and guiding everywhere at once, which means the group activities must have enough inherent structure to operate autonomously, to remain engaging, on-task, and relevant. Some of the simplest models are designed for pairs of students, while other, more complex structures help groups of three to five students work effectively together.

### Buddy Reading/Partner Reading: Primary students pair up and take turns reading aloud to each other, each holding a copy of the same story or article. Whether reading or listening, kids pay close attention to the

written text, and can question each other's readings. In a variation, an older child reads with a younger one, modeling more grown-up strategies.

**Lab Partners:** In any class that involves experimenting or making, teachers can put students in pairs and give them interlocking assignments that require joint observing, writing, reading, discussion, problem solving, or making. Though lab partners are already common in science classes, too often they are filling out convergent, right-answer lab workbooks rather than genuinely exploring and constructing meaning.

**Dialogue Journaling:** Pairs of students engage in written conversations about the content of the curriculum, which might be a book both are reading, a scientific process they are exploring, or a historical period under study. On a regular schedule, students write and exchange notes with one another (and occasionally the teacher), carrying on a discussion that might otherwise have been done orally. Written conversations can be held during class time, so that, contrary to an out-loud discussion where most people silently await a turn that never comes, everyone "talks" at once, in writing.

**Say Something:** Reading highly conceptual content-area text requires that students stop at various points in their reading to demand clarity, sort out confusion, and discuss ideas, issues, and/or vocabulary. In this strategy, students are invited to read with a partner, and agree on a place to stop reading and "Say Something." At this point, the partners take a few minutes to talk about what seems important, to make connections and predictions, and to react to ideas. "Say Something" helps students make sense out of difficult material and value their own thinking and insights.

**Peer Response and Editing Groups:** Ongoing groups of three to five students regularly meet and offer feedback, guidance, and advice to each other as fellow authors. Some peer writing groups meet regularly, while others gather only when convened by a member with a draft ready for response. Some jot comments and edits right on photocopies of class-mates' drafts; others stick to verbal feedback.

**Group Investigations:** Multiple student-research teams investigate different aspects of a larger topic, which can be either a student interest or a curriculum mandate. The process starts when the whole class discusses, responds to, and divides up a large topic, jigsawing the pieces out to smaller task groups for investigation. This model is a direct descendent of John Dewey, with an assist by Herbert Thelan (1967).

**Literature Circles:** In this school equivalent of adult book discussion groups, students choose their own books and discussion partners, set their own reading and meeting schedule, and find ways of sharing their readings with others. Students use structured note taking or journaling strategies to capture their responses as they read and to guide their discussions while they meet.

These models are formal, tried-and-true structures, each with its own history and professional literature. But there are countless other collaborative learning structures, informal home-grown ways that teachers put students together to learn. What these teachers have found (once they got used to the noise) is that students have a great deal to learn from each other. Collaboration can even turn the taking of a multiple choice test into a learning experience where students are able to debate the correct answer, support their answers to their peers, teach others what they know, and learn much about themselves as teachers and learners.

Once the power of peer collaboration is recognized, teachers want to harness it to all kinds of previously solitary activities. At the Best Practice High School in Chicago, one of the key features of our curriculum is a school-to-work internship program where each student goes to an apprenticeship one morning a week. Shelley Rosenstein-Freeman, the internship coordinator, has placed students in fifty-one different sites around the city, including museums, hospitals, community organizations, and schools. During the first year, some students attended their internships in groups, while others worked alone. We were powerfully struck by the difference. The kids' real-world job experiences were far more meaningful when they shared and processed the experience with classmates, on the bus coming and going, in dialogue journals, and back at their advisory groups. We were reminded that kids learn best when they have other people with whom to debrief and reflect upon the challenges they face together. We felt so strongly about the shared experience that we decided to make no future solo placements—everyone now has at least one fellow intern to think and talk with.

## Making Collaboration Work: Community and Structure

All these models of collaborative grouping, formal and informal, can work in a variety of classrooms, but each requires preparation, troubleshooting, and management. The activities grow faster and stronger in classrooms where community is already valued and nurtured, and they in turn contribute to the development of more interpersonal connections and closeness. Teachers who want to build their curriculum around small group experiences make certain that the process of collaboration is not left to chance. These teachers carefully grow classroom cultures that support cooperation, where students are powerfully encouraged and rewarded for helping each other to learn.

In a second-grade classroom in one of Chicago's toughest housing projects, teacher Angie Bynum has established an atmosphere where students understand that working together and helping each other is everyone's most important responsibility. Students' desks are arranged in sets of four, and these small groups work together in literature circles, in peer editing, and in all other work of the day. Ms. Bynum reminds students to go to each other when they are stumped. Her motto is "see three before me." She'll interrupt nearly any classroom activity to announce: "Everyone, I want you to give James a big hand, because he just helped Vivian finish her math project!"

Cooperation, not competition, is the glue that holds this classroom community together. The hand-built culture of respect permeates Ms. Bynum's classroom, enabling students to work and learn collaboratively. These seven-year-olds run their own thirty-minute book discussion groups every day (not to mention other group activities) with little or no direct supervision from Ms. Bynum. They constantly surprise visitors who assume that "these kids" can't handle the responsibility of working in autonomous small groups.

Cooperation also requires structure. Classrooms with effective subgroups are usually well-structured places where students follow carefully developed norms and routines, and where working together is not a disruptive departure but rather business as usual. The activities in which students engage are often authentic and include some form of demonstration of knowledge and competence. Students learn to depend on one another and, in addition to receiving grades and evaluating themselves, are often asked to reflect on how well their groups worked together.

At Addison Trails High School in Addison, Illinois, the culminating activity for an interdisciplinary course that combined English, Social Studies, and Biology was an Education Fair. Groups of freshmen demonstrated their knowledge in student projects set up around the gym; the projects dealt with the rainforest, the effects of drugs, recycling, the Vietnam war and many other real-world topics. Students, parents, and judges were invited to ask each of the presenters questions and listen to their presentations. In this exciting (and noisy) setting, it was obvious to see how much could be accomplished by students when they work together. Student teams had conducted interviews, performed experiments, gathered data, developed videotapes, written reports, and built exhibits to demonstrate their expertise. The gym was filled with the exciting products of learning. In this room, the power of collaboration was palpable.

We think John Dewey was right. Students do need to work and think together, because well-structured collaborative experiences help young people to learn deeply, to really understand, to share knowledge, to ask important questions, and in some cases to take action. If we believe that learning is thinking, then students need to have rich experiences, interesting questions to pursue, large blocks of time in which to pursue them, and others with whom to think.

In this chapter, six teachers show how they provide just such collaborative experiences for their students. In the first of two Variations, Steve Wolk describes an extended team research project that began with some mathematics content, but quickly invited his middle schoolers to reach out across the curriculum. Then, Dagny Bloland recounts a unit that not only immersed teams of eighth graders in different historic schools of architecture, but also spoke to multiple intelligences, generated an original musical play, and even satisfied a new state-mandated fine arts requirement.

Next come three Step by Step stories. The first is an excerpt adapted from Harvey Daniels' book *Literature Circles: Voice and Choice in the Student-Centered Classroom* (1994). Literature circles are small, student-led book discussion groups that meet regularly in the classroom, modeled on the book clubs that many adult readers attend in libraries and living rooms. Taking collaboration Step by Step, Diana Jones, Kelly Naperschat, and Lois Wisniewski tell of their ambitious multiage, cross-school science unit, in which older students coached groups of younger ones through a series of experiential stations. Finally, Harvey Daniels shows how centers or learning stations fit into the larger picture of small group activities, both as a structural alternative to whole-class teaching and as a way of grouping clusters of kids around particular materials or experiences.

# Further Reading

Cohen, Elizabeth. 1986. *Designing Groupwork: Strategies for the Heterogeneous Classroom*. New York: Teachers College Press.

Daniels, Harvey. 1994. *Literature Circles: Voice and Choice in the Student-Centered Classroom.* York, ME: Stenhouse.

Girard, Suzanne, and Kathlene Willing. 1996. *Partnerships for Classroom Learning: From Reading Buddies to Pen Pals to the Community and the World Beyond.* Portsmouth, NH: Heinemann.

Glasser, William. 1986. *Control Theory in the Classroom.* New York: Harper & Row.

Hill, Bonnie Campbell, and Nancy Johnson. 1995. *Literature Circles and Response.* Norwood, MA: Christopher-Gordon.

Hill, Susan, and Tim Hill. 1990. *The Collaborative Classroom: A Guide to Co-operative Learning.* Portsmouth, NH: Heinemann.

Johnson, David, Roger Johnson, Edythe Holubec, and Patricia Roy. 1991. *Co-operation in the Classroom.* Edina, MN: Interaction Book Company.

Samway, Katharine Davies, and Gail Whang. 1995. *Literature Study Circles in a Multicultural Classroom.* York, ME: Stenhouse.

Samway, Katharine, Gail Whang, and Mary Pippitt. 1995. *Buddy Reading: Cross-Age Tutoring in a Multicultural School.* Portsmouth, NH: Heinemann.

Sharan, Yael, and Shlomo Sharan. 1992. *Expanding Cooperative Learning Through Group Investigation.* New York: Teachers College Press.

Spear, Karen. 1987. *Sharing Writing: Peer Response Groups in the English Class.* Portsmouth, NH: Boynton/Cook.

# Variations

## Student Survey Teams: Asking Questions, Seeking Solutions

STEVEN WOLK

About a month ago, near the end of summer, I received a letter from Elizabeth, a seventh-grade student who had been in my class last year. Here is part of her letter, reproduced with her permission:

> Before I came to Burley [School] I really didn't care about what happened in the world. Nobody ever taught me how important it was to know what happened around me. That way I would know how I would be safe and how I wouldn't. I never really knew. But you taught me that we should know how much violence and racism and poverty is going on and destroying our world, and especially our future. At my old school my teacher would never ask me how I

felt about these situations. You did. You actually made me think about them.

I do not include Elizabeth's wonderful words as a boost to my ego, but rather as the sweetest form of authentic assessment a teacher could ever ask for. This article is about one of the projects that our classroom community of seventh graders undertook last year and that contributed to Elizabeth's (and, I believe, the rest of the class') thinking about social issues like racism, violence, and poverty, among many others. For lack of a better title, I call the project "Social Issue Surveys." The basic idea is to have the class form small groups, choose a social issue that interests them, write a survey about it, give their survey to a selected population, analyze the survey responses, and then communicate their results in some form of visual presentation, usually a graph. Although you could say that this is a math project, you will see that the project was multidisciplinary, or what James Beane (1993a) calls "integrative." I also need to emphasize that the ideas and the content presented in this article may appear to apply mainly to older kids, but I consider them to be important and possible for all students—even, as famed kindergarten teacher Vivian Gussin Paley (1992) shows, for five year-olds. Before we get to the specific project, however, a little background information is necessary.

Throughout my teaching career I have called our classrooms democratic. That's because they are not my classrooms, but rather a physical space, a wide variety of experiences, and a curriculum that is owned and created by all of us, teacher and students together as a community of learners. A democratic classroom, however, is not just about the methods of our learning. It is not just about the underlying concepts of teaching and learning—such as constructivism, developmentalism, collaborative learning, and learning in a social context—that direct my thinking as a teacher and that establish the philosophy of our classroom environment. To me, a democratic classroom is equally about the content—or the knowledge—that children have access to and the knowledge that is made an important part of our classroom experience. The knowledge that Elizabeth wrote about in her letter has its roots in critical theory (Freire [1970] 1993; Giroux 1983; McLaren 1994) and the sociology of knowledge (Berger and Luckman 1967; Bowers 1984), and can lead to what many call "critical literacy."

Critical literacy means helping children to see the power, the politics, the ideology, and the interests in knowledge, language, and images; it means helping children to be critical readers of text, of society, and of "reality" itself; it means nurturing in children skeptical and questioning habits of mind; it means empowering children to take a lifelong role in what is supposed to be a participatory democracy; it means helping children see that racism, sexism, xenophobia, economics, violence, environmental issues, and politics all effect our lives on a daily basis; and possibly more than anything else, critical literacy continues the vision of John Dewey by promoting the conscious effort to transform our society and our world and to make it better, more humane, more just, and more caring. Critical literacy and transformative pedagogy is a way to realize the hopes and the ideals of a democracy. Patrick Shannon (1995) writes:

> A [critical] question-centered approach to education breeds active learners. But to participate actively in civic life, we must become more than active learners. We must approach the social world as a created, transformable reality that was put in place and is maintained according to human interests. If the social world is a human artifact, then it is changeable through the acts of other human beings. This concept is not too abstract for children to comprehend. (108–109)

It is fair to say that Shannon's notion of a "question-centered" approach to schooling is a way of life in our classroom. I believe there are far more questions in life than "answers," so I want to nurture in my students the idea of living a life asking questions and seeking solutions.

It is important to emphasize that the freedom to think for oneself and to share thoughts and knowledge within a critical perspective is not only absent from most classrooms, but actually proscribed by strict, predetermined curriculums designed and written by people who have nothing to do with schools. Such curriculums prescribe "teacher-proof" programmatic materials like textbooks and workbooks, and, as Linda McNeil (1988) has shown, underscore the primary emphasis of school: to maintain order and control. Through our Social Issue Survey project, I hoped to bring "forbidden" issues into our classroom and to empower my students to become agents of change, to live their lives in ways that help make our world a better place for everyone.

# Writing and Giving the Surveys

The class first broke into nine self-selected groups of three. After a day or two of group discussion, each of the nine groups had their topic: racism, poverty, the O. J. Simpson trial, women in the armed forces, television, gun control, illegal drugs, freedom of speech, and prejudice. In hindsight, we had too many groups. It wasn't easy finding nine different populations to give the surveys to, so we ended up giving several surveys to the same populations. When I do this project again, I'll either increase the group size to four or five, (making five or six groups) or, even better, take the kids outside of school and into the community to find enough populations. Last year, the surveys were given to various classes in our school and to the teachers. When I did the project in a previous year, one group sent their surveys home with students for parents to complete.

In order to write a survey, we first had to look at some surveys, then talk about what a survey is, decide how to create one and what demographic information to ask for, and discuss the issue of anonymity. Some of this information was communicated through mini-lessons—ten-minute presentations I make to the entire class. However, much of this information was either taught or expanded while we did our work. This is a critically important point. Most of our class time is not spent listening to me teach about survey writing and graphing so that students can then go home and write a survey and make their graphs. Rather, the vast majority of our time together is spent learning by doing and learning through spontaneous interaction as a natural part of a highly social classroom environment.

We spent time looking at the difference between open-ended and closed-ended questions, and the strengths and weaknesses of both. There's an enormous difference between asking someone, "Were you ever the victim of prejudice?" and asking someone to "Write about a time you were the victim of prejudice." The surveys took a good deal of time—about two weeks—to draft, revise, edit, and type. It's important for children to learn that creating something of quality takes time, and if we don't practice this in school we're tacitly teaching the exact opposite. Some groups even did research to write their survey. For example, Jaime, Adam, and John wrote a survey on poverty. In order to help them get a better understanding of the issue, I showed them statistics for poverty in an almanac, some of which became a part of their survey (see Figure 3.1). Maria, Javier, and Jose had to research the Constitution for their survey on gun control, as did Nick, A. J., and Pablo for their survey on freedom of speech.

At various times throughout the project we discussed and did journal writing on related topics. We asked critical questions and searched within ourselves for possible answers. Where do our opinions and beliefs come from? Who and what shapes our opinions? (We came up with our family and friends, the media, movies, music, businesses and corporations, religion, and advertising.) How and why do we change our opinions?

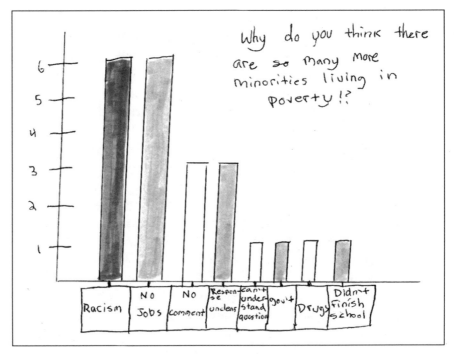

**Figure 3.1** One team's bar graph depicting answers to a survey question.

And, would it be a good thing if we all had the same opinions? This final question was of particular interest. Many of the kids thought that it would be good if we all had the same opinions—as long as the opinions we had were their opinions!

## Analyzing the Surveys and Communicating the Results

Just as writing the surveys took time, so did analyzing them. After a few mini-lessons on mathematical computations (such as turning fractions into decimals), different types of graphs, and using a calculator, the students worked together in their groups performing the necessary computations for the four questions of their choice (two open-ended and two closed-ended) that I required each group to analyze. Once again, most of my "teaching" of these math concepts and skills was done in one-on-one or group conferences while everyone was scattered all over the room doing their work. There are two reasons why I keep whole-class instruction to an absolute minimum: first, research and my own experience as a student confirm that listening to a teacher lecture is one of the least successful ways to learn; second, all of the students are at a different developmental place in math, so it only makes good sense to individualize teaching and learning through short conferences. That way I can help students with exactly what they need most. Also, as a true community of learners, I'm not the only teacher in our classroom. The students can teach each other.

One of the most critical issues raised by this project is the subjectivity of surveys and knowledge in general. When we read about a survey in the newspaper or hear about one on television, it so often has the appearance of truth and objectivity. Actually, it is anything but. Not only are the responses of surveys open to interpretation, but the original selection of questions, the selection of the respondents, and the form the survey takes all bias the results. Note that the results are filtered through and delivered to us from yet another source, such as a newspaper that gave its own interpretation. In analyzing their surveys, students had to talk in their groups and make conscious decisions regarding their interpretations of their population's responses. This was especially difficult with the open-ended questions. When responding in a narrative format, people using different language may mean the same thing or using the same language, may mean different things. Or people may use language that's just plain unclear. Throughout the process I tried to help the kids see how subjective this knowledge is and understand the power survey creators have in bringing "knowledge" to our society that is so often falsely (and subconsciously) accepted as being as truth.

If we had the time, I would have had each group complete a written analysis of their survey, possibly from a demographic perspective. Since all of the surveys asked the respondents their age and gender, it would have been interesting to look at possible patterns of responses. Some of these patterns were obvious and came up in formal and informal discussions. For example, Elizabeth, Pedro, and Andro, who did their survey on women in the armed forces, asked the question "Do you think women should be included in combat?" and did two graphs comparing the responses of males and females. While only 42 percent of the males responded "yes," 100 percent of the females responded "yes." Comparisons like these led to lively, and at times heated, discussions and brought up yet another important point: the danger of drawing conclusions too quickly, overgeneralizing, or stereotyping.

Before any final graphs were done on poster board, a draft copy had to be completed and edited on paper. Once the poster board visuals were finished, each group made a short presentation to the class, explaining them. From beginning to end, the project took about five weeks.

# Turning Our Surveys on Ourselves

As a final step in our project, I selected one open-ended question from each survey, typed them on a sheet, handed out copies, and had everyone choose one question and write their response in their journal. I wrote too. Once finished, we sat in a circle on the floor, and those who wanted to, read aloud what they wrote for open discussion. Andro chose to respond to "If you have ever been a victim of prejudice, write about it":

> I have been a victim of prejudice many times. For example, I was at [a] school playing basketball with an African American kid and then more African American kids came and started calling me "porkchop" because they noticed I was Hispanic. I don't know how they found out. A lot of people don't think I'm Hispanic. But anyway, they started telling me to get off the court because they were going to play basketball. So I did. I was walking out toward the gate and they threw the basketball right at my back, and started laughing, calling me "spic." When I went home I did not tell my mom anything because I thought she would make a big fight about it. And anyway, I didn't want anything to happen to me or anyone.

# Toward Meaningful, Integrative, Critical Learning

Was this really a "math" project? It would be difficult for me to say that it was. We certainly spent a lot of time doing math. But we also spent a lot of time discussing and writing about a wide variety of issues affecting our society, which would place the project in social studies (as would the constitutional implications of issues like gun control, freedom of speech, and women in the armed forces). We also did a lot of writing, including drafting, revising, and editing the surveys, as well as journal writing, which would place the project within the scope of writing. The project involved reading, talking, listening, analyzing language, and a host of other activities and ideas that come about as a natural result of spontaneous self-directed learning in a social context. The answer here should be obvious: this project wasn't really a "math" project at all, but rather a life lesson, where we were presented with a constant stream of overlapping ways to think about and make sense of knowledge and the world.

Aside from that, the real strength of the project was in what Elizabeth wrote. The project helped raise her consciousness of the world. It tacitly communicated to her that these concepts are valuable and that they're just as important to learn and think about as are reading, writing, math, and science. Hopefully Elizabeth will apply these ideas to her own life and will become a critical and informed thinker, asking questions, seeking solutions and, in the words of Maxine Greene (1988), searching for possibilities of what "could be."

# Studying Architecture Collaboratively: A Cognitive, Affective, and Kinesthetic Experience

DAGNY D. BLOLAND

Early one morning last September, I was looking out the window of my classroom and thinking about my struggle to integrate fine arts into our fully packed, gifted-track curriculum. Then I realized that a solution was literally right in front of me. Whitney Young Magnet School is located across the street from the Jackson Boulevard Historic District, a beautiful, block-long stretch of Italianate townhouses that have been lovingly maintained and sensitively restored. They are shaded by mature trees and fronted by pretty gardens fenced with wrought iron. Looking at this lovely prospect, it occurred to me that the solution to the fine arts mandate was a unit on the history of architecture. We could use the Jackson Boulevard Historic District as an example of one style of architecture and study it as part of what was to be a very ambitious project: a three-week unit on the history of architecture from Egypt to the present.

It took two months to develop the unit fully, but some elements of it were clear from the beginning: My first personal goal, beyond those of the state mandates, was that the students would enjoy the project. I wanted them to become aware of buildings as created objects, to think about the people who built them and who lived in them, and to take pride in the city of Chicago as a living museum of great architecture. My second goal was to make it a hands-on unit. The students would have to construct and create as well as study, so that they could experience architecture cognitively, affectively, aesthetically, and kinesthetically.

Whitney Young's principal, Mr. Powhatan Collins, offered his enthusiastic support for the project. After I spoke to him, my first stop was the Chicago Architecture Foundation's Archicenter, an incredible resource for field-trip docents, three-dimensional kits, and books. Academic Center Program Director Roger Prietz generously helped me find a source for three-dimensional architecture puzzles as well as for the $400 it took to pay for all the materials. Our curriculum coordinator, Mrs. Paula Herron, provided the invaluable suggestion that the students could create a fabric hanging incorporating the styles of architecture they were studying. Ms. Theresa Yanek, our fashion design teacher, donated the fabric and the space in her classroom to assemble the hanging. Then, quickly recognizing my complete lack of aptitude at sewing, she very kindly offered to sew the pieces together during her lunch period. Our school library/media center contributed resources as well. I identified ten styles of architecture for study: Egyptian, Greek and Roman, Islamic, Gothic, medieval domestic, Renaissance, Federalist and Georgian, Victorian, Italianate, and modern. I regreted the heavy emphasis on European architecture, but I needed to work with styles for which resource materials and three-dimensional models were readily available.

With all of these components in place and our guest speakers and field-trip chaperons arranged, my students and I began our architectural odyssey in the middle of November. There are one hundred eighth graders in our program, divided among my four language arts classes. I split my smallest class among the others to create three architecture groups, named the Burnham, Sullivan, and Wright groups. Within each group were ten design teams of three to four students each, with each team studying one of the ten styles of architecture I had identified. Several days before the unit began, I surveyed the students briefly to see if anyone had a favorite style of architecture he or she wanted to study. Very few students expressed any preference at all; they simply did not have the background information to make a choice on what was for most a somewhat arcane subject. Students who expressed a strong preference were given their chosen style to work on; the others were simply assigned into design teams based on my desire to create a productive mix.

On Monday, Tuesday, and Wednesday of the first week of this three-week unit, the students met in design teams during language arts with the assignment of becoming experts on the style of architecture I had given them. Each design team was asked to prepare an oral report for the end of the unit and to design a fabric square showing a two-dimensional model of a building done in their architectural style. It was an unusually industrious time. I had explained the state's fine arts mandate to them and told them that we had sincerely tried to find the most interesting possible way to fulfill it. They enjoyed reading the richly illustrated architecture books from our library and from the Archicenter, and they loved working in small groups on a communal, concrete product that would be displayed prominently in one of the halls of our school.

Next came the day-and-a-half-long field trip, during which the three groups experienced: (1) a guest lecture from a husband-and-wife team of architects who were the parents of one of our students; (2) a slide show history of Chicago; (3) a walking tour of the Jackson Boulevard Historic District, led by a Chicago Architecture Foundation docent; (4) a tour of Hull House, a social service agency founded by Jane Addams, to show the students the social conditions of the school's neighborhood during the 1880s and to let them see the interior of a Victorian home; and (5) a half-day marathon model-building session in which design teams built small models in their chosen architectural style, either from Archicenter kits or from three-dimensional puzzles.

The following week, which included Thanksgiving, was devoted to other activities. During that week, each student had the following written assignment: "Imagine that you are living in the Jackson Boulevard neighborhood sometime in the latter half of the nineteenth century. In a short introductory paragraph, identify a year and an architectural style for the building you are occupying. Tell whether you and your family are rich or poor, what the wage earner(s) does or do for a living, and whether you have servants or are a servant. Using graph paper, design a floor plan for the place where you live. Include the kitchen and every other room your living space would have. Attach your floor plan to your composition. Now write a two- or three-page diary entry telling what you did on an ordinary day. Include details you learned about how people lived. Make it concrete, specific, and real."

During the last week of the unit, the design teams finished their fabric squares for final assembly and presented their oral reports. As part of the evaluation, I asked each team to sketch a building in the style they had studied, and I constructed a simple matching test, listing the styles and their sketches. Out of one hundred students, only one student confused two items. Everyone else got everything right. Of course, I don't imagine that my students will always remember the specific characteristics of all the building styles, but I would be delighted if some could recall the major outlines of the style they had studied most intensively.

The important part of this unit for me is the idea that architecture is now a part of their felt experience. The next time they encounter architecture as an idea, they will have a schema in which to put the information. Even if they never study the subject formally again, I like to think that one student's final written comment may speak for others. "I never used to look at buildings," she wrote. "They were just things to walk in and out of. Now when I walk into a building I ask myself what patterns I see, and what the architect was thinking. Buildings are real for me now." That was just what I was hoping to hear.

# Step by Step
## Preparing Students for Literature Circles

HARVEY DANIELS

Every day, in classrooms all across America, most students meet in some kind of small groups to work on reading. Among these groups are found a wide variety of structures, ranging from traditional teacher-dominated, round-robin reading all the way to genuinely collaborative, student-led book discussion groups called literature circles. Unfortunately, the growing popularity of literature circles (or book clubs, or readers' groups) has led, in a few places, to the superficial renaming of old-style skill-oriented basal reading groups as literature circles. While this kind of "word magic" is not unusual in education, it does cloud the picture for dedicated teachers who are trying to deeply understand and fully implement the real thing. "Literature circles" is not just a trendy label for *any* kind of small group reading lesson—it stands for a sophisticated fusion of collaborative learning with independent reading, in the framework of reader-response theory.

So what makes a genuine literature circle? What are the distinctive features of this special structure? While some of the defining ingredients of literature circles may be intentionally omitted when students are first learning the activity or when the group is applying lit circles to some mandated curriculum, authentic and mature literature circles will manifest most or all of these key features:

1. Students *choose* their own reading materials.
2. *Small temporary groups* are formed, based upon book choice.
3. Different groups read *different books*.
4. Groups meet on a *regular, predictable schedule* to discuss their reading.
5. Kids use writing or drawn *notes* to guide both their reading and discussion.
6. Discussion *topics come from the students*.
7. Group meetings aim to be *open, natural conversations about books,* so personal connections, digressions, and open-ended questions are welcome.
8. In newly forming groups, students play a rotating assortment of task *roles*.
9. The teacher serves as a *facilitator,* not a group member or instructor.

**Figure 3.2** Marianne Flanagan's students at Chicago's Metcalfe School meet regularly in literature circles.

10. Evaluation is by *teacher observation and student self-evaluation.*
11. A spirit of *playfulness and fun* pervades the room.
12. When books are finished, *readers share with their classmates,* and then *new groups form* around new reading choices.

Obviously, many of these features are different from—even contrary to—the usual reading lessons in school. So the question arises, how can teachers prepare students to join in this welcoming, student-centered, but very different kind of activity? Students who are already veterans of other collaborative group activities or who are accustomed to open-ended book discussions may be able to jump right into lit circles with little formal preparation. But for those who need more background, teachers may want to invest a couple of weeks in showing students how to successfully run their own book groups.

To find a model of such careful and thorough training in literature circles, we could do no better than follow Barbara Dress into a classroom. Barbara is a former teacher and reading consultant for District 15 in Palatine, Illinois. She recently took early retirement so that she could consult on lit circles with teachers in Chicago and suburban schools. With Sandy King's third graders at Marion Jordan School, Barbara worked for two weeks, about forty-five minutes a day. Sandy's kids were in great shape to start literature circles—their reading and language arts program is rich and literature based. Sandy reads aloud to kids daily, they have an active writing workshop, and the kids think of themselves as real authors. With Sandy and me observing and helping occasionally, here's what Barbara did.

**Day 1:** Barbara greets the kids, who are wearing name tags to facilitate her quickly learning their names. Graciously, she asks if anyone has ever heard of "literature circles." No one has any actual experience, but this doesn't stop third graders from speculating on the definition. Barbara welcomes everything and jots key words on the overhead. She then incorporates kids' ideas and language into an overview of the activity.

She tells the kids that they will be working for two weeks on this project, taking one step at a time. She also tells them they will be reading several great stories this week and a good book next week. The rest of this session is given to the story "The Flying Patchwork Quilt" by Barbara Brenner. Barbara gives each child a photocopy, and then she reads it out loud, slowly and dramatically, stopping a couple of times to invite kids' predictions and clarifications. When she's done, she invites students' comments and responses, and a lively whole-class discussion ensues. Barbara has done her job for this day, which was simply to get acquainted, build some trust, share a good story, and model for the kids the delight of rich discussion topics.

**Day 2:** Today, and for each of the next few days, Barbara will be introducing students to one of four discussion jobs outlined on "role sheets" (reproduced on pages 81–84). These roles are used as a temporary support device to help kids set purposes for their reading, to make sure they capture their responses as they read, and to guarantee that they will have plenty to talk about when their groups meet. After this training period, Sandy's students will transition into open-ended reading logs, where they jot down all kinds of responses to their reading, and bringing these notes to their discussion groups.

Today, Barbara also wants to help kids learn the role of *discussion director*, as she's adapted it specially for this class. Before handing out that role sheet, she talks to kids about open-ended questions. Referring to the story from yesterday, she asks kids to remember or think of some possible questions about the story. As kids offer suggestions, Barbara makes a distinction between "fat" and "skinny" questions. Skinny ones can be answered in a word or two, she explains, leaving nothing more to say. "Fat" questions, on the other hand, you can say lots and lots about. There aren't necessarily right answers to these questions, Barbara says, and everyone can have different things to say about a *really* fat question.

Now she gives out copies of the discussion director (DD) role sheet and another photocopied short story. She invites kids to read the story, think of two or three really "fat" questions about it, and jot them on their role sheet. This time, kids can read the story several different ways. Mrs. King is reading it aloud in one corner, so those who want (or need) to have the story read to them can go there. Alternately, groups can pick one of their own members to read it to the others, and one group elects this option. Other kids read silently. A couple of partners sit on the floor reading alternate pages to each other. As kids begin to finish, Barbara reminds them to jot some fat questions on their DD sheets.

Next, kids go into their groups and meet for ten minutes or so, sharing and discussing their fat questions. Barbara, Sandy, and I circulate, available to help, but not really needed. The kids have plenty to say. For the last few minutes, we gather as a whole group again and Barbara takes sample questions from each group. As always, she skillfully praises and shapes, making sure kids understand what kinds of questions a good discussion director brings to a group.

**Day 3:** Today, Barbara teaches kids the role of *passage master.* Using a third story, she follows the same pattern as yesterday, first explaining the basic idea of the role, and then helping kids brainstorm good examples. One important skill for passage masters (and word wizards, coming up tomorrow) is being able to locate things quickly in the text, so Barbara spends a good deal of time showing kids how to mark on their role sheet the page and paragraph of passages they want to share.

Now, the kids read a story as passage masters. When they're done, they meet in their same homogeneous, four-member groups to try out the role. There's plenty of noise, of course, as kids read aloud their favorite sections. When they finish meeting, volunteers from different groups share examples of what passages they picked and tell why. There is further discussion about the problem of locating their passages. Tomorrow's session will provide more practice on this. Again, Barbara gently and subtly shapes kids' responses, reinforcing contributions that genuinely fulfill the passage master role.

**Day 4:** Today, Barbara teaches kids the role of *word wizard.* She follows the same pattern, first explaining the role, then helping kids practice it by thinking of noteworthy words from yesterday's story. Finally, she sets them to reading another new story with the WW sheet in hand. When they're done, the kids meet in their groups and try out the role. When they finish, Barbara asks volunteers from different groups to share examples of the words they focused on.

**Day 5:** Today, Barbara teaches kids the fourth (and most popular!) role in this set: the *artful artist*. She talks about responding to the reading with a picture instead of with words, and gets kids talking about the importance of the illustrations in favorite books. She stresses that whatever pictures they chose to draw as illustrators do not have to depict actual events or scenes in the story, but can represent personal thoughts, feelings, or connections—even abstractions or designs. Then she goes over the official artful artist role sheet, gives kids one last story to read, and they go to work. Because of kids' pride and care in their artwork, this role sheet takes a little longer than the others to prepare, and Barbara has to work to get them back to their groups. Gradually, kids return to their same-role groups and take turns sharing their graphic responses to the reading. When they are done, Barbara asks volunteers from different groups to show examples of their illustrations. Barbara asks kids to tell what conversations sprung up around the pictures, so they get the message that the drawings are to extend the discussion, not just for decoration.

**Days 6–10:** Now it's time to put the literature circles together. So this week Ms. King's third graders will read a whole novel, meeting daily in their groups—the same four-member groups that trained together, role by role, last week. The book, selected by Barbara for its wide appeal, is *The Chocolate Touch* by Patrick Catling. A takeoff on the King Midas tale, this is a genuinely funny story about a young boy who suddenly develops . . . well, the title gives it away.

Each day's session is divided into two roughly twenty-minute parts: reading time and group meetings. During the reading time, kids are free to read the assigned chapters (about fifteen big-type pages per day), work on their role sheets, or (if they have already finished both, which is rare) read something else. Kids who are slower readers need all the reading time they can get; some are doing part of the reading at home, a few with help from a parent or sibling. All kids have to budget their time so that they will be ready to play their assigned role.

When groups meet, Barbara and Sandy circulate to observe, assist, and help solve problems. Since it is a good, involving book, kids have plenty to say, and the discussions go well. The kids discuss about one-fifth of the book each day, and on Friday, there is a general whole-class conversation when everyone reflects back over the two-week learning process. The kids are pleased and proud of themselves, and a bit sad to say goodbye to this dynamic white-haired lady who has brought such a special treat into their classroom each morning.

Barbara, who is an inveterate educational tinkerer, is already talking about all the things she will change the *next* time she models literature circles in a classroom. She's thinking maybe she should introduce the artist role first, since it is the kids' favorite, and it helps the students who aren't fluent writers to enter their group on an equal footing. But for Ms. King's kids, the job is well done. They "get it." They understand the system, and—most important—they love it.

Mrs. King is impressed, too. As the year goes on, she uses literature circles steadily, as a regular and recurrent part of her classroom schedule. Since the training period is now over, kids pick their own books and move among constantly reforming groups, and much less teacher intervention is needed. The role sheets Barbara used at the beginning of the year have long since been abandoned in favor of open-ended reading logs, in which students store their ideas, questions, reactions, doodles, and connections for upcoming lit circle meetings. A few months later, Sandy looks back and writes: "There is a lot of discussion going on and kids love the freedom they have to choose. The kids are more accountable for what they read, they know what to look for while they read (they monitor their comprehension, so to speak), and they really enjoy it!"

## DISCUSSION DIRECTOR

Name _____

Group _____

Book _____

Assignment p _____ –p _____

You are the **Discussion Director.** Your job is to write down some good questions that you think your group would want to talk about.

1. _____

_____

_____

2. _____

_____

_____

3. Why . . .

4. How . . .

5. If . . .

## PASSAGE MASTER

Name _____

Group _____

Book _____

Assignment p _____ –p _____

You are the **Passage Master.** Your job is to pick parts of the story that you want to read aloud to your group. These can be:

—a good part          —an interesting part
—a funny part         —some good writing
—a scary part         —a good description

Be sure to mark the parts you want to share with a Post-it note or bookmark. Or you can write on this sheet the parts you want to share.

### Parts to read out loud:

| Page | Paragraph | Why I liked it |
| --- | --- | --- |
| ____ | _____ | _____ |
| ____ | _____ | _____ |
| ____ | _____ | _____ |
| ____ | _____ | _____ |
| ____ | _____ | _____ |

## WORD WIZARD

**Name** _____

**Group** _____

**Book** _____

**Assignment p** _____ **–p** _____

You are the **Word Wizard**. Your job is to look for special words in the story. Words that are:

—new  —strange  —interesting  —hard
—different  —funny  —important

When you find a word that you want to talk about, mark it with a Post-it note or write it down here.

| Word | Page | Why I picked it |
|------|------|-----------------|
| _____ | ____ | _____ |
| | | _____ |
| _____ | ____ | _____ |
| | | _____ |
| _____ | ____ | _____ |
| | | _____ |
| _____ | ____ | _____ |
| | | _____ |
| _____ | ____ | _____ |

When your group meets, help your friends talk about the words you have chosen. Things you can discuss:

How does this word fit in the story?
Does anyone know what this word means?
Shall we look it up in the dictionary?
What does this word make you feel like?
Can you draw the word?

From *Methods that Matter: Six Structures for Best Practice Classrooms* by Harvey Daniels and Marilyn Bizar. Stenhouse Publishers, York, ME.

## ARTFUL ARTIST

Name _____

Group _____

Book _____

Assignment p _____ –p _____

You are the **Artful Artist.** Your job is to draw anything about the story that you liked:

—a character
—the setting
—a problem
—an exciting part
—a surprise
—a prediction of what will happen next
—anything else

Draw on the back of this page or on a bigger piece of paper if you need it. Do any kind of drawing or picture you like.

When your group meets, don't tell what your drawing is. Let them guess and talk about it first. Then you can tell about it.

From *Methods that Matter: Six Structures for Best Practice Classrooms* by Harvey Daniels and Marilyn Bizar. Stenhouse Publishers, York, ME.

# Strengthening Muscle Knowledge Through Peer Interaction

DIANA JONES, KELLY NAPERSCHAT, AND
LOIS WISNIEWSKI

> I had fun learning about muscles with you. It is hard learning those scientific names for those muscles. Now I can almost talk to my 10th grade brother at his level. I liked being in the newspaper. I am kind of a class celebrity. Thanks.

Learning for a lifetime! That's everyone's goal. But what specific techniques can teachers use to help students learn material for more than just a class period? We have found that student mentoring coupled with the integration of course content through an interdisciplinary project makes learning not only enjoyable but relevant. Our students in McLean County District 5 joined in an interdisciplinary activity that paired biology freshmen with fifth- and sixth-grade students. The primary objective of the two and one-half hour "mini-field trip" was to learn the names of selected muscles, how muscles work, how muscles are attached to bones, and how muscles become fatigued.

Each freshman was responsible for a specific younger student. They were to assist this student throughout the entire time that the elementary students visited the high school. Elementary students arrived at 9:00 A.M. ready to meet their peer teachers. Students were divided into four separate groups (twenty-four per group) and spent twenty-five minutes in each center with a five-minute passing period. While at each station, the younger students, assisted by their high school peer teacher, participated in different activities that enhanced their knowledge and understanding of muscles and muscle action.

# The Muscle Centers

**The Gymnasium:** Freshman biology students prepared exercise routines using music and Dyna-bands (elastic bands approximately one meter in length). Prior to teaching them to the younger students, they had an opportunity to practice their routines in front of their peers earlier in the week. All students were given a Dyna-band to work through the exercise movement with the group leader so they could feel the muscles being worked through exercise. Freshmen then presented the exercises to the younger students and showed the muscles that each exercise would work. Once the individual exercises were learned, the students completed their three-to-four-minute routines to music like "YMCA," "Twist and Shout," "Drive My Car," "Pump Up the Jam," and "Get Ready for This" High school students worked in groups of four developing their routines. Three groups presented their routines during each twenty-five-minute period.

### The Weight Room:
High school students had been taught the correct procedures for utilizing the universal weight equipment available at the school. They were also given an opportunity to learn which muscles are used when lifting small hand weights (free weights were off-limits). When the younger students were taken to this station, they had an opportunity to utilize the equipment to learn the muscles responsible for a particular action. Students were given a weight room report sheet with the various exercises listed so that they could write down how many lifts they could achieve with a given machine. "My favorite station was the weights. I like working with all those machines. Before the trip I'd never seen those kinds of machines before! I loved that station even though I couldn't lift some of the machines, that's because I'm kind of a wimp."

### The Laboratory:
"Thank you for showing me all the cool stuff there. The best thing there I thought was the dissected frog." The science classroom was set up with a survey-style laboratory experience. Students could circulate through each station in their own time frame. Students were informed that preserved specimens were located in several areas, and that if they were uncomfortable they could bypass the activities at that station.

> Station 1: Students could draw and look at smooth, skeletal, and cardiac muscles that were displayed under the microscopes.
> Station 2: The muscles of the lower leg of a frog were exposed. Students were given an opportunity to discover the movement of a limb in relationship to the shortening of a muscle. Specifically, students looked at the origin, insertion, and action of the gastrocnemius muscle while working through the appropriate action by shortening the muscles in question.
> Station 3: The muscles that were used in the exercise stations were exposed and pinned out on a cat specimen. Students were informed that the cat's muscles were very similar to those of the human and therefore a worthwhile study.

Station 4: A long bone of a cow was cut lengthwise so as to expose all of its internal features. Students had an opportunity to see the epiphyseal plate, spongy and compact bone, and the different types of marrows. Tendons, ligaments, and cartilage were also visible.

Station 5: Bones at this station were treated with acid or baked. The bones in the acid showed students that bone has collagen which is very flexible once the calcium is removed. The baked bones showed how brittle bones become when minerals remain but collagen is removed.

Station 6: Rehab and reconstruction: Students could use different grades of exercise putty to determine which finger was the strongest while learning that damaged muscles have to be rehabilitated. An artificial hip joint was on display so students could get an idea of the capabilities of technology in repairing damage to certain joints. The journal *Orthopedics Today* was available so other technologies could be viewed as well. Lastly, ergonomically correct pencil holders were available (donated by the return-to-work program at a local hospital) for students to test. Each student was given one of these to take back to school for continued use.

Station 7: Students hypothesized the name and location of a series of disarticulated bones. Models of the human skeleton were available to assist students.

Station 8: The X-rays available for student viewing allowed students to locate various structures on the X-ray film as well as to determine the existence of several common abnormalities. X-rays also gave students an opportunity to determine which types of structures can be viewed with an X-ray.

When students completed the activities they chose, each one received a photocopied drawing of the muscles from one particular area of the body to color. Each segment would then be put together and sent back with them to their school. Thus a full-size, student-made human torso, complete with individual muscles, could be displayed on the bulletin board.

## The Computer Laboratory: "That computer was fun. I can't believe my left arm is stronger then my right." Students were given an opportunity to utilize the electromyograph probes while completing an experiment on muscle fatigue (to see which arm would fatigue faster). After

formulating their hypothesis, they were assisted in recording data. Data was collected for 180 total seconds wherein students counted the number of times they could squeeze a tennis ball in 10-second intervals. After completion of the first trial, students repeated the test with the other hand. Students then graphed and analyzed their data and drew conclusions. Students were also hooked up to the electromyograph so they could receive a computer printout of their muscle action.

# Feedback

The student feedback received following the day's events was very positive. Freshmen students admitted to feeling stressed by the increased responsibility of teaching others. Of course, they knew that to be an effective teacher, they had to learn the material more thoroughly. They responded that they felt they had taken more time to adequately prepare for learning muscles and muscle function because they had to utilize this information while teaching others. This heightened awareness increased the learning that took place, and most agreed that this activity was one that they would remember participating in. More important, they felt that it also helped them to learn the material better and longer than more traditional learning activities. How wonderful for a high school student to receive such positive responses from their young peers:

> I really want to thank you for helping me to understand everything at all of the stations. I also want to thank you for teaching me the names of the muscles and helping me to remember them. I still do remember them. The two stations I enjoyed the most were Dynabands and the weight room exercises. I think you did great and you were the best partner. I know that because the kids in my class were talking about their partners and you did better then the rest!

From an observer's perspective, it was rewarding to witness the growth and maturity exhibited by the freshmen involved. Circulating throughout the sessions, we could see it was obvious that a tremendous amount of teaching and learning were taking place. This was further substantiated upon viewing the videotape of the events. The high schoolers were excited and proud when they realized that their young partners were actually learning the muscles that the big kids were teaching.

The elementary students were incredibly excited to be in the high school environment. "I wanted to thank you for taking me around your school and teaching me about biology. That was my first time in NCHS. Thanks to you, I'm looking forward to going there." They listened intently, and the twenty-five-minute sections seemed well suited for their attention levels. Students actively and readily participated in all of the activities designed for the day. A small number of participants did opt out of viewing the stations with preserved specimens. Females and males appeared to be equally interested in the activities planned. We were happy to see that at an age where gender begins to play a role in female attitudes toward math and science, these girls were willing to work through all of the math, science, and physical education activities with uninhibited commitment and enthusiasm.

When the younger students returned to school, they took some time to express their feelings about the field trip by writing letters to their "high school teacher" for the day. Many students mentioned the different areas that were their favorites. The letters provided significant feedback regarding the overall value and interest level in each of the planned activities. "Thanks for teaching more about muscles. My favorite center was dyna-bands. That skinned cat was neat though. EMG is also fun. I took my test yesterday. I hope I got a good grade. It wasn't that hard for me though. I enjoyed going to NCHS."

# Follow-Up

Students at the elementary level will continue to receive information on muscles throughout the school year. A bulletin board display including pictures from the field trip as well as the completed human torso was set up in the gymnasium. Students will focus on one muscle a month, which will be highlighted throughout various exercise techniques during their physical education classes. Lastly, the music routines done with Dyna-bands were videotaped and are being used within the curriculum at both the fifth- and sixth-grade levels. Selected fifth and sixth graders will then be used as mentors for younger students who will use Dyna-bands later in the school year.

The peer teaching and integrated models used to teach human musculature stimulated student interest and motivated students at both levels to learn and apply information to their own bodies. Additionally, this opportunity provided students with relevant experiences that promoted the enjoyment of both learning and teaching.

Thank you for helping me learn about my muscles. I had a great time. That cat smelled bad! My favorite part was weight lifting. It was really fun. Now I know a lot more about muscles than I used to. I had a fun time with you. P. S. It was awesome!

# Centers and Stations: Decentralizing the Classroom

HARVEY DANIELS

In Chicago, where we work, there are still a few of those heartbreaking, old-style classrooms left, the ones with the desks screwed to the hard oak floor in straight rows. Sometimes there's even a little platform for the teacher, a step up from the student level, which makes the blackboard (and it *is* black, not green or white) more visible to all. Those immobile cast iron desks, frozen in six rows of six each, are exhibits in a museum of passivity, emblems of an era when the pedagogy was as fixed as the furniture. What a profound architectural-educational metaphor. The floor plan screams out "Sit down. Shut up. Eyes on me. Keep your hands to yourself. Stop fiddling!"

Of course now, in Best Practice classrooms, we *want* students to fiddle around; we want them to get up and go learn something, to engage with materials, touch things, wrestle with ideas, talk to each other, make stuff, and show what they found out. This kind of learning requires variety and flexibility in the ways students, materials, and equipment are deployed around the classroom. In order to do Best Practice, teachers must be able to subdivide and decentralize their space, to create and re-create the learning environment, not just in elementary but also in secondary classrooms.

## Spaces for Learning

So what exactly are centers? At Joseph Landis School in Cleveland, Debra Kunze runs a second- and third-grade classroom that has a rich assortment of centers. The last time we visited, she had five stations up and running: (1) a writing center where students could pursue their own writing projects; (2) a math center in the form of a store with many priced items to be purchased and toted up; (3) a measurement center at which students tested various attributes of water, including volume measured by different metric and conventional containers, temperature as measured in Fahrenheit and Celsius, etc; (4) a "geosafari" center where students used a rudimentary computer game to find the location of countries around the world; and (5) a physics center focused on simple machines, with assorted materials for building bridges and then testing their strength. While Ms. Kunze's centers were creative and varied, they were also equipped with mostly makeshift items; Landis is an under-funded inner-city school serving poor kids, and it doesn't have an extra dime for "real" hands-on materials.

The children, well accustomed to the procedures of their daily hour of center time, deployed themselves without fuss to their respective areas. They knew what to do at each station from Debra's orientation session earlier in the week. It was quiet in the writing center, as children opened folders and bent to their papers. Elsewhere, kids talked quietly about the work at hand. We were particularly struck by the way the simple machines center had captivated some of the kids, and especially Herbert, who was trying to build a bridge that would support a weight hanging underneath. His brow knitted as he tinkered with different support systems, tested his experiments, watched the bridge collapse, and then started over, trying new structural supports, piling on the weights, watching the bridge go down again, and then starting over with a new design wrinkle.

Jean Piaget would have loved to watch Herbert at work. This center was constructivist learning theory in action. Herbert was in the process of reinventing, and owning for himself, some principles of physics that no lecture, worksheet, or textbook could ever transmit. And he was learning these principles by doing, by playing with real stuff. Well-designed centers like this one are a key way that teachers can make student-centered, hands-on learning come alive.

So here's a more formal definition: Centers or learning stations are special spots in the classroom where the teacher has set up curriculum-related activities that students can pursue autonomously. Usually a classroom has multiple centers, enough so that when thirty kids fan out to them, there are not too many at each—five or six stations is about average among the teachers we've worked with. Centers are used during part of the day, indeed, in many classrooms there's something called "center time" that might occupy an hour of the schedule. Centers are often set up in cycles; that is, the teacher sets up a crop of centers, and the students visit them over a week or two. Then, perhaps after a pause for other activities, the teacher creates another set and the cycle begins again. Rotation is integral to centers—over the cycle, all students are supposed to work their way through all centers—sometimes visiting each one several times. During center time, the teacher is typically supervising, roaming, solving problems, serving as a resource, and when time permits, doing some observational assessment of students at work.

There's tremendous artistry—and lots of teacherly sweat equity—in the design of centers that both embody key curricular concepts and support kid-run inquiry. Centers require the teacher to think up activities, gather (translation: buy or scrounge) the equipment or supplies needed, design an inquiry process, develop kid-friendly instructions, create the necessary charts or handouts, drag everything to school, and hope the janitor helps to carry it all in. Because setting up good centers is so demanding, it's not surprising that there are so many poor ones out there: "writing centers" where kids merely copy text, "science centers" where they fill out ordinary worksheets, "math centers" where students do the odd-numbered problems and leave them in an envelope for the teacher to grade. These are not true centers but ambulatory seatwork, and are not worthy of the trouble to set them up.

To be worthwhile and genuine, centers must have several key ingredients in place:

- *Something to learn or discover.* Centers are not for review or assessment; they are for learning. Teachers must design stations so that kids can have some kind of "aha" experience there, however modest—like Herbert, with the bridge. Teachers can design centers that are applications or extensions of previously taught concepts, ones that illustrate topics currently being studied during other parts of the school day, or stations that preview upcoming topics, offering the teacher a chance to base future activities on kids' responses to early samples.
- *Some kind of interaction.* Many centers feature tasks that students do individually, though this can mean that students end up waiting while the kid ahead of them finishes the solitary task. One alternative is to design centers so that four to six kids can work simultaneously. Even better, recognizing that kids generally do arrive at centers in groups, and that talking is a good way to externalize one's thinking, the station can incorporate ways for the kids to work and talk together.
- *A tangible outcome.* Learning stations should provide students with something to take away from each stop around the room, whether this is a sketch in their journal, a completed puzzle, or a computer disk with saved Internet bookmarks. Some centers also ask kids to leave something behind—posting their results from an experiment on a chart that becomes part of the station's data, leaving a poem for others to read, or making an entry in a log that stays in the center to be read by subsequent visitors.

In order to make centers work, the teacher must choose and put into place management procedures to cover several concerns.

- *Scheduling students into centers.* In some classrooms, kids simply vote with their feet, going to whatever center they're interested in on a given day. This approach has the advantage of being casual and spontaneous, but can of course lead to clogs in some corners of the room. Other teachers ask kids to sign up in advance, say the day before, listing their center preferences in priority order, so that overcrowding problems can be worked out beforehand. Still other teachers, often those just beginning with centers or those with rambunctious youngsters, will build a schedule themselves, assigning students to a rotation through the centers. Though this approach deletes a bit of the student voice and choice, it can create optimal combinations of kids and prevent off-task groups from travelling through the stations together. Debra Kunze runs a daily center lottery; kids draw from twenty-five popsicle sticks, five for each station, to guarantee the random (and indisputable) assignment of kids to centers.

- *Instructions.* Because students are supposed to do centers without the teacher present, the instructions posted at the stations become critically important. More than one teacher has become a human ping-pong ball, with kids crying out for the clarification of unclear steps or procedures from all six centers at once. Like Ms. Kunze, many teachers make it a habit to walk kids through the centers on the first day they are introduced, previewing the directions for each.

# Centers for Older Students

For many of the six structures featured in this book, the versions used with children of all ages are basically identical. A reading workshop in high school will probably use the same procedures and activities as one in the primary grades: though the kids might be twelve years apart in age, you'd still see teacher modeling, mini-lessons, conferences, peer editing groups, sharing time, and publication opportunities. Centers, on the other hand, may begin to look quite different as students get older, though their underlying aims and deep structures will be the same. In fact, some people assume that centers are a little-kid activity that's supposed to be phased out as kids move toward adolescence. And if the practices of most middle and high schools are any guide, this misunderstanding is all too prevalent.

The secondary classroom can benefit from the same spatial flexibility and decentralization that is practiced in the lower grades. Two recent phenomena have combined to show the teachers of big kids that stations are for them too. One is cooperative learning: by setting kids to work in collaborative group investigations or peer editing groups, teachers have already started rudimentary forms of centers. And then there's the computer. The arrival of computers in classrooms, not just in labs, has almost forced teachers to invent ways that some kids can be using the computers while others are doing something else. The classroom computer often becomes the first center—now what will the other four or five be? The door to the multitasking secondary classroom is kicked open!

What kinds of centers can you have within and beyond the high school classroom? To begin with, in some classes—science, art, physical education, home economics—centers are already happening. In these subjects, teachers are trained to organize stations where pairs or small groups encounter structured laboratory experiences. Too often, these centers are identical—that is, all six groups in the home economics class are making the same brownies, each in their own little kitchen. If this were elementary school, the centers would probably feature different recipes, with students being invited to create innovations and variations on bar desserts. At Best Practice High School, our physics teacher Arthur Griffin sometimes offers labs where everyone does the same thing, but at other times he sets up multiple stations, where kids work through different aspects of, say, the refraction of light.

Secondary centers don't need to be contained within the four walls of a single classroom, nor do they have to be invented and supplied by one lonely classroom teacher. We can assign students to "centers" throughout the building, ones that don't need to be created anew, and which are already manned by others. These include, of course, the library, the computer lab, the tutoring center—as well as sites like a school telephone where interviews can be conducted, the classroom of another teacher with needed expertise, or an off-campus research site arranged in advance. If students are pursuing a broad and meaty inquiry—perhaps as part of an integrative, interdisciplinary unit—it is natural to think of the school as a building full of centers where they may go to work on different aspects of the inquiry. As with younger kids, there need to be management structures and operational controls in place to answer questions like: Where are you going? Why? With whom? What product will come out of this? When? How long do you expect this segment of the study to take?

At Best Practice High School, we have developed a variant of centers called "choice time," which happens once a week on Wednesday afternoons, after students return from their service internships around the city. During this time the faculty sets up eight to ten learning centers based on student requests, and kids sign up to attend the center of their choice. Lately, some of the popular ones have been chess, singing, drama, computer art, photography, and special help in physics. Each "center" consists of a room in the school, provided with the needed equipment (like chess boards) and one adult who is knowledgeable about the activity at hand.

Even though decentralized classrooms are an important tenet of our school philosophy, the local board of education hasn't been much help equipping them. When we started BPHS two years ago, we requested six-person tables and chairs as our baseline furniture, instead of separate student desks. But there weren't any tables to be had in the city's huge school furniture warehouses, because hardly anyone uses tables, because the board buys desks instead. Understand? We didn't either, but we still needed tables, which we ended up buying out of our of measly Chapter 1 funds.

But we spent the money willingly, because the ability to flexibly arrange our students was critically important to our curriculum, both practically and philosophically. Space matters. We have to subdivide the classroom. Kids must multitask. If we cannot set up situations where small groups of kids can meet, sit, lay stuff out, and work through materials, how can we offer an active, experiential curriculum?

# CHAPTER 4

# Representing-to-Learn

HUMAN BEINGS HAVE probably used writing to understand the world ever since the first alphabet, clay tablet, and stylus were invented. Over the past twenty years, many American teachers and schools have embraced a modern incarnation of this phenomenon called *writing-to-learn*. Developed by and elaborated by teachers like Peter El- bow (1973) and Toby Fulwiler (1987), writing-to-learn has become a minimovement with a broad literature and a wide following, especially among interdisciplinary college programs.

More recently, we have begun to see that putting down *words* is not the only way for students to engage, construct, probe, and store knowl- edge. Many other representational strategies that are commonly classified as art—drawing, sketching, mapping, drama, movement, song—turn out to be equally powerful cognitive levers, used either alone or in combina- tion with words. But, hey, me draw? Dance? Act? The minute we invite teachers to have their students engage ideas artistically, we run into rampant art phobia. The anxious cry "But I can't draw" resounds, and the size of the movement shrinks.

Everyone seems to accept that writing, especially edited discursive writing, is a normal and necessary school undertaking. But art is an extra, and a nervous-making one at that. So in this chapter, let's talk about writing as a tool of learning first. Later, we'll see how the arts add another constellation of representing activities that students can use in any subject across the curriculum.

Writing is not just one of the "language arts." It is also a form of thinking, a way of engaging and acting on information. As we discussed in Chapter 1, all contemporary learning theories share one precept: in order for students to remember information, they must act on it. Writing can be a way of acting on information, manipulating, challenging, ex- ploring, and storing it. However, for writing to have this cognitive power, the words students write must be original. Copying isn't exploration. Filling in worksheets does not count as writing-to-learn. Even taking notes in class can be mere transcription, with the transcriber's brain idling in neutral. Such closed-ended, right-answer exercises are really just obedience rituals, and do not involve constructing meaning. Unfortunately much of the writing done in American schools still does not tap the higher-order uses of writing. Writing even continues to be used as a punishment in some classrooms. On the floor of a Milwaukee school, a colleague recently found a sheet of notebook paper with the phrase "I will not talk in art class" written one hundred times.

Sometimes teachers outside of language arts are a bit suspicious about the exhortation that they should use more writing in their history, physics, or physical education classes. They suspect that English teachers are trying to invade their subjects, conscripting them to teach stuff that should have been covered during English. Well, the skepticism is understandable, but we can pledge that writing-to-learn really isn't a clever turf grab by wily language artists. Rather, it is a real gift—a gift of pedagogy.

That's because writing can also be seen as a teaching method. Writing activities are one instructional option teachers enjoy, just as they may elect to have students read a book, listen to a presentation, conduct an experiment, watch a videotape, or join in a discussion. Of course, inviting students to write does not exactly seem like a radical new choice on the pedagogical menu—after all, book reports, term papers, and written exams have long been a staple of many classrooms, grade levels, and subjects. The trouble is that these traditional kinds of writing assignments are tightly convergent, solitary, and mostly done out of class.

Instead, students need more open-ended, well-coached, in-class writing experiences. If writing can actually help people think—sort through, weigh, comprehend, and save information—it should be used *during* class, while information is flowing. And if writing can be used to share learnings, to represent and embody ideas, we need to involve the class as collaborators and as audiences for each other's writings. Again, we need to rebalance, cutting down on lockstep writing assignments done alone at home with no coaching and submitted to no audience other than the teacher's in-box. In their place, teachers need to tap the tool of writing to help students connect with the content of the curriculum, and with each other, here and now.

Now, let's add art to the picture; in fact, let's notice that art is already present. As teachers have explored and used the repertoire of WTL strategies, they notice that many of the most powerful "writing" variants—like clustering, mapping, or webbing—actually combine words with some kind of drawing or graphic element. When you divide a journal page into two columns, or array ideas in two overlapping circles, or begin to draw arrows between concepts, you are using spatial and artistic, as well as linguistic, strategies to help you think. From there, it is a short step to recognizing the value of purely graphic forms of journaling and other writing/drawing combinations.

# Journals and Genres

There are two main types of representing-to-learn, one especially useful for constructing meaning and the other for sharing it. The first, *journaling*, involves short writings or drawings that help students move into, through, and beyond the content of the curriculum in any subject. While they needn't be literally contained within an official journal, notebook, sketchbook, or learning log, these entries have several features in common: they are short, spontaneous, exploratory, expressive, informal, personal, unedited, and ungraded. Typically these drawings/writings are completed in two- to five-minute bursts before, during, or at the end of a lesson or class session.

While these entries are typically not collected or graded by the teacher, they are systematically *used* during class, as a springboard to activity. At the start of class, students may jot down questions on the topic of the day; these are shared aloud and then become part of the official agenda. Or the teacher can begin the class by reading aloud a few "admit slips," in which students have offered their open-ended reactions to the previous night's reading assignment. Often, whole-class discussion can be sparked by the varying responses. In the middle of a presentation, the teacher can stop and ask students to sketch a graphic or picture that represents their understanding of the topic, and share these with a partner. Or at the end of class, students can write "exit slips" explaining what from the day's lesson has been most confusing or difficult for them, and the teacher can then draw on these writings to plan the next day's class. For homework, students may exchange their dialogue journals with their partners, continuing an ongoing written conversation about the subject of the class, whether it is science, literature, or history. As these examples suggest, journaling can truly be a teaching method, not an English (or art) invasion. The prompts and structures for journaling are genuinely generic, and can be applied to any subject.

Representing in *genres* is more formal and extensive. In writing, we invite students to use the whole range of conventional forms—mysteries, sonnets, laboratory reports, editorials—to embody and share their thinking about the content of the curriculum. In contrast to journaling, which is quick and unedited, genre writing is substantial, considered, and polished. While in journals, we don't worry about inconsistencies or informality, in genre writing we work hard to meet the norms and requirements of the form we have chosen. While journaling is mainly a tool that helps us think, with writing used as a kind of crescent wrench of the mind, genre writing is for sharing with others. It's not just for finding out what we know, but for offering what we know to some kind of audience by embedding our ideas within the conventions of a carefully crafted form.

Most teachers are already familiar with the range of options for genre writing. However, when we move from written to artistic genres, very few classroom teachers possess a repertoire of activities to help kids represent their learning. Indeed, many teachers feel reluctant and unsure about the process—or the validity—of bringing art from the margins of schooling to the center. This reticence runs deep. As Arnold Aprill, director of the Chicago Arts Partnerships in Education (CAPE), explains, most Americans (including school teachers) have had their expressive impulses shamed and silenced in school, stunted by scores of prescriptive, do-it-right "art" assignments: "Here's a doily and a sheet of red construction paper. Make a heart just like the one on the board." While we know that very few teachers had good experiences with writing in school, even fewer had their artistic sensibilities nurtured and developed. Clearly, if a teacher is a wounded artist (or writer), she is highly unlikely to devote much classroom time to activities personally connected with uncertainty, discomfort, embarrassment, and failure.

Beyond their own fears, teachers also raise sincere questions about the legitimacy of arts activities. Is acting out a story really a valid representation of understanding? Wouldn't writing an essay be more meaningful? Isn't a poem about using the microscope a little less academic than a well-organized list of directions? And isn't drawing your response to a historical figure just the easy way out, compared to composing a reasoned argument and supporting your interpretation?

Questions like these reflect a couple of issues. For one, they reveal the pressure teachers feel about grading, about finding ways to score and rate and classify their students. Perhaps because they have more practice at it, many teachers are capable of assigning and defending grades on student writing, but feel at a loss when required to hand out grades for a readers' theater performance or a mosaic mural.

But even more important, teachers' reluctance about the artistic representation of learning shows us how little the idea of "multiple intelligences" has actually penetrated our school culture. In recent years, practically everyone working in education has enthusiastically genuflected to Howard Gardner's (1983) concept that human beings don't have just a single type of intelligence, but rather a combination of eight different kinds of "smarts"—linguistic, mathematical, musical, spatial, kinesthetic, interpersonal, intrapersonal, and environmental. The key implication of this reasonable and well-supported theory is that schools must extend kids' existing areas of intelligence, while helping them develop their weaker ones. Pedagogically, this means students should be encountering, processing, and representing ideas through a dramatically widened range of instructional activities. The connection with the arts is apparent: they offer established practices, media, materials, and conventions for making learning more kinesthetic, more spatial, more musical, and in many ways, more inter- and intrapersonal.

At the Center for City Schools in Chicago, the dozen of us who are full-time teacher-consultants have been working hard to become more multiply intelligent, to grow our own repertoires of classroom arts activities. Many of us came to this as reading and writing specialists, graduates of the Illinois Writing Project who are now supposed to help other teachers develop integrated curriculum in their Chicago schools. As we have tried to get past our own insecurities and learn new strategies, we have worked with several CAPE artists, people who divide their time between doing art and working with teachers and kids in school. We have also worked with technology gurus who have enabled us to see the art of making and demonstrating meaning through the creative use of computers. For now, we'll just share two of the promising activities we've learned from these special colleagues.

## Two-Minute Videos

Virtually every American school—and many individual classrooms—now possess video cameras. Unfortunately, no one seems to have any idea what to do with them. Camcorders can be hard to work with: they're breakable; the kids push buttons before they know what they do; it's hard to get good sound in noisy classrooms. But video artist Dierdre Searcy has taught us a truly simple structure she calls "Two-Minute Videos," which neatly solves these problems and potentially applies to any subject in the curriculum. All you need to make two-minute videos is a subject (the solar system, racism, photosynthesis—what's in your curriculum?), some old magazines and scissors, and a video camera on a tripod.

Working in pairs or small groups, students first review and discuss

## 8

At Best Practice High School one student internship involves designing, building, planting, and tending a community garden (p. 174).

Students draw on geography, English, and art to design their own island nations (p. 25).

L

Joining in prairie restoration with urban-naturalist Pete Leki (opposite top), students encounter science, social studies, research, writing, and art in an urban dump (p. 177).

Farragut students integrate mathematics and art to create a mural depicting the consequences of gang violence. A second mural (opposite page) explores the alternatives to gang involvement (p. 110).

As part of their family history study, African American, Hispanic, and Asian students join with newly-immigrated Russian children to explore each others' heritage and culture through partner portraits and group collages (p. 46).

Exhibitions provide audiences and culminating experiences across the curriculum.

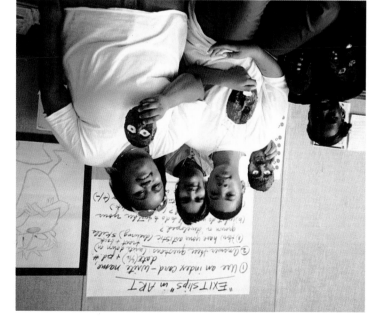

From masks to computer graphics, Best Practice High School students represent their learning in artistic as well as written forms (p. 102).

the ideas they want to represent. Then they leaf through some magazines, seeking images that can somehow convey their big ideas and main points. They cut out these pictures or graphics, and then start arranging them on a tabletop, seeking a good sequence. Next they write a script, essentially a caption to go with each image. Usually this script will include words to be read into the camera microphone by one or more students, but it can also include sound effects or bits of music. When they are ready, each group brings their pictures and script to the stationary camera "studio." They hang the first image on the wall, push the camera shutter, and read the script segment. Then they stop the camera (this is called "pause editing" in the video business), put up the next visual, get ready, turn the camera on again, and read the second script segment. And so on. When they are done, students have a smoothly edited, professional-looking two-minute video that can be as solid, informative, entertaining, or provocative as their script and images allow.

## Hypermedia Stacks

A second promising art form involves another piece of underutilized school technology: the computer. While school boards are relatively quick to invest in hardware, software purchases and teacher training tend to lag behind, so computers end up being used for mundane drill programs and record keeping, and teachers don't use them to invite kids' expression and develop their multiple intelligences. But at their best, computers can be used for sophisticated forms of multimedia authoring—a new and exciting genre of art.

One such program is Hyperstudio, which allows students to create nonlinear, audience-directed multimedia presentations. In other words, kids can create something like a Web site, where their audience is offered text, sound, graphics, music, photos, and video clips in combinations and sequences that visitors select for themselves as they make choices, following forks and branches designed by the author. Working with our colleague Jeff Flynn of Voyager Computing, elementary and secondary students around the Midwest have developed a wide array of Hyperstudio stacks on a wide variety of topics. At Lincoln Park High School in Chicago, each of Madame Breen's foreign language students created a stack of images about a chosen French artist, reading the text aloud in English, in their own first language (including Polish and Spanish in this class), and, of course, in their very best French. Sharon Flynn's middle school class in Dexter, Michigan, read Felice Holman's novel *Slake's Limbo,* about a homeless teenager living in a subway tunnel. Moved by the book, the kids created hypermedia stacks that included artwork, music, and kid-written and performed raps addressing issues of urban fear, violence, and loneliness. In Lisa Hahn's first-grade room at Gifford School in Elgin, Illinois, her reading recovery students use simple hypermedia stacks to document their own reading, while teachers use their stacks to conduct miscue analysis. Across town at Eastview Middle School, John Case has his science students creating stacks that explain angles of measurement using graphs, sound, and visuals.

Multimedia authoring stands at the other end of the complexity spectrum from the two-minute videos described above. While kids can be up and running with Dierdre's videos in one day, Hyperstudio is a tricky program that requires some training and experience. (There are simpler commercial programs, like Wiggleworks, designed for younger users, and some general programs like Claris Works have primitive multimedia features built in.) But for true Hyperstudio authoring, there's a steep learning curve; if you work at it an hour a day, you may need a couple of weeks to become proficient and start creating satisfying products.

At Best Practice High School, we ask Jeff to come in every year and teach kids the program over a couple of days, followed by plenty of over-the-shoulder coaching. Our students realize that creating Hyperstudio stacks is a demanding artistic challenge. Unlike traditional writing, which uses only words, multimedia authors may select from words or pictures or video clips or sounds in creating a text. Even more complex is the fact that the order is not fixed; the author must provide for a "reader" who can jump through the ingredients in any sequence. Indeed, one of the special responsibilities of a Hyperstudio author is to offer the audience lots of genuine and attractive choices.

These two strategies are emblematic of a whole range of arts genres and forms that teachers can adopt and use, provided that they experience them personally first and have a chance to get past their old "I'm not an artist" thinking. When art-shamed adults make their own two-minute videos or hypercard stacks, it can be a truly transformative experience. Teachers are often stunned to hear themselves saying: "I *can* do this!" Many pull a pedagogical U-turn; they can't wait to bring the arts activity that terrified them half an hour ago into their own classrooms.

Matching the breadth of the topic, this chapter ranges widely. We start with two Variations. First we hear how one active parent and school council member, Pete Leki, was able to bring his fascination with the Chicago River to students at Waters Elementary and Amundson High School. Pete visited a few classrooms at both schools and simply invited young people to write and draw their experiences with rivers—either the one in the neighborhood's backyard, or ones they had grown up with back in Mexico, Bosnia, or Mississippi. Beginning with a book collecting these special stories and artworks, the children, the teacher, and Pete gradually developed a commitment to ecological studies that has since become an official schoolwide theme at Waters School. Then we shift about fifty blocks south to Farragut High School, where Charles Kuner and Steven Cole found that mural making could help students to represent their thoughts about the gang wars plaguing their neighborhood. Not only did the mural project allow students to probe and express their views of gang violence, it also invited them to apply their knowledge of mathematics, history, and art. A telling detail about the impact of this project: while the first muralists chose to depict the negative consequences of gang membership—death, injury, imprisonment—the next year's group looked at the blank wall opposite the original mural and decided to fill it with images of a gang-free life.

In the Step by Step section, we begin with an inventory of twenty-three notebook entry prompts, brief activities that invite students to use drawing, writing, or combinations of the two to engage ideas and connect with content. These strategies are generic in the proudest sense: they are adaptable to any almost subject matter or age level. Finally, Steve Zemelman shows how very young writers can produce an example of their own favorite genre—the big book. With careful teacher guidance, the whole class coauthors and produces its own volume, even as the kids are learning how to read from other, "real" big books every day.

# Further Reading

Anson, Chris, and Richard Beach. 1995. *Journals in the Classroom: Writing to Learn.* Norwood, MA: Christopher-Gordon.

Bayer, Ann Shea. 1990. *Collaborative-Apprenticeship Learning: Language and Thinking Across the Curriculum K–12.* Mountain View, CA: Mayfield.

Calkins, Lucy. 1990. *Living Between the Lines.* Portsmouth, NH: Heinemann.

Claggett, Fran, and Joan Brown. 1992. *Drawing Your Own Conclusions: Graphic Strategies for Reading, Writing, and Thinking.* Portsmouth, NH: Boynton/Cook.

Countryman, Joan. 1992. *Writing to Learn Mathematics.* Portsmouth, NH: Heinemann.

Edwards, Betty. 1979. *Drawing on the Right Side of the Brain.* Los Angeles: Tarcher.

Ernst, Karen. 1994. *Picturing Learning: Artists and Writers in the Classroom.* Portsmouth, NH: Heinemann.

———. 1997. *A Teacher's Sketch Journal: Observations on Learning and Teaching.* Portsmouth, NH: Heinemann.

Fletcher, Ralph. 1996. *A Writer's Notebook: Unlocking the Writer Within You.* New York: Avon.

Fowler, Charles. 1996. *Strong Arts, Strong Schools: The Promising Potential and Shortsighted Disregard of the Arts in American Schooling.* New York: Oxford University Press.

Fulwiler, Toby, ed. 1987. *The Journal Book.* Portsmouth, NH: Boynton/Cook.

Heller, Paul. 1996. *Drama as a Way of Knowing.* York, ME: Stenhouse.

Hubbard, Ruth Shagoury, and Karen Ernst. 1996. *New Entries: Learning by Writing and Drawing.* Portsmouth, NH: Heinemann.

Isaacs, Judith Ann, and Janine Brodine. 1994. *Journals in the Classroom: A Complete Guide for the Elementary Teacher.* Winnipeg: Peguis.

Moline, Steve. 1995. *I See What You Mean: Children at Work with Visual Information.* York, ME: Stenhouse.

Olson, Janet L. 1992. *Envisioning Writing: Toward an Integration of Drawing and Writing.* Portsmouth, NH: Heinemann.

Page, Nick. 1996. *Music as a Way of Knowing.* York, ME: Stenhouse.

Parsons, Les. 1994. *Expanding Response Journals: In All Subject Areas.* Portsmouth, NH: Heinemann.

Rico, Gabrielle. 1985. *Writing the Natural Way.* Los Angeles: Tarcher.

Robinson, Gillian. 1996. *Sketch-Books: Explore and Store.* Portsmouth, NH: Heinemann.

Romano, Tom. 1995. *Writing with Passion: Life Stories, Multiple Genres.* Portsmouth, NH: Boynton/Cook.

Whitin, Phyllis. 1996. *Sketching Stories, Stretching Minds: Responding Visually to Literature.* Portsmouth, NH: Heinemann.

Worsley, Dale, and Bernadette Mayer. 1989. *The Art of Science Writing.* New York: Teachers and Writers Collaborative.

Zakkai, Jennifer. 1997. *Dance as a Way of Knowing.* York, ME: Stenhouse.

# Variations

## A River of Miracles by Waters School

PETE LEKI

In the city, standing on a school playground carpeted with black asphalt, it's hard to picture the wetlands of the Chicago River that used to linger and sprawl here, under what is now the foundation of Waters Elementary School. Hard to picture cormorants and herons nesting in the reeds; bears foraging the shallows for spawning sturgeon; wolves, elk, and buffalo searching among the little blue stem grasses for a place to nap under the broad canopy of savanna oaks—and the music and prattle of human voices coming from the camps and villages of the Illinois and Potawatomi peoples for whom these grounds were sacred.

This was my son's school. It was my neighborhood. I chaired the Local School Council. I had taken a leave of absence from my job as a water plant operator to finish up a long dormant college degree in interdisciplinary studies, ecology, education, and neighborhood studies. In the winter of 1994, I asked seventh graders at Waters to share their perceptions of and experiences on the Chicago River, which runs through our neighborhood. I asked them to ask their parents for river memories from their own youths and homelands. The students jotted down several possible ideas for stories and finally selected one to work on. I visited their classrooms once a week over about a six-week period, and sat with them in the hall, conferencing on their drafts. The students seemed to enjoy the one-on-one conferencing as much as I did. They read their work to me. Although the quality varied widely, every story had some unique charm to it. April wrote two pieces, one softly poetic with an eerie edge to it. This companion piece, an interview with her father, is staccato, Chicago, a historic artifact:

**Stinky Hole**
*by April Weisgerber*

AW:  Where did you grow up at?

WW:  Armitage and Seminary.

AW:  Where did you hang out at?

WW:  Adam's Park.

AW:  Did you ever hang out at a river?

WW:  Yes.

AW:  What was its name?

WW:  The Chicago River.

AW:  What other name did you call it?

WW:  The Stinky Hole.

AW:  What did you used to do down there?

WW:  Sit and have a couple of beers.

AW:  What kind of beer?

WW:  Budweiser.

AW:  Do you remember anything in or around the River?

WW:  Around there was a paint factory on Cortland. There was a tire factory on Cortland and Southport. And a shrimp house on Cortland and Southport on the opposite side. And that's still standing now till this day.

AW:  Did you ever see any animals?

WW:  Rats and birds.

Peaches was a big girl, always smiling and eating candy. She struggled with her piece. In the end we decided to format it as a poem, full of redundant longing:

**So Nice Over There (Eight Mile Rock, Bahamas)**
*by Peaches Rahming*

The sea is so nice over in the Bahamas.
I wish I was there now.
There is nothing in the water.
Nothing.
It is so blue, it look like the sky.
There is all kind of fish and nice stuff.
Like the pearl conch shell.
It is so nice.
The sand is so nice over in the Bahamas.
The people is so nice over there.
There is no pollution in the water.
I love over there.
That's why I wish I was over there now.

Valeria, a small, quiet girl, surprised me with this vivid piece:

## Piranas Came (Michoacan, Mexico)

*by Valeria Guiterrez*

One day we went to the river and there were other people at the river. And the people there were in the water. And the paranas came where the people were. And the paranas eat the people. And it was so ugly because they take the people's eyes and fingers. The people were crying and yelling for help. And the police came and the people were with blood and so disgusting and were ugly. My family went to the car and brought our stuff back and went to the other river. But the paranas were there too, eating other people. So we went to help the people get out of the water.

Santos was just learning English and had a learning disorder as well. But he shared a real piece of life with us. Notice the pattern of word repetition—*river* in the first paragraph, *mother* in the second:

## Washing Clothes (Cuspala, Mexico)

*by Santos Covarrubias*

My mother washed the clothes in the river. Me and my friends played in the river. The river was in the back of my house. The river was clean. There were rocks in the river. I could walk to the river. I went to the river almost every day. The river was in Cuspala, Mexico. I took a bath in the river.

My mother goes there when she is mad. She was mad because her mother screamed at her. Her mother was mad at my mother because she didn't like her cleaning. That's why my mother went to the river.

Once we were satisfied with the text, we copyedited and I entered the stories into a computer. We asked the students to illustrate their stories or to bring in photographs. I showed them photos from the Ravenswood historical archives of the river in our neighborhood. We looked for their rivers on maps, in atlases, on globes.

Later on, with the help of the Chicago Teachers Center, the collection was published as *Sipi*, the Algonquian word for "river." The book is anchored in our little stretch of the Chicago River, which the native peoples called the Stinking Onion River, but it branches and comingles with waters from around the planet, the headwaters of our community.

The goal of this volume was to introduce our stories, our rivers, and our lives to one another. The river represents the natural world, its diversity and bounty. The clear flowing stream stories told by some of our writers help us to envision our own river, restored and healthy. This is the birthright of every child—to drink, swim, fish, and meditate in clear waters along with all of creation.

I would like to say that the best time to go to the river is to get anger out and think. It's the best place to be alone. I go there when I'm mad. Like when me and my Dad would get into a fight I would just blow it off. Instead of taking it out on my loved ones, I would go down to the river and let the sunshine and the wind soothe my mind and soul. I go there to think. Though it's all dirty and messed up, I think it's a beautiful place. I could get my anger out just by looking at the green water. It looks like my Dad. It's peaceful and wonderful.
*by April Weisgerber*

## The Beginning of Time
*by Jerry Caldwell*

The river was from the beginning of time
It is so muddy and mucky
But it is so beautiful in so much time
Thou shalt think the true beauty of it
is the parasites, bugs, and slime.

All these things I've told you, happened in the river. Me and my family all thought that there was something bad about that river. So we decided to get out of that river. We were on our way out of the river, to another pool, when we saw a sign in the sand close, like two feet away from the river. We read the sign. It said River of Miracles.
*by Janet Pineda*

Once we started telling river stories, we were hooked. Our curiosity about the river inevitably connected us up with the Friends of the Chicago River, an advocacy group just gearing up for elementary school outreach work. Friends took members of our staff and a group of teachers from Amundsen High School (the local environmentally focused high school most of our graduates attend) on a walking tour of the river in our neighborhood. A trio of teachers—in art, journalism, and biology—invited me to work on river writing with their high school students. The art work of one high school student, Davy Bulba, depicting the history of the river, was used to illustrate *Sipi*.

Friends of the Chicago River put us in contact with the Illinois Rivers Project, which coordinates a statewide interdisciplinary river study and protection effort at the high school level. They publish a yearly collection of student writing from the Mississippi watershed called *Meanderings*. The Chicago Academy of Sciences also looked to the school for a partnership as it opened its Water Wonder exhibit that spring. Along with the Friends of the Chicago River, they were networking with agencies, advocacy groups, and schools to do watershed protection and organize summer conferences to develop an elementary school rivers studies curriculum.

The Nature Conservancy's Mighty Acorns project, a joint venture with the Cook County Forest Preserves, came to us like some fairy godmother and offered to take classrooms of students out to prairie restoration sites (five students to one Acorn volunteer), to explore, learn, and perform stewardship tasks like pulling weeds, cutting brush, and collecting seed. Our fourth through sixth graders will return to the site each season over a three-year period to root their identification with the Sauganash Prairie. Jullietta Thornton, an art consultant hired by the school, received a grant to try out her Potawatomi project, a hands-on study of native plants, wigwams, dream catchers, medicine pouches, and our ancestor people who lived here for centuries.

Finally, the governmental agency charged with control of the Chicago River system, the Metropolitan Water Reclamation District, answered our inquiries about support and cooperation by saying, "This is the phone call we've been waiting for." At a get-acquainted meeting we discussed the whole realm of possibilities for river exploration and study at the middle school level: water quality monitoring and testing on their barge-lab, fish surveys, river trips to scout out illegal dumping, and neighborhood campaigns to stop the disposal of oil, toxins, and antifreeze in street sewers.

Since then we've written and received grants from the City's Urban Greening program to re-create a savanna oak community at the south end of our school ground, an area that somehow escaped entombment in asphalt. A log circle is in place for storytelling. Raised planting beds arranged in two circles are reserved, one for each class. This sacred place makes it easier for teachers to access nature. The beauty and vigor of the place has discouraged vandalism.

So the river theme was only the beginning of a vision of land and community-based learning. It seemed to me that the river and the nearby prairie lands were calling out to our school for a meeting. We were lucky to have such a rich place to study history, ecology, social issues, math, and science. We seemed blessed to have nearby resource institutions ready and willing to offer staff development and technical and material resources to our faculty. Waters Local School Council embraced this opportunity for community-based, experiential, meaningful, hands-on learning. Our marriage to the river and prairie were written into our school improvement plan in May, 1994.

But that doesn't mean teachers could immediately implement programs and use all the resources offered. Sometimes we construct enormous possibilities in our minds, while the people who have the responsibility of carrying them out are busy thrashing through the big and small traumas of daily school life in the city and the cascades of changes brought on by reform, the council, and our new principal, Tomas Revollo.

But the call seemed too strong to ignore. We in the council were slowly learning the importance of focusing on a few changes at a time: to allow change itself adequate time and resources and an honorable title in school renewal. Our link-up with the Best Practice network of the Center for City Schools has convinced me of the primacy of the process. The power of Best Practice methods for teaching, writing, and reading are modeled in staff and parent development sessions. Reading and writing workshop formats and collaborative experiences allow students, parents, and staff time to discover themselves, the person next to them, their community, and their place in the world.

I know that rivers and prairies will have a place in that discovery because they are speaking to us so clearly and insistently. The mighty burr oaks that guard the south end of the playground, the night heron cruising over the river against the western sky, the rogue carp thrashing and spawning in the weedy shallows. Discovering, maybe inventing, our community is the reason I came to Waters with my son Jamal in the first place.

> Then, later on, we were sitting in the dry dirt, our butts were crushing some leaves. One of my friends told us to "Look. Look at the seagull." It took me a few seconds to realize that the seagull held a fish in its claw. Then it dropped it. Another seagull swooped down and stole the floating fish. I was so surprised. It didn't know that these birds hunted. I thought they just eat junk food that we litter on the streets and sidewalks.
> *by Albert Vo*

Q:  How did the Mississippi affect your thinking pattern?

A:  It didn't really have much affect on me other than when looking into the water I seemed to be able to think more clearly.
*by Vincent Crowder*

Spending some time with the children in their classrooms, producing this modest but beautiful piece of community self-reflection, our book, called *Sipi,* is both process and end all in one.

# Going to Scale: Muralists Use Art and Mathematics to Decry Gang Violence

CHARLES KUNER AND STEVEN COLE

Recently we joined in a cooperative student project involving our Art and Ethnic Studies classes. The unit combined literature, history, art, and math, and we think it could serve as a model for other team-teaching efforts across disciplines. The concept was to design and produce a mural depicting the consequences of gang activity, a very real problem for the students and the community served by our school.

In preparation for this project, the students read and discussed Luis Rodriguez's autobiography, *Always Running: La Vida Loca* [The Crazy Life]: *Gang Days in L.A.* Students chose four specific images from the autobiography to illustrate the central theme of gang warfare. The images chosen by the students were (1) gang members hanging out; (2) a drive-by shooting; (3) a funeral; (4) a cemetery. Then the class was divided into four groups with each group depicting one of the images. It was determined that the images would be sequential and would tell a story. We also decided that the images would be separated by borders and would not blend in a panorama, as in the classic mural style.

To prepare for the mural, the entire wall of Mr. Kuner's room was drawn to scale (1 in. = 1 ft.) on big sheets of white paper. The area was divided by Mr. Cole into four frames with approval of the students. Three rectangles side-by-side composed the top two-thirds of the wall, while one long rectangle filled the bottom third. This composition was determined after students explained what they wanted to put in each of the four pictures. The cemetery naturally called for a long, low, horizontal space. Consequently, this image was placed under the other three, unifying them.

Each group then drew a picture that fit in its respective space on the scale drawing of the wall. A square grid was drawn on each small picture. The lines of the grid were one inch apart. Large sheets of white paper were taped together into four rectangles that were now the actual size of the four pictures that would make up the mural. Students consulted the scale drawings to measure these large rectangles. The paper rectangles were too big to fit on the art tables, so each was worked in halves and fit together on the wall. This presented the problem of making sure that the two halves fit together so that an image begun on one half would continue on the other half without interruption. Paying careful attention to the scale drawings became crucial.

The small-scale drawings for each of the four parts of the mural were then drawn at actual size, which was twelve times the size of the scale drawings. To do this, the students drew a grid made up of one-foot squares to correspond to their small-scale drawings, on which a grid of one-inch squares had been drawn. To make an exact enlargement twelve times the size of the small drawing, they drew the large squares to look as much as possible like the small squares, working square by square.

After the large images were drawn in pencil, the lines were gone over with black marker or paint. The main outlines were finished mostly in black or gray on the white paper. Red was the color most often used in addition to black and gray. We thought that too many colors would brighten the look for such a sober message. This way it was more dramatic.

We now had all the pieces done. They next had to be fitted together on the wall just like the original scale drawing indicated. Here we discovered a few errors in measurement, and some of the images did not line up when put next to one another. Corrections were made and all pieces were adhered to the wall with mounting tabs from the hardware store. The pieces were first taped on the wall with masking tape to see if all was well. When we were sure it was right, we took off the tape and put in the permanent mounting tabs (see Figure 4.1 and page 4 of the color insert).

At the completion of the project, the students were proud of what they had accomplished. The mural will stay on the wall of room 416 as a testimonial to what African American and Hispanic American students can accomplish together when working toward the common goal of creating meaningful images.

Recently, a second mural was created on the opposite wall of Mr. Kuner's room. This time, the mural was painted directly on the wall rather than on white paper. Its content also contrasted with the first mural. This one illustrates the positive consequences of *not* joining a gang (see page 5 of the color insert).

**Figure 4.1** Detail of mural depicting the consequences of gang involvement.

The second mural was another cooperative student project involving Mr. Kuner's human relations class and Ms. Olga Gonzales' art class, with special assistance from Mr. Cole. While the first mural took us approximately four weeks to complete, this one took us about six weeks. This time the mural was composed of seven panels, each panel illustrating a benefit of avoiding gangs, such as getting a good education, a satisfying career or job, and so on. Students were divided into seven small groups, each group responsible for creating an image for their wall panel. While this was going on, other students were given the responsibility of measuring the wall and dividing it into seven panels. As each student group completed their panel, we teachers watched the obvious pride on their faces when they saw their small drawings come to life, enlarged on the wall.

We can sum up this two-year mural project by simply stating that the student muralists learned not only how to work together in order to accomplish a larger goal, but also how to become teachers of a sort. They left their legacy and commentary for future Farragut students to absorb and reflect on. They proved that art can be a powerful teaching tool in any subject area.

# Step by Step

## Jotting and Sketching: Twenty-Three Ways to Use a Notebook

HARVEY DANIELS

Old-time, pre-Best Practice schooling emphasized the *reception* of ideas. Teachers told, delivered, explained, lectured, presented, demonstrated, and talked. The job of students, by and large, was to receive, hear, listen, watch, catch, or somehow absorb ideas teachers expressed. Education embodied the popular T-shirt slogan: "Don't just do something—sit there!" Not uncommonly, school days consisted of a nonstop stream of teacher expression and student reception. Of course, the process of student reception was notoriously imperfect, leading to endless control battles and elaborate punishment/reward systems of extrinsic motivation.

Today, modern learning theory, the mandates of subject matter experts, and common sense tell us how backward this paradigm was. Students, not just teachers, need to express ideas, act on information and knowledge, and construct meaning. Passivity isn't wrong just because it's boring; it is wrong because it doesn't work. All the major learning theories—behaviorism, information-processing, cognitivism—agree: for learners to internalize ideas, they must act upon them. Knowledge cannot remain external, inert, untouched. Learners must do something with information: connect it, draw it, weigh it, manipulate it—metaphorically, they need to grab ideas by the throat and demand that they make sense.

Happily, there are plenty of writing and drawing activities that can help students to engage and explore subject matter in just this way. The best of these activities translate across subject fields and grade levels, helping students to move into, through, and beyond the content of the curriculum. In a moment, we'll review an inventory of twenty-three such activities. But first, a bit of definition. We want to be clear that journaling or notebook activities are different from genre writing and formal art assignments in several important ways. Here are eight key contrasts:

*spontaneous* vs. planned
*short* vs. lengthy
*exploratory* vs. authoritative
*expressive* vs. transactional
*informal* vs. formal
*personal* vs. audience-centered
*unedited* vs. polished
*ungraded* vs. graded

Journaling or notebooking involves short, spontaneous, exploratory writings, often done amid or between other activities. This form of representing is tool-like: we use jotting or sketching as a device that organizes, channels, and gives extra leverage to thinking. These thinking tools work best when students can be informal, tentative, colloquial, loose, and personal; when experimentation and risk taking are invited; when the demands for revising and the risks of grading are eliminated; and when the products are frequently *used* in class, as contributions to an ongoing exploration of content.

We stress these contrasts to make it clear that the two types of representing-to-learn—journaling and genres—are quite different, though equally important. Elsewhere in this book we honor the value and importance of students' producing artworks and writings that are carefully planned, substantial, and polished; products that speak effectively to others, that observe the conventions of their genre, and that are ready to compete in the public arena of ideas. For now, though, we are talking about another category of representing—much more personal and transient—that is also vital to the development of powerful thinkers.

# Sample Activities

## 1. Start-Up or Warm-Up

The first 3–5 minutes of class time each day are regularly set aside for students to do a quick segment of writing on the topic of the upcoming lesson. This can be the same question each day (reflections on my reading, questions I have this morning, highlights from the homework, etc.) or may be in response to a specific daily question or quote put on the board by the teacher. This activity works especially well to begin a class, since it causes students to break social contact, look down at their writing, tune in to the lesson, gather thoughts, and get centered. The "investment" of a few minutes of class time helps students to clear their minds of previous issues, activate their prior knowledge, and prepare to join in the upcoming topic.

## 2. Freewriting

In "focused freewriting," students simply write as fast as they can on a given topic for 2–3 minutes, to tune in to what they know, to surface their knowledge. The teacher's instructions must expressly invite "sentences, phrases, notes, jottings—whatever helps you to get thoughts down quickly." Because the goal of freewriting is spontaneous, quick jottings, teachers are careful not to say, "write a paragraph." For many kids, this command is rooted in detached, unengaged writing. This and the next three activities are variants of brainstorming that are especially useful for introducing new topics or units.

## 3. Listing or List-Storming

This is the written version of brainstorming. Here, the student quickly jots a list of words or phrases reflecting whatever they know—or think they know—about a given subject, without editing or second-guessing themselves. Later, lists can be used in many ways: pairs or teams can compare and discuss their lists; frequency tallies for certain items can be totaled and announced, and so on.

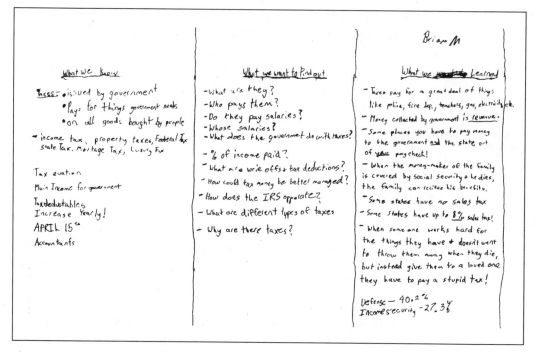

**Figure 4.2** One student's K-W-L brainstorming on the topic of taxation.

## 4. Fact/Values Lists

When a new topic with a strong values dimension (e.g., AIDS, nuclear war, slavery) is being introduced, students begin by making two lists side-by-side: on the left, facts about the topic, and on the right, attitudes, beliefs, values, or opinions they have about it. As the lesson proceeds, students can validate their facts and explore their values.

## 5. "K-W-L"

When a topic is being introduced and investigated, students make and use three lists that guide the inquiry (see Figure 4.2). At the start of the unit, each kid divides a piece of paper into three columns, sideways. In the left column, each student lists all the things they *Know* about the topic. Then these are shared aloud and a whole-group list of "Knows" is compiled. Next, in the middle column, everyone writes down some things they *Want* to know. Then these are shared aloud and a whole group list of "Want to knows" is also compiled. Then the class pursues its questions as the unit unfolds. Toward the end of the unit (perhaps days later) kids return to fill in their third columns with things they *Learned*, and these are again the subject of a wider class discussion and review (Ogle 1986).

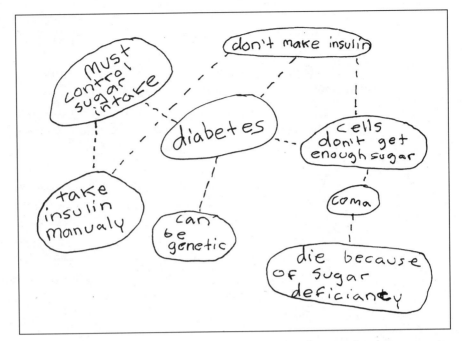

**Figure 4.3** Clustering can help students to map and remember key concepts.

## 6. Graphic Writes

Drawing and writing are branches of the same cognitive tree, and for many students the graphic mode better fits their learning style. There's always room for doodling ideas, cartooning the subject being studied, making sketches, maps, or diagrams of important concepts. Below are a batch of graphic/drawing strategies, all of which combine words with pictures.

**Clustering:** A special form of representing-to-learn using a kind of right-brained outlining developed by Gabrielle Rico in *Writing the Natural Way* (1985). Students put a key concept, term, or name in a circle at the center of a page and then free-associate, jotting down all the words that occur to them in circles arrayed around the kernel term, in whatever pattern "seems right" (see Figure 4.3). Often clustering reveals unrecognized connections and relationships, and is great for surfacing prior knowledge or recollecting "lost" information.

**Semantic Maps:** Maps or diagrams of ideas that help us to remember terms, concepts, ingredients, or relationships. These maps help kids to chart content or knowledge in order to plug it into their brain, or memorize it. Clustering is helpful for retrieving the map later on.

**Mindmapping:** This raises the idea of mapping to the level of art. The principle: if you really want to remember something—like a set of terminologies or a complex concept—it helps to make a careful, craftsmanlike, artful illustration of it. This strategy can involve considerable time making a unique and personal map.

**Story Maps:** Diagrams or maps of the events in a story or narrative, often done chronologically. This can apply to both literature or to historical narrative.

**Venn Diagrams:** When subjects—books, concepts, people, countries, and so on—have certain attributes that are *alike* and others that are *different,* kids can use two or three interlocking circles to display the contrasts and similarities.

**Timelines:** Another familiar combination of graphics and writing, applied to chronology. Works best when cartoons or other illustrations are added.

**Drawing/Sketching:** This is the graphic equivalent of freewriting. Students do original drawings to illustrate ideas found in their reading, discussion, and inquiry. Drawing can be used to probe passages or quotations in reading materials, and labels or captions can be mixed with lines and forms (see Figure 4.4).

**Cartoons:** Another combination of words and drawings, cartooning can either be a quick response or a fine-art form, depending on the time devoted to it. This can be a key strategy to help getting reluctant writers to get words on a page—in balloons or captions.

## 7. Written Conversation/Dialogue Journals

Talking informally in writing about course content with the teacher and/or other students provides a private, two-way channel of communication, typically developing into an exchange of information about both academic an interpersonal issues. If written conversation is to stand alone as a regular class activity, the teacher will have to make significant efforts to institutionalize it (perhaps by initiating the first notes, by installing a mail box, by doing much modeling, and by responding promptly and fully, etc.). As this gets to be a regular activity, it blends into learning logs

Theater of Marcellus

**Figure 4.4** Drawing helps students visualize ideas, even in Latin class.

(see below). Either the teacher or another student must respond to each letter/entry; Post-it notes limit the burden and also save the surface of students' work from markings.

## 8. Learning Logs

Learning logs could appear anywhere on the list, and in a sense are the natural culmination of doing lots of notebooking/journaling activities. You've got to save all this stuff somewhere! As teachers become committed to journaling, they want to make it an official, regular, consistent, and predictable part of their courses. They also need a place for students to store all their drawings, lists, clusters, admit slips, and freewrites. Many teachers have formalized this approach by asking each student to keep a continuous notebook or learning log throughout the class. While some specific topics may be set by the teacher, the essential idea is for students to be making regular journal entries on a variety of class-related topics—three, four, or five entries per week, some in school and some at home. This document becomes a special place where the subject-matter learning of the course is both accomplished and reflected on. We prefer a loose-leaf format, so that students can remove and share one entry without having to hand over their whole spiral notebook to someone else. Index cards, admit slips, and any other odd-sized entries can simply be pasted or stapled on a loose-leaf page and added to the notebook.

## 9. Exit Slips

Instead of teaching "bell to bell," teachers save the last 3–5 minutes of class for students to do a short piece of writing or drawing representing their response, summary, or questions about the day's session. The teacher may collect and study these herself, and use them to plan future lessons. Exit slips can be a great diagnostic tool for the teacher, and a natural source of quick-review highlights during the next class—the teacher can read a few sample exit slips from the previous day aloud (without names, probably) to commence the lesson.

## 10. Admit Slips

Upon entering class, students hand over their "tickets"—short writings on a preassigned topic, such as three suggested discussion questions for today's class, a sketch of a character or historical figure appearing in our reading, or a summary of the previous night's reading assignment. To begin class, the teacher may share some or all (with or without names attached), or admit slips may be passed out randomly among students to be discussed in pairs or groups (see Figure 4.5).

## 11. "Stop-n-Write"

Too often in presentations, teachers feel a need to plunge on and "cover the material," when in fact students would benefit greatly from an occasional pause for them to reflect on their thoughts. Some possible focusing suggestions: what I'm thinking right now; what I grasp up to this moment; questions that are bugging me. This pausing to draw or write provides kids a chance to consolidate what's been learned so far and prepare to go on (see Figure 4.6).

## 12. Poetry

Many different genres of verse are adaptable to quick-draft or content-area writing: haiku, limericks, bio poems, diamantes, and the like. The ones with simple and clear-cut formulas seem to work best.

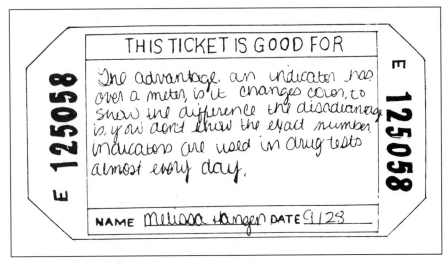

THIS TICKET IS GOOD FOR

E 125058

E 125058

*The advantage an indicator has over a meter, is it changes color, to show the difference the disadvantage is, you don't know the exact number, indicators are used in drug tests almost every day.*

NAME *Melissa Hangen* DATE *9/23*

**Figure 4.5** Admit slips are used at the beginning of class to start discussion or group work.

## 13. Dialogues

A good way to ensure students grasp both sides of complex issues is to have them write dramatic dialogues between opposing characters, personages, historical figures, points of view, scientific traditions, and so on, giving students practice articulating ideas while learning.

## 14. "Faction"

Students can create a pieces of fiction that depend upon a solid understanding of facts studied in a course. Examples: writing imaginary scenes from history or from novels. You cannot create a "missing chapter" of *Huckleberry Finn* or write plausible corridor gossip from the Constitutional Convention unless you know the material. Roving reporters can interview Pythagoras, Madam Curie, Hitler, and so on. All these "factions" invite illustration, of course.

## 15. Definitions

Sometimes it is valuable to focus on certain key words in vocabulary-heavy content areas. Some basic approaches: freewriting on the key word or key term; predicting definitions of the central vocabulary of a lesson; drawing with concrete poetry using key words from the subject matter.

## 16. Paraphrases

Paraphrasing means writing precise summaries of key ideas, concepts, procedures, processes, events, quotations, demonstrations, or scenes. Yes,

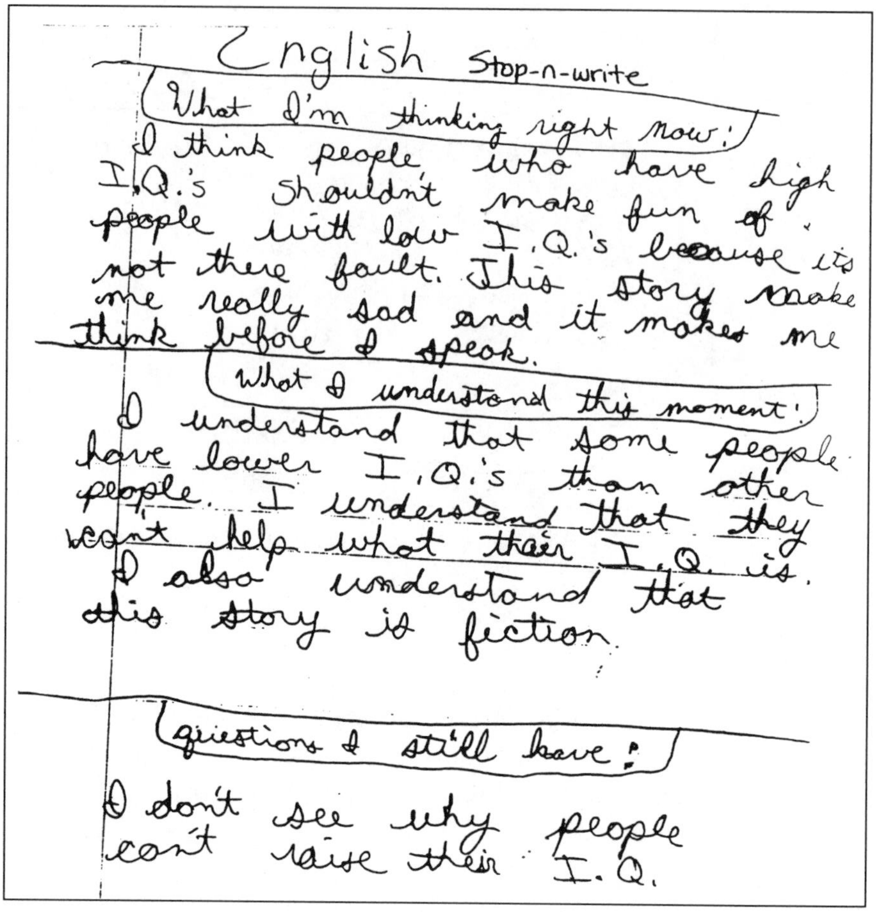

*English Stop-n-write*

*(What I'm thinking right now:)*
I think people who have high I.Q.'s shouldn't make fun of people with low I.Q.'s because its not there fault. This story make me really sad and it makes me think before I speak.

*(What I understand this moment:)*
I understand that some people have lower I.Q.'s than other people. I understand that they can't help what their I.Q. is. I also understand that this story is fiction.

*(questions I still have:)*
I don't see why people can't raise their I.Q.

**Figure 4.6** When teachers give students time to stop and write, they can reflect, consolidate, and predict.

you can even have kids write summaries of textbook sections. Though this activity is a bit dry, it can be more palatable and useful if done in pairs or teams rather than solo. The "side talk" that goes on while kids try to boil a chunk of text down to its elements is often worthwhile. One of our teacher friends has each student create their own cartoon character (e.g., "Biology Baby") who "writes" each summary (see Figure 4.7).

## 17. Predictions

The teacher stops students at a key point in a reading, an activity, or a lecture and invites them to quickly write or draw what they think will happen next, and then discuss their predictions in small or whole group settings.

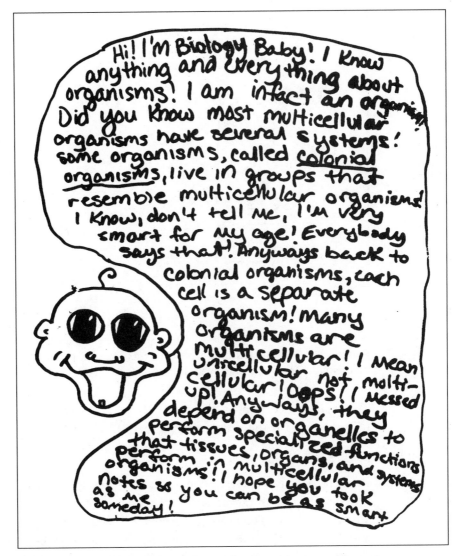

**Figure 4.7** Even paraphrasing the textbook can be energizing when your personal cartoon character speaks for you.

## 18. Dialectics/Double-Entries

Students divide note cards or journal pages in half, thirds, or quarters, and then use each space for a different kind of writing or drawing. In one kind of double-entry journal, the left side is used for factual note taking during reading, lecture, or activity—while the right side is used for personal reactions and questions. In mathematics, one side can be used for doing calculations and the other for explaining in words how the student attacked them. Many math teachers report that if students

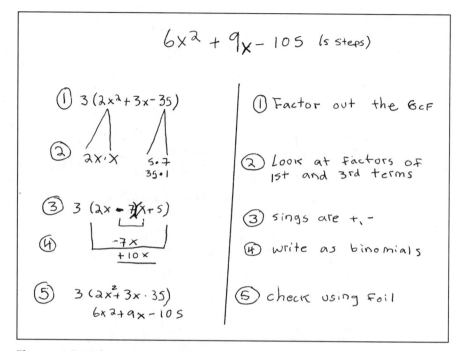

**Figure 4.8** Dialectic journals invite students to work problems both in mathematical symbols and everyday language.

can explain a concept in these two languages—symbolic and English—they really grasp the ideas (see Figure 4.8).

## 19. Metacognitive Analysis

In metacognitive analysis, the student writes to describe her/his own thinking process in the subject, perhaps up to the point where difficulties are encountered. For example, showing how a math problem is tackled and worked through up to the point where the student becomes stumped. One teacher we know gives full credit if the student can explain clearly in prose "what I would need to be able to do to complete this problem successfully."

## 20. Instructions/Directions

The "how-to" is one of the most primitive and inherently engaging forms of writing. Classroom possibilities: how to conduct a science experiment, how to build a birdhouse, how to hem a skirt, how to plan a battle strategy, how to solve a quadratic equation. Notice the natural audience possibilities. A realistic performance assessment would be: can a reader do this task, based upon the instructions given?

## 21. Observation Reports

Science labs have always offered a special and valuable kind of composing experience: reporting data from the close observation of physical objects, processes, phenomena, and events. This sort of writing can be extended to data gathering and observational reports in a number of other subject areas and formats. Social observation (ethnography) and interviewing are subtypes useful in social studies classes, for example.

## 22. Class Minutes

One student is elected (or serves on a rotating schedule) as minute taker for each daily class session, and must produce a set of official "minutes" by the following class. Minutes are either posted in a regular spot or are copied for distribution to the group. Reading and amending these minutes provides an excellent focusing activity for the start of each day's class; having everyone's captive attention gives each student author a chance to shine. In practice, authors usually try to infuse the minutes with as much personality as accuracy will permit.

## 23. Problems, Questions, Exercises

OK, it's the oldest one in the book, and potentially deadly if mishandled, but . . . students can write their own discussion, study, essay, or even exam questions, mathematics word problems, or science experiments on the material being covered. This can replace dull, rote, end-of-the-chapter questions or workbook banalities with questions that students originate because *they* identify them to be worth considering.

# Variations and Extensions

Any of these twenty-three activities can be made collaborative. One of the best ways to help students to externalize, verbalize, and further organize their thinking is to work with one or two other students in actually creating writings or drawings together. This may be done by pairs or small teams, and it works especially well on a quick paragraph, short observation report, or a simple diagram.

Any of these short notebook entries can be treated as rough drafts, as first steps toward longer, more polished genre writings or artworks. Sometimes we call these "upgrades." Any piece begun in one of the above activities can be pushed toward a more formal, audience-centered product. In fact, this program of frequent, exploratory daily journaling is almost guaranteed to create an inventory of seed ideas, some of which students will be eager to develop further.

# How to Help Your Kids Compose and Publish a Whole Class Big Book

STEVEN ZEMELMAN

The favorite literary genre of many early primary children is the "big book." These huge, two-by-three-foot books are designed to help teachers re-create the intense closeness of reading on a parent's lap. Big books are so large that the teacher can hold one up to a group of children who are sitting on the rug in front of her and, metaphorically, put every one of them in her lap as she reads aloud. The best big books include plenty of rhyme, big illustrations, predictable stories, and language patterns that young children can follow and pick up. Some are simply enlarged versions of established classics (*Goodnight Moon, Who Is the Beast?*) while others have been written specifically to be big books (*Mrs. Wishy-Washy, The Best Book for Terry Lee*). Once kids get into big books, they usually want to write (and read) their own, and so, along with some teachers from the Disney Magnet School in Chicago, I developed the following pattern for helping primary kids create and "publish" their own big books.

1. *Introduce a Mini-lesson.* Introduce to children the concept that every story includes a problem or conflict. Use a read-aloud or two to illustrate this—*Wilfred Gordon McDonald Partridge, Thundercake, Owl Moon*—just about any of your favorite picture books will work just fine. Because this is a powerful concept that students can use throughout their schooling to think about literature, it's well worth taking time to help them become comfortable with it over a period of days or weeks.

2. *Brainstorm* **possible problems for the class big book to focus on.** Ask the kids to think about problems they might like to write stories about. Then go around the circle several times and record all the ideas on a chalkboard or flipchart. Often, kids who don't volunteer right away have an idea by the second or third round. You might wish to star the ideas that are mentioned more than once, to spread the recognition and begin to focus on the topics held in common in the class.

3. **The group votes to *choose one idea* for the class book.** Several rounds of voting may be required for narrowing down the list since, especially

with younger kids, each person will at first tend to vote for his or her own suggestion. This process can be challenging, because some children will be disappointed their idea wasn't chosen. It's good to reassure the class that this is really a list of excellent story ideas for the whole year, and that everyone will also get a chance to write his or her very own piece for the next project.

4. *Identify a variable and a refrain* for the predictable pages. Most big books for early readers are built around repetition, so the book can be structured by figuring out what event or aspect can be repeated with variations on a number of pages. For example, in a story about a lost pet, the variable might be the numerous places where the children search for the animal. Depending on the age level, the kids may need your help determining this variable. Once it's set, they'll have no trouble brainstorming lots of choices and then deciding on an appropriate refrain. For the pet story, our class listed lots of places to look—up a tree, under the bed, in the cafeteria, and so on. The refrain on each page was then easily created: "But he wasn't there!" The group also wanted to identify the pet, so it became Green Star, the dog.

5. **Small groups go to work to** *create the middle pages.* Even though there's more to plan, it's good to do some concrete work at this point. Divide the class into groups of three, so each group can create one page. If possible, each group should have at least one strong writer. The tasks for the groups are as follows:

1. Choose one of the variable options.
2. Decide what the words will be for the page.
3. Pick one writer to draft the words on a half-sheet of butcher paper or chart paper.
4. Assign the other two kids to draw and color the illustration on the upper half of a full sheet of paper (this allows all to work simultaneously without getting in each other's way).

Depending on the children's age, writing experience, and purpose for the book, you may decide to use the children's writing as is or to prepare a large-size, computer-printed, teacher-spelled version of the words. If it's just for the class and the children are beginning writers, the most encouraging approach is to use the children's own spelling. If the book will be used for other children to practice their reading, it's legitimate to create a "publisher's" version. To honor the children's efforts, their original versions can be included on the pages as well.

**6.** *Brainstorm a beginning and an ending.* We still need some parts for our story, so it's time for the group to brainstorm some more. How will the story start? What initiates the problem? And how will it end? For our example, the children creating the lost pet big book decided the dog ran away because his owners weren't taking good care of him. Then they brainstormed where he would be found, for the ending. It helped the thinking to point out to the kids that the dog's hiding place would relate to why he ran away in the first place. Our group overwhelmingly chose the principal's office for the ending—a revealing insight into first graders' need for order and authority.

**7.** *Groups draft* **the beginning, ending, and other needed pages.** Divide the class into groups of three again. Assign (or help kids choose) one group to create the first page, one for the last page, and other groups to create a title page, an "about the author" page, a back page "advertisement" for the book, and so on, to involve as many groups as you have as well as to acquaint them with the various elements of a published text.

**8.** *Put it all together.* Tape the wording sheets onto the picture sheets. Bind the pages together at the top or sides, using individual notebook rings or other flexible fasteners. Then include the rereading of the big book as a regular option during sustained silent reading and other open choice work times. Finally, inspire other classes to create their own books and trade them around the building for reading practice. The children will all be extremely proud that their books are being regularly used to help others learn to read.

## Some Helpful Mini-lessons for Getting Started

1. Have kids develop a list of their own topics for writing. Do your own first to demonstrate.
2. Guide students in using journals to develop good topics. For example, events, people, or issues that come up repeatedly over a period of time can be given separate sections in the journal and the student can go to that section whenever an additional thought on the topic comes to mind. Once a number of entries have been collected, it will probably be easy to use some of them, or parts of them, as the core of a more formal written piece (see especially Lucy Calkins' *Living Between the Lines* [1990] for more on this subject).
3. Help the class to set some work-time behavior rules—and state them as positives. For example, "Use your twelve-inch voice when conferring with a partner," rather than "Don't talk loudly." Ask the class to make a list of things a student can do if he or she is finished with a

draft, or stuck, or waiting for a conference—this will help keep kids productive. Put these lists up on posters, so it will be easy to refer to them when students need reminding.

4. Help kids to develop their own list of goals for improvement, which will go into their folders and will be consulted during assessment conferences. Then demonstrate how a writer can use the list to self-evaluate his or her own work and continue working on it before submitting it to the teacher.

5. Teach kids how to respond with a brief description of what they're working on (the topic, what stage they're at, and whether they need help today) during "status of the class" meetings so that you can get a quick read on how students will be using their time during the workshop period, and who will be needing help from you.

6. Teach kids how to work with you when having a teacher-student conference. They should be prepared to respond to three questions that you'll ask them before you read anything they've written: (1) What is your piece about? (2) What stage are you at in the work? and (3) What help do you want from me? Help them to pick out one important thing in the writing that they'd like to improve—and to ask for a conference after they've done this preparatory thinking.

# CHAPTER 5

# Classroom Workshop

O NE OF THE MOST powerful instructional metaphors to emerge in recent years is the idea of the classroom as workshop. Under this model, elementary and secondary classrooms are no longer merely locations where information is transmitted. Instead, they become working laboratories or studios, where genuine knowledge is created, real products are made, and authentic inquiry pursued. The classroom workshop is the pedagogical embodiment of constructivist learning theory; in a workshop, students and teachers together reinvent whatever field of study they are engaged in.

The workshop model is simple and powerful. It derives from the insight that children learn by doing, and that in the past schools have simply failed to provide enough time for doing math, science, reading, writing, art, music, and history. It recognizes that kids need less telling and more showing, that they need more time to *do* learning, and less time hearing about what particular subjects might be like if they ever engaged in them.

The idea of the workshop as an educational institution has centuries of rich tradition. Through much of human history and across the world, the crafts-shop, where a master craftsperson coaches and mentors apprentices, has been a traditional and effective mechanism for both schooling young people and producing useful artifacts. In the context of making real stuff, learners observe demonstrations by the master practitioner and try out the trade with feedback and close supervision. The production isn't pretend, it's real—the workshop isn't a separate institution like a modern school, set apart to prepare learners for later entry into the real producing world. Instead, the workshop is part of the real world now, and its participants are immersed in a whole, genuine process. At the same time, we don't need to romanticize the ancient workshop; many of them probably were authoritarian places where apprentices were rigidly controlled and offered precious little "voice and choice" in their education. For us today, the challenge is to translate the most valuable structural features of the workshop method to contemporary education.

Of course, the crafts-shop idea is not entirely new to modern education. Some subject fields like art, science, home economics, physical education, and other "doable" subjects have a long history of workshop learning, although they usually call it the laboratory or studio. Teachers of these subjects know a great deal about the value of modeling versus presentation, about working with real materials, about guiding and coaching students, and even about managing student work in small groups. Too often though, even in these inviting subjects, the workshop opportunity is squandered when the classroom is harnessed to convergent, right-answer outcomes and low-level exercises, rather than truly exploratory, meaning-creating experiences.

We have to thank language arts teachers, who have been experimenting with the classroom-as-workshop idea over the past fifteen years, for inventing many of the procedures needed to adapt the workshop model to modern schools. Educators like Donald Graves, Lucy Calkins, and Nancie Atwell helped solve the inherent management problems of workshops by developing new, clear-cut roles for both teachers and students. They created the operating structures and training processes that make a workshop work—and make it easily transferable across subject fields. Following on their accomplishments, teachers in other fields have generated more models, such as *History Workshop* by Karen Jorgensen (1993) and *Science Workshop* by Wendy Saul and colleagues (1993).

Thanks to this long history and these creative contributors, we now have a contemporary version of the workshop-style, learning-laboratory classroom, and it looks like this: students in the workshop choose individual or small group topics for investigation, inquiry, and research using long, regularly scheduled chunks of classroom time for doing the work. They collaborate freely with classmates, keep their own records, and self-evaluate. During workshop time, students take responsibility for the whole learning process, from topic selection all the way through producing and sharing meaningful results with others. Teachers take on new roles, too, modeling their own thinking, investigating, and authoring processes, conferring with students one-to-one, and offering well-timed, compact mini-lessons as students work. In the mature workshop classroom, teachers don't wait around for "teachable moments" to occur—they make them happen every day.

Workshops meet regularly—every day if possible, at least once a week at an absolute minimum. A defining element of the workshop is choice:

students choose their own phenomena for investigating, topics for writing, books for reading. They follow a set of carefully inculcated norms for exercising that choice during the workshop period. They understand that all workshop time must be used on some aspect of the inquiry, so when they complete a product, a piece, or a phase, they aren't "done" for the day: instead, students must begin something new, based on an idea from their own running list of tasks and topics, or seek a conference with the teacher. While there are regular, structured opportunities for sharing and collaborating in a workshop, students may also spend much time working independently and autonomously.

Teachers who value the workshop ethic often create hybrids that fit their particular settings and curricular parameters. Julia Charlesworth, who teaches English at Lake Forest High School in a suburb of Chicago, has developed an interesting way of combining reading workshop with literature circles. Here is how she explains the process to her students in a handout:

> Reading workshop and literature circles give you the opportunity to *have more choice and control of what we read and study in English class.* Workshop provides significant class time to *just read*—an activity that is an important and valuable part of your education. Literature circles provide significant class time for you *to share books with your peers through discussion* of the literature where the *topics are chosen by you* and your group and *guided and supported by me.* I hope you will find this academic freedom stimulating and fun, and that you will use the valuable time to explore your interests, expand your horizons, and to challenge yourself as a reader, thinker, and writer.
>
> Along with this academic freedom of choice and control comes added responsibilities. Reading workshop and literature circles will only be successful if everyone lives up to the *following responsibilities:*
>
> - Always have a book to read.
> - Keep the literature circle discussions interesting and fun for you and the group.
> - Use the class time responsibly.
> - Come to the literature circle meetings prepared to discuss and share ideas.
> - Be open to sharing your group's ideas with the rest of the class.

This clever adaptation of the workshop model was implemented within the traditional fifty-minute high school period, and called upon

Julia to use every minute carefully. In reflecting on her ambitious under-taking, Julia says that the workshop worked, and that students really did learn to take responsibility for their learning. As she puts it,

> In genuine, student-driven learning situations, high school students begin to discover and develop their own literate and literary vocabu-lary. They create a pattern of how to approach, read, and understand books. Choice is a very important component in this process, and students can become very uncooperative when that choice is com-promised or threatened in any way by the teacher or by peers. Concrete feedback from the teacher is very important to the process of students learning from and improving performance in literature circles. Feedback needs to be immediate and constant, or students can get off track, not meet expectations, and lose motivation.

Today, pathfinding teachers are beginning to extend the workshop model outward into all corners of the curriculum—establishing math workshops, science workshops, speech workshops, history workshops. Below is a generic schedule for a single fifty-minute workshop session that could happen in any subject:

- *5 Minutes:* Mini-lesson. The teacher briefly demonstrates one element or ingredient of the kind of work students will be pursuing during the upcoming session.
- *5 Minutes:* Status-of-the-Class Conference. Each student announces in a few words what she has chosen to work on during this session, from a list of approved alternatives.
- *30 Minutes:* Work Time/Conferences. Students work according to their plan. Depending upon the rules and norms, this may include experi-menting, researching, reading, writing, talking or working with other students, going to the library, conducting phone interviews, and using manipulatives or microscopes. The teacher's roles during this time are several. For the first few minutes, the teacher may experiment, read, or write to model her own doing of the subject. Then the teacher may manage for a bit, skimming through the room to solve simple problems and make sure everyone is working productively. Then the teacher shifts to her main workshop activity: conducting individual or small group conferences with students about their work, either follow-ing a preset schedule or based on student sign-ups for that day. The teacher's role in these conferences is as a sounding board, facilitator, and coach—rarely as a critic or instructor.
- *10 Minutes:* Sharing. In many workshop sessions, teachers save the last

few minutes for a few students to discuss or present what they have done that day. Math students may show how they applied a concept to a real-world situation, young scientists demonstrate a chemical reaction, social studies teams report the results of their opinion survey, writers read a piece of work aloud, or readers offer a capsule book review.

In most effective workshops, teachers and students set quotas and due dates. Even as students enjoy the autonomy of self-directed study, they are also accountable for regularly producing work and meeting deadlines. For example, in typical writing workshops, students are encouraged to start many different pieces of writing. But, on a regular schedule (weekly for younger kids, every three weeks for older ones) they are required to select the one most promising piece and take it through a full publication process: careful revision, multiple teacher and student conferences, scrupulous proofreading and polishing, and "publication" of the final draft within the group. Other quotas agreed upon by students and teachers often involve a distribution among genres; while some repetition is permissible, at some time during the year all students are required to produce polished pieces over a specified range of genres— poetry, drama, exposition, argument, and book reviews.

The workshop method is naturally linked with some key assessment practices. Since students are working on different topics, either individually or in teams, the teacher needs a system for recording students' choices and monitoring their day-to-day work. Because conferences are a key ingredient of the workshop, the teacher typically develops a simple system for jotting down the highlights of these conversations. With students working on many different materials at once, generating all kinds of notes, drafts, clippings, and sources, it becomes vital to have portfolios for storing all the different artifacts as they are created. Later on, ingredients of the portfolio may also be used for showcasing finished products and looking back to assess a cycle of workshop activity.

Though the workshop model is undeniably powerful and effective, implementing it can be a real challenge for teachers. The structure itself violates the expectations of many students, administrators, and parents; it seems to compete for time with the official curriculum; and it often contradicts teachers' professional training and their own childhood experience in school. Nor do students always take smoothly and effortlessly to the workshop model: on the contrary, implementation can be bumpy, tricky, and slow, even for dedicated teachers in progressive schools. Because the structure is unfamiliar and complex, smart teachers give plenty of time to training. They begin by explaining the structure to students long before commencing the workshop. Joanne Hindley, whose book *In the Company of Children* (1996) provides a superb picture of a workshop-based third-grade classroom in New York, spends one whole month preparing children for workshop. She reports that by the time the month of orientation (and build-up) ends, her students can't wait to write.

When the workshop is first begun, teachers keep the time short—it can always be lengthened later as kids become more independent. To help with the start-up, they may bring in an extra adult or some workshop-savvy upper-grade children from down the hall. In the early days of workshop, teachers keep the structure simple, limiting kids' choices as needed to get the work started. For example, if having a peer conference is an available option right from the first minute of the workshop, many kids will automatically choose to talk with a classmate instead of producing something to conference about. So teachers install temporary rules: "Work by yourself for the first twenty minutes. After 9:15 you can have a kid conference if you want." This and a hundred other adaptations show how teachers move from the promising metaphor of the crafts-workshop to the manageable reality of classroom workshop.

All the trouble and training are worth the effort. When the workshop starts to work, it turns the traditional transmission-model classroom upside down: students become active, responsible, self-motivating, and self-evaluating learners, while the teacher drops the talking-head role in favor of more powerful functions as model, coach, and collaborator. The classroom begins to embody the ideals of Best Practice, becoming genuinely—and manageably—student-centered, authentic, collaborative, and challenging.

In this chapter we hear from two teachers who are pioneering their own Variations of the workshop/studio/laboratory method. Dale Halter describes his conscious attempt to transfer the workshop model of Graves, Calkins, et al., directly into his sixth-grade mathematics classroom in suburban Des Plaines, Illinois. Dale's article shows how mathematical understanding and communication, two aspects of mathematics that were emphasized by the National Council of Teachers of Mathematics *Curriculum and Instruction Standards* (1989), can be brought to life in a workshop situation. In Dale's well-organized classroom, student mathematicians are working on many different projects and investigations at the same time, sharing their results with each other.

Karen Dekker takes the workshop model into the world of poetry, using a blend of freedom and structure to evoke some remarkable verse from her middle schoolers. Karen builds community with her burgeoning poets by beginning the workshop with lots of reading and sharing of favorite poetry, while she serves as a model by sharing her own poems with the group. Her students discover that they enjoy writing poetry and that for many of them, poetry is a special and liberating form of expression.

In the Step by Step section, Harvey Daniels writes about conferences, the heart of the workshop. Many teachers have demonstrated that student-teacher conversations can be the most important way of mentoring students in a workshop. Harvey details twelve kinds of conferences that promote student responsibility and growth. Jeanne Heinen, who teaches at a Chicago high school for special education students, tells how she began with a short stretch of sustained silent reading time, and started growing toward a reading workshop. Jeanne takes us through the nuts and bolts of establishing her workshop, showing how she and her students created the norms they needed to function together. Jeanne's story reminds us that every workshop is different, and that every one of them is always growing. The workshop is never done, but is always evolving.

# Further Reading

Allen, Janet, and Kyle Gonzalez. 1998. *There's Room for Me Here: Literacy Workshop in the Middle School.* York, ME: Stenhouse.

Atwell, Nancie. 1987. *In the Middle: Writing, Reading, and Learning with Adolescents.* Portsmouth, NH: Boynton/Cook.

Avery, Carol. 1993. *. . . And with a Light Touch: Learning About Reading, Writing, and Teaching with First Graders.* Portsmouth, NH: Heinemann.

Brown, Cynthia Stokes. 1994. *Connecting with the Past: History Workshop in Middle and High Schools.* Portsmouth, NH: Heinemann.

Graves, Donald. 1983. *Writing: Teachers and Children at Work.* Portsmouth, NH: Heinemann.

Harwayne, Shelley. 1992. *Lasting Impressions: Weaving Literature into the Writing Workshop.* Portsmouth, NH: Heinemann.

Hindley, Joanne. 1996. *In the Company of Children.* York, ME: Stenhouse.

Hubbard, Ruth Shagoury. 1996. *A Workshop of the Possible: Nurturing Children's Creative Development.* York, ME: Stenhouse.

Jorgensen, Karen. 1993. *History Workshop: Reconstructing the Past with Elementary Students.* Portsmouth, NH: Heinemann.

Rief, Linda. 1992. *Seeking Diversity: Language Arts with Adolescents.* Portsmouth, NH: Heinemann.

Saul, Wendy, Jeanne Rearden, Anne Schmidt, Charles Pearce, Dana Blackwood, and Mary Dickinson Bird. 1993. *Science Workshop: A Whole Language Approach.* Portsmouth, NH: Heinemann.

Zemelman, Steven, and Harvey Daniels. 1988. *A Community of Writers: Teaching Writing in the Junior and Senior High School.* Portsmouth, NH: Heinemann.

# Variations

## A Community of Mathematicians

DALE HALTER

Like English, mathematics is a language. People use mathematics to make sense out of the world and to communicate what they think and know. NCTM's *Curriculum and Instruction Standards for School Mathematics* (1989) put heavy emphasis on two particular aspects of mathematical power: understanding and communication. This language-oriented view of mathematics calls for some changes in our vision of teaching and learning. It seems reasonable, then, to look at the best theory and practice already developed for language education and think about applying those principles to our teaching of mathematics.

One method that has been extraordinarily successful in many language arts classrooms is the reading and writing workshop. Many teachers are already familiar with this popular model; Nancie Atwell, Donald Graves, Lucy Calkins, Steven Zemelman, and Harvey Daniels have all written extensively about workshop. In this article, I want to discuss how I have adapted and translated some principles and techniques of workshop to teaching mathematics in my own sixth-grade mathematics classroom.

The following assumptions have guided my explorations of the mathematics workshop. In this special community of mathematicians:

1. Students learn to use mathematics to create meaning for themselves and others. Rather than only learning about the discrete skills involved in mathematics, specific skills like adding and division are taught in the context of the students making meaning in real-life applications.

2. Students spend time talking and writing about mathematics for real audiences and for real purposes, because understanding and communication are so closely linked. The purpose of mathematics is to understand the world and communicate that understanding; school mathematics must have that same purpose.

3. Students relate the mathematics they use in school to their everyday lives, and to other school subjects (social studies, music, science, physical education, etc.).

4. Students have a great deal of choice in what they study. They confer with the teacher to determine what investigations or reports they will

work on, and what mathematical concepts those projects will involve. The teacher and students also decide how the results of the work will be reported, and to what audience (an oral report to the class, a poster in the hall, a letter to the P.T.A., etc.). Within this context of real mathematics work, the teacher finds opportunities to help students develop the specific skills they need and the curriculum requires.

5. The teacher is a fellow learner and mathematician with the students, as well as an expert resource and coach.

The math workshop encourages students to work together, using mathematics to understand their world. The teacher works alongside the students, encouraging them to become more sophisticated in their mathematical skills and understandings and in their ability to communicate mathematically. This atmosphere is designed to resemble a community of mathematicians dealing with real-life mathematical situations and problems.

With these principles in mind, the teacher's goal is to help students create this community in the classroom. Reaching that goal is a complicated, interesting, and invigorating task; of course, there is no one way to do it. What follows is my own approach to beginning the year in a mathematics workshop. It is not a plan for a whole year of teaching, but rather an example of the kinds of activities that have been used to get one classroom community started.

## Beginning the Year: A Survey

I start the year by asking my sixth-grade students to fill out a survey of their attitudes toward and experiences with mathematics (see Figure 5.1). This survey looks very similar to the reading and writing surveys Nancie Atwell published in *In the Middle* (1987). Two purposes are served here: I get to know something about the kids' attitudes and history as math students, and they begin to get a sense that this math class is going to be about what they think, that their ideas will have an important place in our classroom.

## An Initial Investigation

Our upcoming year of mathematics workshop will be filled with students doing mathematical investigations and reporting their results to the class (and to other audiences when appropriate). In order to help them get prepared for this kind of work, I begin an investigation with the whole

## Mathematics Survey

Name _____

For the first seven questions, circle the number that best shows what you think or feel about the question.

1. Do you like math?
   Not at all                                    Very much
   0    1    2    3    4    5    6    7    8    9    10

2. How good are you at doing math?
   Not at all                                    Very much
   0    1    2    3    4    5    6    7    8    9    10

3. Do you get good grades in math?
   Not at all                                    Very much
   0    1    2    3    4    5    6    7    8    9    10

4. Do you use math outside of school?
   Not at all                                    Very much
   0    1    2    3    4    5    6    7    8    9    10

5. In school, how often do you learn new things in math?
   Not at all                                    Very much
   0    1    2    3    4    5    6    7    8    9    10

6. Do you use math in other subjects in school?
   Not at all                                    Very much
   0    1    2    3    4    5    6    7    8    9    10

7. Outside of math class, is math important?
   Not at all                                    Very much
   0    1    2    3    4    5    6    7    8    9    10

Please write a brief answer to each of these questions:

8. What does it take to be good in math?

9. What do you do best in math? Why?

10. What kind of math is most difficult for you? Why?

11. When is math the most fun to do? Why?

12. How do teachers know when a student is good at doing math?

13. In general, how do you feel about math?

**Figure 5.1** The math workshop begins by seeking students' mathematical autobiographies.

class together. One simple project students have found engaging begins with the question, "How long do you think our class would stretch if we laid down in the hallway end to end?" Students work in groups to make an estimate; then they tell their estimate to the class and explain how they reached it. We then go out and lie down in the hallway to see how long we are. This leads to discussion of what an average sixth grader's height is. It also helps students deal with problems involved in adding, multiplying, and dividing using feet and inches (or centimeters and meters).

This first whole-class investigation gives the students a framework for going about similar projects on their own and in groups. This height project can lead into an inquiry in which the class describes the "average sixth grader." Students think of ways to describe themselves, and then each student chooses one attribute (age in days, eye color, distance of home from school, etc.). That student's job is to gather information about that attribute, describe the "average student" in a mathematical way, and present the results to the class. While each student is responsible for a report, students may also work in groups, which act as support and give feedback to the individuals on how their reports are coming. The culminating event for each student is a report to the class, which can include visual and oral presentations of the information (what attribute I studied, what information I got, and how I found the average). My students usually make "average student posters" to hang in the hallway for Parent Orientation night.

# ▲ A Typical Unit: Measurement

In the math workshop, one unit of study might focus on measurement. Students begin by discussing why and how people measure things. After making a list of their ideas (and the teacher's), students are formed into groups. The students' tasks can be explained as follows:

## Your Measurement Projects

In our last class discussion, we listed many things that people measure. Some of them are listed for you below. If you think of other things people measure, add them to your list. That list can help you decide on projects you want to do.

THINGS PEOPLE MEASURE

1. Length (6 inches, 10,000 miles)
2. Area of a flat surface (900 square feet)
3. Volume (one quart, 50 cubic feet)

4. Time (three hours, 1/10 of a second, 500 years)
5. Speed (55 miles per hour, 186,000 miles per second)
6. Loudness (25 decibels)
7. Heat (98.6 degrees Fahrenheit, 1 degree Celsius)
8. Work (800 foot-pounds)
9. _____
10. _____

As you work through this unit, your group needs to do the following things:

1. Each member of the group must do an individual measurement project. This project will use one or more types of measurement. You will do the measuring and calculating necessary to describe whatever you have selected, and report to your group (and maybe the whole class) on what you measured and how you did it.
2. Your group will also work together on a group project. This will be like the individual project, but everyone in the group must help do the measuring and calculating. Everyone in the group must also help present the project to the class.
3. During this unit the whole class will work together on some mini-lessons. Every member in the group must participate fully in these lessons. Your participation may include leading lessons for the class, if you wish.

As the students think about possible subjects for individual and group reports, they may need help in the form of suggested topics. While it is ideal for students to come up with their own ideas, it is also natural for mathematicians within a community to ask each other for ideas. Below are some measurement questions that kids have pursued at our school; certainly every school or community presents a wealth of similar possibilities.

1. How many cement blocks were used to make (our classroom, the gym, etc.), and how much do they weigh?
2. How much air is there in this room (the hallway, etc.)?
3. How much area is there in a (football field, baseball park, tennis court, soccer field, etc.)? Which sports use the largest areas?
4. How much garbage does our lunchroom throw out per (day, week, month, school year)?
5. Develop a rating system to judge the performance of basketball players. Use that system to rate the Chicago Bulls (or your school team) for several of their games.

6. Develop a lesson to teach something about measurement (measuring to the nearest quarter inch; cups, pints, quarts, gallons, etc.). You might choose to teach our class or some other class in the school, such as our first-grade buddies.

7. How big is our playground (perimeter, area)? How much of it is blacktop, grass, stones?

8. How thick is a piece of paper? Are all types of paper the same thickness?

9. How fast do people grow? How tall are students of various ages at Orchard Place School?

10. How does the temperature change as we go from fall into winter?

11. How far would you go if you walked continuously for (one day, one week, one month, one year)?

12. How many stones are there under the swings and slides on our playground?

13. How much work does it take for our class to walk upstairs from the lunchroom?

14. How long does it take for the average person to perform some task?

# Organizing the Mathematics Workshop

If the idea of students working on different projects and investigations in a mathematics workshop sounds valuable for students, it can also sound difficult to manage. If you are familiar with workshop in a reading and/or writing context, you will see how I have adapted the familiar structures of a literacy workshop to mathematics. Here are some suggestions of organizing techniques, many of which I've borrowed from colleagues who are running successful reading and writing workshops.

## Five Minutes: Status-of-the-Class

Status-of-the-class is a simple procedure teachers can use to make sure that every student has something productive to do. The teacher starts the period by asking each student to say very quickly what they will be working on that day, and where they are in their project. Typical student responses in a mathematics classroom might be: "I'm going to measure the hallway so that I can figure out its area" or "I'm finishing the poster about the speed of cars in front of the school" or "I need to talk to you about what I should do next in my project." Status-of-the-class gives the teacher an idea of who is making good progress and who needs immediate attention. It calls on the students to be responsible for determining what they will do and for making progress each day. It also helps students get ideas by hearing about each other's projects, difficulties, and activities.

## Five to Ten Minutes: Mini-lesson

After status-of-the-class, the teacher might lead a short mini-lesson on some topic appropriate to the type of projects the students are currently working on. Typically these take five to ten minutes near the beginning of the period and are used for a wide variety of purposes. The teacher might use mini-lessons to teach about different ways to organize and present data. The teacher (or the students) might teach lessons on a particular kind of computation that is difficult for a number of students.

These mini-lessons provide one important opportunity for the teacher to "deliver the curriculum." If many students are working on games, the teacher might briefly present key concepts about probability. If they are working with measurement, mini-lessons about standard units, margin of error, area, and volume might be appropriate. The students' real-math work helps them grasp the concepts and helps them see why and when basic math skills are used. In general, these mini-lessons can help the classroom community participate in a shared set of experiences and develop a common vocabulary for their mathematical discourse.

## Thirty-Plus Minutes: Work Time

After the mini-lesson, students work independently and in small groups. This working time takes up most of the class period. The students use this time to plan investigations and carry out various kinds of research, measurement, and calculation. They organize their results into coherent final presentations (written, oral, or both) for their classmates and other audiences. During work time, the teacher meets with students to guide and advise them and to assess their progress. The teacher might make anecdotal notes about students' progress and difficulties, or use a checklist to record observations. This time provides an excellent opportunity to see exactly what a student needs to learn and to provide specific individual or small group instruction.

## Ten Minutes: Sharing Time

Sharing is an important and enjoyable time for most students. During this time, a few students will explain to the class what they have done (finished or in progress), and ask their classmates for feedback. Individual students or groups can tell the whole class what question they are studying, what they have done so far to figure it out, and what they plan to do next. They can also ask for advice on how to go about the work. Feedback from the class is officially limited to what the presenter needs and requests.

Important learning takes place when students share their work this way. Students learn from each other's reports, and the reporters learn, too. I have seen more than a few students work most of the way through a project incorrectly, only to realize their mistake when they prepare to tell their classmates what they have done. Students need a wide array of such "publishing" opportunities, chances to communicate their mathematical ideas. This can be done either through oral presentations in class or in writing, with posters to be hung in the halls, chapters in class magazines, or letters to outside agencies or individuals. A rich assortment of these outlets for sharing provides students with many opportunities for the kind of discourse so highly recommended in the NCTM standards.

# Conclusion

Together, the teacher and students in a mathematics workshop can build units around such topics as time, money, games, numbers smaller than one, or anything else of interest to them. As they do this, the teacher will find appropriate places to teach the skills and knowledge the students need—as defined by the district curriculum or the national standards. The key is designing mathematics classes that are about what the students think and know and that respect and use their real-world mathematical experiences and knowledge. Then mathematics learning takes place in a context of real mathematical work.

One very important difference in the workshop approach is that the teacher serves not just as a presenter of mathematics, but as a colearner, a model, and a side-by-side participant as students work. By joining in investigations alongside our students, we honor their work; we naturally demonstrate how adult learners tackle mathematical questions; we gain firsthand understanding of the rewards and difficulties of the kids' work; and we receive a wealth of teaching opportunities. Best of all, it gives us a chance to celebrate real-life mathematics, to show how math is really a tool for understanding subjects that are important to all of us.

Many of us learned a language like Spanish or French when we were in high school, but have lost that language because we haven't used it since then. Sadly, this is the same experience many people have with mathematics. It becomes a strange, abstract, lost language spoken only in school, and too many students leave it at the door at the end of every school day. In the same way, "school math" can seem so unrelated to things students know in the real world that they leave all their common sense outside the door when they enter math class.

Mathematics workshop is one attempt to bridge this gap, to connect the in-class language of mathematics to the outside world, to everything else our students think, know, and do. It is a way of turning our math classes into communities of active, independent learners and mathematicians.

# Poetry Workshop

KAREN DEKKER

My initial reason for starting poetry workshop with my sixth graders was simply to help students enjoy the reading and writing of poetry. I was afraid that, like me, many of them would have had poetry "ruined" for them by the objective and analytical way it is usually approached in school. While some students had already had such negative experiences with poetry in school, others had gotten a positive start in their elementary school years or at home. So for the most part, my students seemed eager to spend a seven-week period reading and writing poetry.

Over the course of our poetry workshop, the children and I discovered the many benefits of reading and writing poetry together. The most important of these was that we grew very comfortable sharing information about ourselves with one another. We learned about fascinating and meaningful moments in each other's lives, moments that otherwise might not have been shared. Also, by being immersed in reading and writing poetry, my students began to understand and appreciate some of the different approaches that poets take in expressing their ideas. They thought about and discussed "what worked" and "what didn't work" in a variety of poems, and especially in poems that they had written themselves. We had time to make mistakes, take risks, and reflect on what we had written. Having that time was critical to our success.

## A Scaffolded Approach

For the first several days of workshop, the students and I just relaxed and read poems. I asked students to bring in favorite poetry books from home, and I checked out about thirty-five poetry books from our school's resource center. We shared poems we enjoyed and told of our reasons for picking the poems. I began the workshop in this relaxed way in order to show students that poetry does not have to be dissected or analyzed. It can be enjoyed at an intuitive, affective level. The students loved having class time to explore a variety of poems.

During the next phase of our poetry workshop, I tried to do several things. Initially, I designed assignments for some beginning poems. For example, I assigned a "noise poem" (Koch 1974), in which I asked students to listen carefully to sounds they heard around them or to imagine sounds that might be heard in different parts of the world. The students might also think of noises that would not literally be heard (e.g., "the bustle of growing wheat") to incorporate into their work, thus introducing the notion of figurative language. They were also asked to begin at least some of the lines of their poems with "I hear" or "I listen to," an introduction to the use of repetition within poetry. I read them portions of "Song of Myself" by Walt Whitman as a model for their noise poem, and we discussed the sounds that he "heard" and wrote about. After these prewriting mini-lessons, the students were given class time to write their poems. They were able to share their writing with their peers as they worked, and I wandered around the classroom and observed their work in progress. As I do in my regular writers workshop, I would write along with the students at least part of the work time.

I chose this more regulated way of beginning our poetry unit to give some of my hesitant students the confidence to try writing poetry. This structure helped many students to feel comfortable and to believe that they could write poetry. It also helped them to recognize, experiment with, and focus on specific poetic strategies that they could later use in their own poems.

Next, I began giving the students broad themes about which to write. We wrote poems about family, community, memories, childhood, and so on. Before writing poetry about any of these themes, we would read and discuss three or four poems that dealt with each respective theme. This helped students to see the range of approaches that could be taken in "handling" a given topic. I saw this phase as a more independent, open way of writing; the students worked from "big ideas" that I had assigned, but they picked their own specific subjects about which to write. They also had the freedom to choose a form that worked for them.

Toward the end of the seven weeks, I gave students time to write poems on topics of their own choosing. When doing this unit again I would invite students to write about self-selected topics throughout the unit. Many students wrote extra poems—heartfelt and important pieces —on their own, which helped me to see that they craved and could handle choosing their own themes right away.

## Becoming a Community of Poets

Reading poetry aloud gave students the opportunity to share experiences and learn about one another. We wrote "looking back" poems, which focused on a person, a place, or an experience from the students' past, after reading poems from Cynthia Rylant's *Waiting to Waltz*. We read about Beaver, the small town where the speaker in the poems grew up, with its "Kool-Kup" and "Moon-Glo Motel." The children then shared their own descriptions of small towns they had visited. I talked about Gott's Corner, near the tip of the thumb in Michigan, with its gas station/grocery store and bar; the town that literally is a corner. Our discussion ended up lasting for about twenty minutes, as we compiled a list of notable features of these small towns and discussed why they were memorable. In hearing stories of cross-country family drives and long-lost relatives who were visited in small towns, we learned a lot about one another. Again, poetry became a way to bridge different students' experiences.

While I learned a lot about the students from their writing and conversation, I wanted them to learn about me, too. It did not feel right to ask them to share themselves if I held back. I also thought I could use my writing to model possible approaches or "takes" on some of the assignments. Moreover, writing with the students, I could better gauge what they were experiencing and remind myself of the difficulties and rewards in writing poetry.

When we had class time to write, I wrote with the students. I shared my first attempts and very rough drafts of poems, just as the students shared theirs. The class seemed to enjoy learning about my childhood experiences. I wrote a poem called "The Stranger Doings of Mother Nature" in an effort to model how the arrangement of words on the page can help to convey meaning in poetry or give emphasis to certain ideas. It was a poem about a frog-catching experience at my grandparents' farm:

**The Stranger Doings of
Mother Nature**

After what seemed like hours
of patient
stalking,
he caught two frogs:
Bubba and the (little one).

An empty Folgers can
still carried the bitter scent
and we poked
breathing   holes
in its plastic lid.

Next we added David's frogs;   Anger
shook
                the
can.

David's heart-
breaking cry,
a cry of
disbelief and sorrow.

The only movement:
the rapidpulsingofitsthroat,
and bulging
from Bubba's belly,
the outline of the
tiny
frog
David had worked so hard
to catch.

I think that my students were disgusted by what happened in this poem ("Bubba was a cannibal?!") but loved it. I could almost see them re-defining me as I told them about my frog-catching escapades. Why shouldn't they see me through my writing in the same way that I am permitted to see them? In his reflection on the poetry unit, Peter wrote: "You made it a lot of fun with all of the different poems, and I like the ones that you wrote, especially the 'Cannibal' one. That was funny. Thank you!"

# Use of Models

Much of the research I read on teaching poetry to adolescents stressed the use of models to help children learn to write more effectively. Often, I used the poems of published writers when introducing an idea or an assignment. For example, when the students wrote poems about people within their community, we first looked at poems from Edgar Lee Masters' *Spoon River Anthology* and discussed his approach. Sometimes, if I completed an assignment before the students, I would use my own writing as a model. I only did this in conjunction with other models, though, as I did not want students to feel limited by my versions.

For example, when the students wrote *calligrammes* (shape poems determined by their subject), I used Jean Streich's "America the Beautiful" and Guillaume Apollinaire's "It's Raining" as models, as well as my own poem, entitled "The Neighborhood Crows":

The Neighborhood Crows

| c | c | c | c | c | c | c | c | c | c | c | c |
|---|---|---|---|---|---|---|---|---|---|---|---|
| a | a | a | a | a | a | a | a | a | a | a | a |
| w | w | w | w | w | w | w | w | w | w | w | w |

A line of crows balance upon the telephone wire, black on black, chattering endlessly, of grey skies and food supplies, in their crackling caws for all the neighborhood to hear.

The calligramme assignment was a popular one; the playfulness of the form is meant to be shared, and I was glad to be a part of the excitement. Writing poetry with my students afforded me the opportunity to move out from "behind the desk" and be a participant in the learning.

# A Heightened Sense of Language

Poetry distinguishes itself from other types of writing in many ways. It is intended to be read aloud, words/lines are arranged on a page in a deliberate manner to convey meaning, and each word within a poem contributes to the poem's meaning. Yet there are aspects of good poetry that overlap the definition of good prose as well. In our study of poetry, we learned that four strategies are key in writing effectively: (1) using specific sensory details; (2) using "unforgettable language" (Fletcher 1993); (3) presenting the familiar in unfamiliar ways; and (4) writing strong endings. We practiced these strategies in mini-lessons, and the students referred to them when reading poems, responding to each other's writing, and writing their own poetry. While these strategies helped students write more effective poetry, they are equally useful in other types of writing as well.

## Use of Specific Details

The students began to see the importance of using specific details in their writing, rather than more general, abstract thoughts. Jessie wrote a poem that described herself, at the age of four, sitting in her father's closet, smelling his shirts, when what she was really writing about was the fact that she missed her dad when he went away on his frequent business trips. Kate described her old neighborhood as one of those "'Can-I-borrow-a-cup-of-sugar?' neighborhoods." Chris wrote about how he "danced on a windowsill" instead of simply saying that he put forth a lot of effort to entertain an old man at a nursing home. Liz described "carrying on in a southern accent" and remembered her words: "Better get the horses and wagon ready / if we want to get to Oregon before spring" in recalling an experience playing make-believe in the woods. Instead of explaining that his father is blind, Heath wrote that his father "has not seen a sunrise since he was a child." Big ideas are conveyed through small details, and many of the students did this effectively in their work.

In addition to "writing small," students became more aware of using sensory details in their poetry to help readers better understand their experience or more vividly picture an aspect of their poem. Carol wrote of her walk along a beach, referring to the "rough, barnacle-covered rock" and the "suction of the recently uncovered sand / not wanting to let go." Greg told of the "sounds of the night crickets, about to fade away" as morning approached at his grandmother's house. Kim wrote of the "sour and fiery taste" of blood within her mouth after an accident. Emily wrote of the "smooth white paint / covering the bannister at every inch," one of her only memories from her first house. Rachel described the ocean as "waters cloaked in black, their funeral attire." Kate described the way "pebbles scatter, as an angry boy walks home / after a hard day at school." Nearly all of the students incorporated sensory details into their poems. They understood, by listening to each other's poems, the way specific details of sight, sound, taste, or smell impact a reader.

## Unforgettable Language

Similarly, the students worked on using "unforgettable language," images that stay with the reader and awaken him to a fresh way of seeing something. One of the most effective ways of creating unforgettable moments in a poem is through drawing comparisons. As a class, we spent time reflecting upon similes and metaphors used in poems. The students even wrote their own metaphor poems, wherein the object that was being described was named only in the title. The students then guessed what each other's poems were a metaphor for. In describing a mitten, Rebecca wrote the following:

> A small pocket of warmth,
> protecting from the
> cold
> icy
> chill,
> A lost soul on the ground,
> never to be found.

And Zach wrote of a cat:

> A perfectly oiled machine
> sleek
> yet
> temperamental
> a reliable friend
> fast starts
> precise turns
> quick stops
> can go on until its fuel
> runs out.

Students incorporated similes and metaphors frequently into their own writing. In one poem, Anita described herself using metaphorical language: "Like a Spanish Rose, / but an American Daisy" and as being "Red as fire / on a Sunday night." MacDara wrote, "We entered the old gates that creaked / like fingernails on a blackboard." Nikki described going to the Twisted Christmas concert where "the mosh pit looked like jumping beans" and the music "roared like an angry tiger." Rachel created an entire noise poem that was an extended metaphor:

**kitchen symphony in c major**

> I think I will do nothing for a long time but listen
> listen to the great
> symphony
> of my house at dinner.
> the orchestra begins with the
> banging of pots and pans,
> followed by the rushing water from the
> faucet and
> the bubbling soup, hot on the stove.
> I listen to the great soprano,
> my dog,
> singing with her howling and barking
> that becomes a muted snarl.
> the whirring of the lettuce spinner,
> the dicing of the pears, and
> the tinkling of the silverware in the drawer
> form a trio that softens to the soup, now faintly
> bubbling.
> I hear the rustle of the white damask tablecloth

> being laid on the dark, cedar table,
> and the crackle of the lit candles.
> the clinking of the ice in glasses
> serve as the fairy-like bells that end this
> kitchen symphony in c major.

Unforgettable language extends beyond the use of similes and metaphors to any word or image that makes the reader pause and rethink the idea. For example, Meredith, in writing about a man she saw trying to paint over graffiti at the train station, wrote: "The many coats of paint smell of / frustration and unanswered questions." For me as a reader, that was a powerful way to communicate the senseless destruction. Kate wrote about her elderly, rollerblading neighbor, describing her as "a seventy-year-old woman of the nineties." Again, her words speak more than what is written; they focus on numbers and contrasting images, which add a playfulness to her poem.

Part of getting students to use unforgettable language is helping them realize when they have communicated an idea in a truly original and thought-provoking way. As a reader of their poetry, I tried to catch them expressing an idea effectively and explain to them why their line or image worked for me. Ralph Fletcher (1993) encourages teachers to become mentors to young writers, recognizing that "a mentor builds on strengths, often seeing more in a student's work than the student sees." For example, when Chris read his poem about a dangerous sledding experience to the class, I pointed out the action verb he used in the following lines: "Racing down the icy slope / coping with the scattered trees." We talked about the fact that "coping" is not generally used in the context of sledding; usually it refers to dealing with stress or daily problems. That made it a fresh way of referring to the fact that Chris was doing the best he could to avoid the obstacles that lay before him on the hill. When I asked Chris if he had given a lot of thought to using that word in his poem, he laughed and said that it had just popped into his head. By raising the students' awareness of the effectiveness of certain words or images, I wanted to encourage them to seek out opportunities to say things in unique and interesting ways.

The students became increasingly conscious of the diction used in their poems. As Kim wrote, "One of the poems I think I did well on was the noise poem. I enjoyed thinking and listening just to catch the perfect sound in words. My favorite line in this poem is '. . . the crystal flake, hitting the soft white snow.'" Jessie wrote: "I improved a lot on my ability to find my mistakes and find better words that sound more in line with my poem. For example, sometimes when a word didn't seem to fit exactly what I was saying, I would look in the thesaurus and try to find a better meaning for my ideas." I was glad to see my students becoming aware of language, not only for the sake of writing poetry, but for the carryover to other types of writing as well.

## Presenting the Familiar in Unfamiliar Ways

Throughout the poetry unit, we discussed the concept that poetry seeks to make the familiar unfamiliar. Poems help us to see a person, a place, an event, or an object with new eyes. One student wrote that she had "never done a kind of writing that took a look at something and took it deeper than it already was, that looked at something inside and out. For example, I looked at a flower and saw a rainbow captured in the soft, silky lace." In order to foster this type of intense observation and description, the students read Wallace Stevens' "Thirteen Ways of Looking at a Blackbird." While this is a difficult poem, we simply discussed the tone of each of the stanzas and the different ways in which the bird is described or perceived. In some stanzas, the blackbird was frightening; in others, it was a precious creature. In some stanzas, the blackbird was in motion, while in others it was still against a landscape. Borrowing an idea from Kenneth Koch (1974), the students worked in groups to view ordinary objects in five different ways. They then worked independently to create a poem that presented an object of their choice in five different ways. Rebecca did an especially sophisticated job with this assignment:

**Five Ways of Looking at the Wind**

1
The music maker,
it whistles and dashes, through, in, and about
leaving the imprint of its coming,
ringing in the ears of an attentive traveler.

2
The different moods of the wind,
changing as often as
the place it is blowing through.

3
The calming breeze,
bringing the sweet smell of spring
and thoughts of the summer to come.

4
The angry rage of the wind,
leaving destruction in its path,
never to look back on the pain it has caused.

5
Against the hazy backdrop of our future,
the wind leads,
the intelligent close their eyes
and let it take them where it will.

The students then wrote poems viewing themselves in at least five different ways. Peter described himself as "A little speck / among the football crowd." Emily wrote of herself: "All she wants to do / is make a difference. / She would never go on, / if she didn't know it was / possible." Meredith described a piece of herself: "Hair as dark and gloomy / as the midnight sky." Heath noted that he is "A boy who eats whatever he wants / because he is only 83 pounds." Ned accurately wrote that he "tries to fit into / new places / like a bird flying south / for the first time." Ryan saw himself as "glued tight to the VCR / like a monkey to a banana." Heather described herself as "A dancer / the only dedicated tapper / in the grade." While the students found it difficult to write about themselves, they were extremely perceptive and sometimes painfully honest when examining the different facets of their identity.

## Strong Endings

The students also worked on writing poems that contained a "twist" or "punch" to keep the reader thinking. We read many poems, such as "Icicle" by David Huddle, which provided a thought-provoking ending, where the message or mood of the poem took a sudden shift. The students caught on to this technique quite easily, wanting to leave the reader to think and rethink their words. Heather's poem shows this:

**Before My Birthday Party**

Every second, I counted
how
much
longer,
hoping the clock would speed up for once.
50s music drifted into the living room and
I smelled the excitement in the air.

I picked up a smooth, purple-and-white-striped hula hoop and
spun it around my waist, to practice for the party.
I thought about how much fun I was going to have,
and then the doorbell rang.

I liked Heather's final line for a couple of reasons. First, the doorbell
ringing seemed to be a call back to reality for the speaker of the poem,
delivering her from her hopeful reveries. Also, the first few times I read
Heather's poem, I interpreted the last line to mean: and then the excitement stopped; the excitement seemed to be the anticipation of the party,
not the party itself.

Another poem with a powerful ending was Kim's:

**Christmas with Eric**

We sat, smelling the Swedish sausages
cooking in the kitchen,
as we all sang St. Lucia.
I saw Eric looking at me, laughing.
His face was kind, full of wrinkles.
As the sausages were passed around,
Helen asked Eric to say grace.
Tears filled his eyes,
as well as those of Florence, his wife.
Everybody, except me, knew
that this would be his last Christmas
with us.

As I read this poem, I began to sense that something was not "quite right"
when tears filled Eric's eyes; still, I wondered if they were tears of joy. The
final lines shed a new light on the situation, and left me marveling at
Eric's composure and his acceptance of death. The poem's ending contrasted sharply with the festive atmosphere at the beginning of the poem.

As our poetry workshop came to an end, I was pleased with the way
in which students began to examine language more closely, to experiment,
take risks, learn from their failures, and build on their successes.

# Step by Step

## Conferences: The Core of the Workshop

HARVEY DANIELS AND STEVEN ZEMELMAN

One of the reasons teachers set up workshop-style classrooms is to make room for regular one-to-one conferences with individual kids. These student-teacher conversations are so fundamental that the workshop model itself is sometimes called the "studio-conference method." As master teachers like Donald Graves (1983, 1994) have shown, even teacher-student conferences as short as three minutes and spaced as far apart as two weeks can have a surprisingly strong impact on students' learning. So, while the structure of workshop has many other beneficial effects, it inherently provides a set of norms by which the teacher can hold brief individual conferences while other students work autonomously for extended periods of time. When teachers institute a workshop for forty-five minutes or an hour a day, they are implicitly swapping the low-intensity impact of whole-class instruction for brief but powerful individual lessons embedded in long chunks of orderly practice time.

Why are conferences so valuable? Why are they worth the trouble to set them up? To start with, conferences obviously facilitate the individualization that educators (and parents) always dream of but find so hard to provide in practice. In conferences, we can talk to each child just about what that person needs at that moment, instead of aiming our teaching at "the middle of the group." Teachers also find that students are more comfortable and self-disclosing in private conversation than in the whole-class setting. Many kids "open up" in conferences, showing far more of what they know and what they need. In a very real sense, conferences are a way of opening a whole separate channel of communication between teacher and students, one that is unexploited in classrooms where the talk is predominantly teacher-to-group.

Ironically, once teachers have created time for conferences, they sometimes cannot think of what to say. Teachers new to workshop-style classrooms ask: "How can I be sure I say the right thing in conferences?" "What happens if I say the wrong thing?" "How can I plan what to say to many different children in a day?" These sincere concerns remind us just how rarely teachers actually talk to individual kids about their work, and how little experience they have in taking up a coaching, rather than a presenting, role. Indeed, teachers who work mainly in traditional,

**Figure 5.2** One-to-one, teacher-student conferences are the heart of the workshop model.

transmission-model classrooms are relatively unaccustomed to having face-to-face conversations with individual kids.

Teachers tend to wonder what information or advice they can deliver in a conference, just as they might decide what information to present in a lecture. But conferences should not be treated as simply another delivery system for teacher presentations—indeed, they are actually quite inefficient mechanisms for distributing information. What conferences uniquely provide are chances for teachers to take on some very different roles—as mentor, coach, and model. Instead of delivering facts, teachers can demonstrate patterns of thinking, habits of mind. With virtually any piece of student work on the table before them, teachers can lead students through the stages of reflection and self-assessment. As an experienced learner, the teacher can show how a researcher sifts and winnows information, creates categories, interprets data, resolves discrepancies; or how a writer combs back through the text of a draft, finding places for revision and improvement, editing and polishing.

The ultimate value of conferences does not lie in what goes on during any one three-minute session, but in what develops over a recurrent series of meetings between a teacher and a learner. When conferences are a regular occurrence, teachers can inculcate the habit of stopping to take stock: to pause amid one's efforts, to review the work to date, to identify strengths and weaknesses, to review possible courses of action, to make choices among possible next steps, and to put one's plans to work—and, after not too long an interval, to pause and reflect once more.

In other words, conferences are private demonstrations of how to think, how to run your brain, how to monitor your work, how to evaluate your products, how to sustain your efforts. In the best of conferences, the teacher does not step in to solve students' problems or make their decisions, but guides them through the process of deciding for themselves, making their own choices, and living out the consequences. Conferences help kids internalize that vital cognitive habit of shifting gears from production to reflection, from immersion to distancing, from doing to assessing. And the key to this cognitive coaching is not advice or information given by teachers, but their presence, patience, and consistency in accompanying students through the process.

## Conducting Conferences

Understanding the deep structure of conferences, teachers can relax about what they say in any one conference, and see themselves more as long-term thinking coaches. The process, the regularity, the developing relationship, the habits of mind are most important. There's not one right conference to have, but many worthwhile conversations to pursue. With any given child, with any piece of work at hand, and at any particular moment, there will always be several "correct" conferences, many healthful and valuable things that a caring, tuned-in adult can say. Of course, some approaches may be better than others, and we could imagine a few that would be ill-timed or even destructive. But by and large, teachers can't go too far wrong as long as they construe the conference as a natural, human conversation between an expert and a novice or apprentice.

Here are some ideas about the mechanics of conferencing, drawn largely from the works of Graves (1994) and Zemelman and Daniels (1988).

- Before you start conferences, explain how they will work, so students know what to expect and can come prepared. Because time will be short, kids need to realize that conferences will probably focus on a single issue or topic rather than a comprehensive review of a study, paper, or reading project. Let students know that conferences are for real, back-and-forth talk, and they should be ready to join in by sharing questions, ideas, plans, or problems. If you think students will have trouble envisioning a conference, act one out in the "fishbowl"—pick one volunteer child, sit in the middle of the room, and have a conference for everyone to hear and discuss.

■ Pick the spot for conferences. Some teachers like to have students come to them at their desk. While this can be convenient, it also reinforces the traditional teacher-student power imbalance, and can make it hard to break off a conference when time is up and a student lingers. A neutral spot elsewhere in the room can be a better choice; a table in the back works well, so other kids looking up will not be distracted. Nancie Atwell, who pioneered language arts workshops in the 1980s, opined that a rolling chair should be standard equipment for the conferencing teacher, so you can swoop up to (and away from) students' desks as needed.

■ Wherever you locate your conferences, sit on the same side of the table with the student, signaling collaboration rather than opposition. Let the student hold the paper and decide to angle it or hand it to you if she wishes.

■ The scheduling of conferences presents a variety of choices, each with advantages and disadvantages. Teachers can allow students to request conferences as they need them, one day or one class at a time, which provides flexibility and maximizes the chance to catch students at their "teachable moments." On the other hand, putting conferences on a regular, recurrent schedule—seeing the same five students every Monday, another five on Tuesdays, and so on—offers the benefit of regularity and predictability. When conferences are held on student demand, the neediest or most dependent students may monopolize the teacher's time, while shier students go days or weeks without conferences. Skillful teachers work around these risks: if their conferences are on a fixed schedule, teachers save ten minutes each day for unscheduled students with immediate needs or "emergencies." If conferences are set up daily by student demand (like a sign-up list on the board), the teacher reserves the right to invite students to conferences herself, especially focusing on those who don't volunteer.

■ Ask questions and help students talk, rather than just studying what's on the desk and giving a comment. Opening questions can help the student start off the conference and explain what she is trying to accomplish. "OK, Jill, tell me what your report is about and what part you're working on right now." Questions can signal the teacher's interest in the ideas, draw students out, and encourage them to consider more information: "I didn't realize a computer could do that. Do you need some special program or equipment?"

- Ask questions that help students see where they are in their work and how they might proceed: "OK, so you are having troubles with your partner. Tell me how these problems started. How could you two sort this out?" Questions can also encourage students to identify the main idea or structure they are creating: "So what is the main thing you are trying to say with this bar graph?" As we wait while students answer these questions, we are letting them work out what they need to take their next steps or improve their work.

- Search for questions students can answer, rather than questions that put them on the spot. Conferences should encourage students, not just prove the teacher is smarter. If the student thinks their project is perfect even though problems are apparent, ask what it is that gives him the most satisfaction with it, or how he thinks a reader will react to particular parts. This can give you valuable information about what the student is trying to achieve, and what approach might help him understand the difference between his own perception and that of an outside reader.

- Wait after asking a question. Give students a chance to think, and try not to jump in immediately. Silence can be a good sign. Remember, we are using conferences to teach thinking, and we must allow students time to think.

- If the student wants to read a chunk of their journal, log, or draft aloud, simple listening can sometimes be a helpful form of conferring. Not only can you offer a response at the end, you can notice (and perhaps won't even need to help at) those lovely moments when the student hears an error or thinks of a revision, picks up a pencil and jots down a correction or a note to herself. This is what it means to be a thinking coach; it is conferencing in action.

- Keep conferences short. Many teachers limit meetings to three or four minutes, which allows them to see a good number of students during each workshop session, often getting to each student once a week. Though at first a three-minute conference can seem almost rudely short, once teachers and students become accustomed to the span and come prepared, both are often surprised how much can be done within these limits. Some teachers can never get comfortable with such short conferences, and so they simply conduct longer ones more infrequently, without reproaching themselves.

- You don't always need to prepare for conferences. At times, it is entirely appropriate to talk with students about work you haven't previously read or reviewed. Indeed, as a coach of the inquiry, research, scientific, or writing process, you don't need lesson plans to ask important procedural questions like: What is this about? What makes you think that? What are your assumptions? What are your problems? What could you do instead? In other words, you can help students stop and reflect without necessarily taking on an expert role.

- Stick to process and thinking issues early in the conference. If you are going to provide information or teach particular skills, do so late in the conference, and limit the amount, so the student will remember those few items clearly.

- Listen and learn from students. Conferences not only help students think, but help the teacher understand how they think, discover what is blocking them, or notice the valuable ideas hidden under surface confusion.

- Tape-record conferences periodically to monitor the process and your own teaching methods. Give your conferencing program some time before judging whether or not it works.

# Basic Types of Conferences

Because conferences are brief and must by necessity focus closely on limited tasks, it can be helpful to think about a few of the different jobs teachers and students can tackle in conferences. Each of the following types could be appropriate in any given school subject—indeed, on any given day, a teacher might be having several of these types of conferences with students at different stages in a project or with different needs as learners.

**Process Conference:** There are lots of great conferences, but this is the basic one, the classic. This conference allows teachers to conduct quick but helpful conversations with students without prereading the work at hand, without preparation, without "teaching" skills, and without offering any advice. Over the course of the conference, the teacher simply asks some version of these three questions: (1) "What are you working on?" (2) "How is it coming?" and (3) "What are you going to do next?" Other than these questions (or your own variations) the teacher doesn't need to say much else except "uh-huh" as the student talks to herself—which is the point. (This interaction is not unlike the sort of psychotherapy in which the therapist does very little talking, compelling the client to take the lead in explaining, probing, and evaluating experiences—with the long-term goal of helping the person become more reflective and self-reliant.) Often in process conferences, teachers find that they will raise one additional question somewhere along the way, something completely contextualized by the student and the topic, something that comes up naturally and unpredictably in the course of the meeting.

### Status-of-the-Class Conference:
This is a whole-group conference held at the beginning of a workshop session, during which each student says aloud what she/he will be working on that day ("I'll be running my statistics on the computer." "I'll be making a diagram for my report." "I'll be revising my draft.") In this conference, each kid makes a public commitment to some specific work, while also letting others know what they're doing, so they can work together on common tasks. Some teachers have students run and record the status-of-the-class, saving themselves from the record keeping.

### Topic Search Conference:
In workshop-style, project-oriented programs where kids actually have a choice of what to pursue, they sometimes need help choosing. The topic search conference focuses on helping the student generate a list of possible interests, and then selecting one promising idea to pursue. Essentially, this is a process of guided brainstorming; the teacher's job is to help the student develop a written list of possible choices. The point is not to struggle toward one idea, but to generate a bunch, a surplus, and then narrow down. The teacher can be the recorder, freeing the child to generate ideas and alternatives, and then handing over the list at the end of the conference. Some teachers bring along another kid or two for more good ideas in topic search conferences.

### Read-Aloud Conference:
When students are drafting a report, paper, or story, they can read a section part of the piece aloud to teacher, as a way of hearing their own work and getting the teacher's reaction and comments. Students are encouraged to pause amid the reading, as they notice problems or get new ideas. Teachers wait while kids make notes about what to do later. One common variation is for the teacher to read a section aloud to the student, again pausing for the student to make notes or changes.

### Summarizing Conference:
One problem that often arises in primary grades is that students want to spend all their conference time reading their work aloud to the teacher. In the secondary version of this phenomenon, students hand papers to teachers, expecting them to use most of the conference silently reading, and then offering a response. As noted above, some of this sharing can be valuable, but there are many other important purposes for conferences. By holding summarizing conferences, the teacher helps students to move beyond the simple hunger for

an audience (or for approval) and begin to reflect more broadly on their thinking strategies and work habits. In summarizing conferences, teachers ask students to tell about, summarize, or paraphrase the work they are doing, instead of sharing samples of it. In these conferences, the written work usually stays in the folder or even back at the desk.

Content Conference: Though many of the types of conferences described here focus on thinking and inquiry processes, content does matter —and teachers are often experts in subject matter. So it is entirely appropriate at times to have conversations officially aimed at discussing and developing the ideas, meaning, or content inside a research project, draft, or report. If the teacher is offering information, sources, or authors to be investigated later, notes jotted by the teacher can help a writer remember things to do later, back at their desk.

Dialogue Journal Conference: This is the written version of conferences, in which students and teacher exchange notes about selected chunks of curriculum on a specified schedule. The most common use of written conversation is reading logs, where students regularly record their responses to class readings in the form of an informal note to the teacher. The teacher responds in kind (on a schedule designed to avoid burnout while providing every student with regular personal notes). In addition to being a coaching conversation, dialogue journals are also a powerful reading and writing lesson, since the teacher is creating a personalized text for each student, modeling skillful adult writing in the process.

Editing/Publication Conference: It is fine for some conferences to be devoted to simple, narrow tasks, such the final proofreading of a draft aimed at a publication or display. Usually, time prevents doing the whole job, so editing conferences amount to a brief stretch where the student and teacher are doing the task together—a paragraph or a page—with the teacher showing how a skilled adult catches and fixes mistakes. A nice version of this for younger kids is the finger-editing conference, useful when the child wants a "perfect" final draft. The kid reads through the piece aloud, as the teacher runs her finger under the text. There are three possible outcomes when an error is encountered: (1) The child recognizes it, stops, and makes the correction herself; (2) The student stops but isn't sure what to do, in which case the teacher supplies the information and the student enters the change; (3) the student doesn't notice an error at all, so the teacher stops her, locates the problem, and asks if she knows what is needed. If the student can make the fix, she does so; if not, the teacher supplies the change.

**Evaluation Conference:** Though many conferences stress the ongoing process of inquiry, searching for revisions and next steps, students also do finish work from time to time. Then, it is appropriate to hold an evaluation conference, with the student and teacher sitting down to review the strengths and weaknesses of a project or piece of finished work. Among the key outcomes of such conferences are specific written goals (entered in the student's course log or folder) for the next project. An important form of evaluation is the portfolio conference, in which student and teacher review a body of work over a span of time. Typically, the student is asked to identify the most successful and most problematic pieces, talking about strengths and weaknesses, and setting plans for future growth. On an even wider scale, teachers with ongoing workshops often schedule quarterly evaluation conferences, which involve students in the grading process. They may ask students to score themselves on a performance rubric, fill out another copy themselves, and then meet in conference to review and reconcile each other's ratings.

**Student's Choice Conference:** One of the trends we hope to see in workshop classrooms is students taking more ownership and responsibility for all phases of their work, including the focus of conferences. In mature workshops, one often hears teachers starting conferences with a single question: "How can I help you?" or "What do you want to work on today?" Then, the student brings up a particular problem or concern in their work, which becomes the focus of a free-ranging conversation. This kind of kid-driven conference may not immediately work with inexperienced students, who don't yet know how to initiate and carry on a true give-and-take conversation with a teacher. Sometimes they first need to experience the range, the repertoire of choices that they actually enjoy, before they can effectively "run their own" conferences. But after teachers have shown them the choices, kids should be charting the course of most conferences.

**Small Group Conference:** While the basic design of workshops calls for individual student conferences, small group meetings can be an important option, as long as teachers stay in the role of thinking coach. The teacher can meet with three or four kids at once, perhaps ones with a common interest or who are teaming on a project. Small group conferences can be a way for the teacher to get to more students when there isn't enough time or when classes seem too big. For teachers new to workshopping, small group conferences may simply feel more comfortable and familiar, since they seem similar to reading groups. The drawback to group conferences, of course, is that the special focus isn't on a single child; on the other hand, in groups children do get a wider audience for their thoughts, and get to hear how other students are thinking and talking about their work.

**Peer Conference:** Teachers are the main bottleneck in scheduling conferences; the number of meetings is limited by the amount of time the teacher has. The obvious and necessary solution is to work toward student pairs or peer group conferences. Once kids have learned from their own individual teacher conferences what kinds of conversations can be held, they can run their own meetings without the teacher present. Students can eventually conduct any of the above types of conferences—topic searching, editing, process, whatever. As students take more responsibility in this area, teachers will need to shift to coaching groups, making sure students keep to the spirit of the conferences at hand, don't regress to bickering or gossiping, or otherwise get off track. Student-led evaluation conferences can be especially tricky and require some special training so that kids neither wound nor soft-soap each other. Smart teachers prepare kids by having them first practice on "training papers" taken from unknown students outside the class, which helps students hone their critical diplomacy before evaluating each other's work.

Conferences, when they are genuine two-way conversations, can develop student responsibility and promote growth. If conferences become teacher-dominated or advice-centered, they can backfire, silencing kids and discouraging involvement. And make no mistake—it can be tough for teachers to stay in this unfamiliar mentor role. Donald Graves says it well:

> How hard it is for an activist to conduct conferences. Everything is reversed. I have to give up the active, nondelegating, pushing, informing role for another kind of activity, the activity of waiting . . . But the rewards, the new energy as the learner teaches me, keep me going . . . The top teachers, I've found, whether in the center of the city, or a rural school, have an insatiable appetite for learning. When teachers learn, children learn. (1983, 127–128)

# Growing a Reading Workshop

JEANNE HEINEN

The simplest version of reading workshop is often called sustained silent reading or SSR for short. Fine, but: How can you get kids to be silent?

To really read? To sustain this silent reading? Knowing the value of independent reading from the professional research as well as from personal observation, I was convinced not to give up on it—even when my high school English freshies show up with reading levels from 2.0 to 6.5, and, in our special school, assorted physical and learning disabilities, as well as the requisite hormones and horseplay. I do not claim unqualified success, but I have worked out some methods to get around many of the stumbling blocks.

At the risk of being "ho-hum" obvious, I cannot emphasize enough three components vital to independent reading time: (1) each student must have a book in front of him; (2) the reading session must be set for a definite amount of time—even as dictated by the audible ticks of an old-fashioned timer; and (3) I must avidly read my own book. Not such a big deal? Right. Plain, simple, effective.

## Set the Stage for Success

Make certain every kid has a book. It sounds silly to say this, but it is crucial. There will be no S, S, or R unless you attend to this. If you are fortunate you can rely on the library. However, sometimes it is difficult to schedule class time there, the collections of books at various reading levels may be limited, and the students may have bad credit ratings with the librarian. It is best to build up your own class library by employing the usual means: department book orders, abandoned treasure troves of old books in the book room or departed colleagues' cupboards and closets, student paperback book clubs (including the "freebie" orders you can earn with points from the student purchases), rummage sales, garage sales, resale shops, used book stores, remaindered copies in bookstores, and so on. Do not overlook the special ed. or L.D. teacher for resources. If you teach in a city school like mine, you may need to have padlocks installed or use a wheeled cart to protect your collection. It's difficult if you move from room to room, but it can be managed. I have even considered buying one of those $39.95 locking videotape storage cabinets and putting casters on it.

Remind kids to bring their books. Type up and distribute a schedule of reading days. Post a large schedule outside the classroom or use a knock-'em-dead neon poster or bright flag to hang on the door on reading days. As the kids pass in the hall they'll get the message to dig into their lockers before coming to class. I know some teachers who insist the books stay in the room, but that cancels out the chance of at-home reading, which I also want to encourage.

Substitute magazines if they do not bring their books. I keep a supply in my room for the forgetful types. It isn't ideal, but at least magazines give kids a chance to read and be quiet. I give them credit for reading an article and convert the columns of print to book-size pages to compute how much they read. I do however, lower their "cooperation" (a.k.a. "behavior") grade for the day, so that forgetting books is not rewarded with the privilege of reading an article about some sports figure's love life during book reading time. By the way, research seems to indicate the emphasis for SSR should be books. On the other hand, why be too fussy when the main object is to get the kids to read?

Be a mind steward. Just as the sommelier in a fine restaurant is quick to recommend wines compatible with various dishes, I have found I need to immerse myself in young adult literature titles and authors so I can direct students to books that will complement and satisfy their reading appetites. I get to know my students and their interests mainly from their journals, so I know it may take awhile to match kids with appropriate reading levels and titles. Usually the recommendation procedure snowballs as students write responses and share enthusiasm.

Choose the reading time wisely. Do not attempt SSR at the very start of a period when students are likely to interrupt and disturb the class as they trail in with tardy passes. If you have them for a double period, get a feel for their learning rhythms and schedule the reading earlier or later as you see fit.

Chart and celebrate their progress. I buy those large gridded wall charts at a teachers' store and list the names vertically and the reading due dates horizontally across the top. I can usually get two classes on a chart. The chart hangs prominently in the room. The grading formula I use for each quarter simply counts pages read: $200 = D$; $270 = C$; $340 = B$; $400 = A$. Some years I adjust down or up, depending on abilities. Even in an Intro class I have been able to require 500 or 600 pages for an A. I expect the kids to read 7 to 10 pages a day, five days a week, for homework, although the reading in class counts toward this goal. Sometimes I only require in-class reading, and then I increase the number of reading days from two to three or even daily.

To monitor comprehension I also require students to keep a written response log on their reading, three-fourths to one full page of notebook paper for every 20 or so pages read. These are turned in twice a week, on Mondays and Thursdays, or Tuesdays and Fridays. I give out sample response sheets (I disagree with . . ., I wonder . . ., I like the part . . ., etc.) and expect the kids to write enough to engage in a sustained discussion. These can be worth up to 10 points. (Five points if they only write summaries of information from the book without interpretation.) I chart these points, too, and curve them for grades. To keep motivation and enthusiasm high, it is essential to record pages and points faithfully every week. I might add here that I have also tried an Alcoholics Anonymous approach at times, where we all sit in a circle and the kids take turns announcing their weekly totals: "Hi. I'm Tiana. I'm a reader. This week I read 65 pages. Let me tell you about my book." (Applause!)

Let them "get down." Reading time is the one time I let the kids create urban sprawl all over the room, with feet on chairs, long legs stretched across rows, young shoulders scrunched down, whatever position is comfortable (though not obscene, hazardous, or conducive to sleep).

## Let the Timer Work Its Magic

For some reason, my students seem to need a continually ticking timer, not a silent electronic one that beeps only when it goes off. I do not fully understand why this is so, but trust me. After I am sure all kids have books in front of them and that paper and pencils (for writing responses after the timed reading period) are ready but not on the desktops, I really get dramatic with the timer. I announce that we are about ready to start and walk about the room holding the timer ceremoniously aloft as I go. For some reason this brings an air of serious formality to SSR. This little metal and plastic totem captures the students' attention. I announce how many minutes we shall read (5–20), turn the time knob with large sweeping motions, and set the thing down in a prominent location with a dramatic clunk. The ticking sounds ripple out across the room with a lulling but forceful message: tick, tick, tick, read, read, read. Maybe ticking replicates a mother's heartbeat (remember the old rhesus monkey-surrogate mother experiment?). All I know is that it has a calming effect and subtly keeps the kids on task. (I do take care to place the timer far from easily distracted kids.)

## Serve as Model

Every article on independent reading emphatically states the teacher must read along with the students. And every time I am tempted to use this time to read papers, do my monthly attendance summary, or whatever, I realize I am undermining my own reading program. The message has to be that reading time is sacred. I have noted many times that my students often do not settle down right away even with the timer casting its spell. I am fully aware that sometimes in their restlessness they do not get serious until they see me becoming immersed in my book. I am reading but still am aware of some noises, shifting, talking. I ignore it all and continue to read. If a sound catches my attention I look up not so much with a scolding expression but one of startled annoyance that proclaims, "Don't bother me. I'm reading." Sometimes I wave my hand down to indicate "Go away. Don't bother me." I let my reactions show as I read. I frown, I smile, I flip back to check something. I know some students are watching me and it's good for them to see a reader in action. Almost always the whole class settles down within a minute or two.

## Try it!

The bottom line on SSR is that with careful but simple precautions and preparations, it works, and before you know it you are running a reading workshop with all of its necessary ingredients. Kids start to think, to keep logs, to share, to explore topics and genres, to adopt favorite authors. As a result, I have seen some of my students' reading levels jump two and three grade levels—just because they were given the time to be readers.

# CHAPTER 6

# Authentic Experiences

W HAT DOES IT MEAN to be a learner in the real world? In life we learn because we are naturally curious and because we have a drive to make sense of the world we live in. In schools, learning does not always tap into our natural curiosity, and learning becomes lifeless, sterile, and quickly forgotten.

Carl Rogers and Jerome Freiberg (1994) talk about two different kinds of learning that fall at opposite ends of a continuum. At one end is the learning of isolated facts and nonsense syllables, which they call "learning from the neck up," and the other end is "significant, meaningful, experiential learning." This kind of learning has a strong component of self-discovery. When a child moves to a foreign country and is allowed to play freely with her companions for hours, she will probably learn the language and be able to speak it with a native accent. "But let someone try to instruct her in her new language, basing the instruction on the elements that have meaning for the teacher, and learning is tremendously slowed or even stopped" (36).

What is it about the first kind of student-centered learning that enables it to stick with the learner? Why don't the more traditional teacher-directed lessons achieve the same results? As we visited classrooms and talked to teachers about projects and activities that were meaningful for their students and for themselves, we began to notice that many of them had the qualities of what Rogers calls experiential learning: self-discovery, real-life experience, the coming together of the cognitive and the affective, and the appeal to natural curiosity. Teachers and students alike find meaning and life in this kind of learning, but in most schools and classrooms, so many elements combine to defeat what we call authentic experiences. Teachers are often bogged down in standardized measures of achievement, bureaucratically prescribed curricula, and knowledge dispensation through lecture, with a complete absence of student choice.

In this chapter, we will look at classrooms where students and teachers are at their highest level of engagement, operating at the "experiential" end of Rogers' learning continuum.

# An Asymmetrical Structure

In this book, we are writing about six important structures or methods that bring Best Practice teaching to life in classrooms. We have been arguing that these methods, when used regularly in a fairly consistent way, will give kids the kind of student-centered, meaning-driven learning that they deserve. However, this particular ingredient—*authentic experience*—is not exactly a method, and was not initially one of the classroom structures we identified when we started writing this book. However, when we began to examine the stories that teachers told us and wrote about, we noticed that many of them had the important element of being somehow real, genuine, or authentic. In these accounts, students were very often engaged either outside the school, or with outside activities brought into the school. This kind of learning seemed immediately recognizable to both the teachers and students as something important and worthwhile. Too often in classrooms around the country, students are asking teachers why they need to study the disconnected pieces of curriculum they are presented with. With authentic experiences, students are not storing their learning to be used "later," but instead are involved in stuff that has meaning for them now.

# Authentic Experiences Take Many Forms

Authentic experiences in schools can be as small as writing a real letter to ask for an autographed picture, and as large as schoolwide projects like planting a garden, setting up a recycling center, or investigating the sources of pollution on a local river. Just as in real life, these experiences are inherently messy; problems need to be identified, complexity needs to be faced, and solutions must be found.

The importance of real-life investigations, both large and small, is recognized by many national subject-matter organizations. The National Academy of Science makes this bold statement: "Inquiry into authentic questions generated from student experiences is the central strategy for teaching science. Teachers focus inquiry predominantly on real phenomena in classrooms, outdoors, or in laboratory settings where students are given investigations or guided toward fashioning investigations that are demanding but within their capabilities" (1996, 31).

This thoughtfully written standards document offers many rich classroom examples to support its call for authenticity. In one example, Mrs. F. helped her third-grade students learn about collecting data and conducting research when she noticed their fascination with the earthworms living in an empty lot next to the playground. Before ordering some earthworms from a biological supply house, she asked students to prepare a proper habitat for worms. The students spent much time examining the natural habitat of the earthworms in the empty lot before creating a similar environment in a terrarium, away from the sun and filled with soil, leaves, and grass.

The students spent two weeks observing the earthworms and recording their behavior before they began to list the questions they wanted to answer. Among the many questions that the students generated were: How do they have babies? Do they really like the dark? How big can they get? How long do they live? Children formed into small groups to decide together which question they would be most interested in exploring. The small groups were given time to decide how they would conduct their investigations and by the following week, the investigations were under way.

The group that chose to investigate the life cycle of earthworms had found egg cases in the soil, and while they waited for the eggs to hatch, they read some books about earthworms to add to their knowledge base. One group was studying what earthworms like to eat and was preparing to test foods. Two groups wondered what kind of environment earthworms preferred, and they were experimenting by varying moisture, light, and temperature.

This authentic scientific inquiry started with the interest and natural curiosity of the students and taught them much more than just stuff about earthworms. They became researchers, gathering data, manipulating variables, asking questions, discovering answers, and asking more questions. The students worked collaboratively, because in the real world science is a collaborative enterprise which is dependent upon the sharing of ideas and discoveries.

This kind of inquiry becomes possible because the conditions that are necessary to support Best Practice are already in place. The classroom is a *community*, students are willing and eager to take *responsibility* for this kind of hands-on experiential learning, and as students learn and grow they have many opportunities for *expression* of what they have observed and learned.

Social studies, like science, is a natural home for authentic school experiences. *Expectations of Excellence: Curriculum Standards for Social*

*Studies,* published by the National Council for Social Studies, asserts that "the social studies are powerful when they are meaningful, integrative, value based, challenging, and active" (1994, 162). These qualities emerge when students are enabled to immerse themselves in real-life thematic inquiries where knowledge is connected and useful both in and out of school. Further, says the NCSS, "Social studies programs should reflect the changing nature of knowledge, fostering entirely new and highly integrated approaches to resolving issues of significance to humanity" (5).

In other words, teachers should develop their curricula around the real issues that people face in the world, helping to immediately connect students to the importance of what they are learning. These connections deepen the learning process and help students to construct a personal meaning about their world. The social studies provide many opportunities for this kind of knowledge building. Students can spend real time learning about democracy by practicing it in their classrooms. Whether through writing a class constitution, setting and implementing the classroom rules, or deciding democratically what they are interested in learning about, students practice the skills that are necessary for adult participation in the world.

To help students build an understanding of themselves and their place in the world, a promising starting point is the investigation of family history. Our colleagues Pat Bearden and Yolanda Simmons have developed a form of personal historical investigation that starts by asking students to interview each other and their families about their roots. They begin with very basic questions such as: Where do my ancestors come from outside of America? Where do they come from inside America? and Where does my name come from? These initial questions send students home to interview their parents and grandparents and are the beginning of a sophisticated investigation into their own families and the events in American history that affected their lives.

Students make time lines of their lives and the lives of their ancestors, and they compare these living histories along parallel time lines of our nation's development. For example, students who find that their ancestors were slaves can read to find out what their lives must have been like. Students whose ancestors fought in World War II read to find out how the war affected their families. Just as in science, these real-life investigations, which start with the interest of the students, can provide a powerful tool for driving the learning deeper and helping all involved to see the connectedness and importance of all of the disciplines of the social sciences, including history, sociology, political science, and geography.

At the new Best Practice High School, one of the most exciting components of our curriculum is the internship program, which provides service and work experience from freshman year onward. These once-a-week placements help young people to face genuine issues about what it means to work, provide them with real-world problems to solve, and open the world of career options for them to explore. When the students were interviewed at the end of the year about the knowledge and experiences provided by the internships that they would not have received in "regular school," they reported that they learned how to deal with adults better, to solve problems on their own, and sometimes to speak to groups. We were surprised to hear that almost all students had learned to operate at least one new machine or piece of equipment. Some had learned to use big office-type photocopy machines, while others operated cameras or video equipment. Perhaps most impressive was our pair of student interns at Chicago's Adler Planetarium, who gradually became trusted to run the five-million-dollar "sky show." Returning to school after one internship morning, these girls bashfully reported that as they switched on the night sky that morning, they had "forgotten to turn off the sun." They were embarrassed, but their teachers were delighted to hear that in their internships, at least some of our students were running the universe.

## Opening the Doors to the School

In order to bring learning to life, it is important to get beyond the four walls of the school, using the world as a learning laboratory and bringing chunks of the world inside. When students are given the chance to leave the building, many important things can happen. At Washington Irving School in Chicago, principal Madeline Maraldi provides buses and blank checks for each class to visit a bookstore three times a year. In this way, the children participate in building their own classroom libraries. Each student is allowed to purchase one book, which is placed in their class-room's library with a bookplate saying "Selected for Washington Irving School by _____." Students experience firsthand the wonders of a real bookstore and the joy of purchasing a book of their choice.

But the door to the school works both ways, and sometimes inviting experiences into the school can be equally rewarding. Students in Bonnie Flannigan's second-grade class at Hendricks School in Chicago invited their grandparents to come to school to be interviewed for an intergenerational unit. Students did a great deal of preparation before the visitors arrived. Interview questions were written, and the students practiced using a video camera in order to tape the interviews. The grandparents served as expert informants, sharing their experiences about growing up and going to school. This authentic experience seemed to be as satisfying and special for the grandparents as it was for the students.

The Chicago Arts Partnership in Education (CAPE) brings real artists into Chicago schools to help students and teachers to find the artist in each of them. Forsaking the residency model of the artist as a transient discipline expert, CAPE artists join with teachers to plan extended, holistic units of study, meeting curriculum standards even as they use the arts as a lever to integrate the curriculum and invite kids' expression. These practicing artists are typically found helping to design and teach units on ecology, community history, or ethnic heritage, working alongside the regular classroom teachers. For students, working and learning with a real dancer, sculptor, or actor helps them know that doing art is a real endeavor that happens both inside and outside the school.

# A Continuum of Authenticity

We started this book with a story about taking students out to sea in an ecology ship. We still realize that not every learning experience is going to include a voyage outside the school building. But authentic experiences can be brought to students in a dozen or more modest ways. The key is providing students with activities that have relevance and meaning built right in, whether they occur inside or outside of the classroom. To begin with, simply inviting students to express their interests and curiosities is a big step toward authenticity. When students are given a voice and some degree of choice, when they are asked to think about how the learning should proceed, it is more likely that they will be able to see the importance in what they are doing.

The teachers in this chapter have discovered many Variations for bringing school to life, creating powerful opportunities for students to build and construct knowledge of and in the real world. Pete Leki, the Coordinator of Parent Projects for the Center for City Schools at National-Louis University, a parent and an urban-naturalist, writes about his experience with students and teachers in the natural world. High school teaching partners Katy Smith, Ralph Feese, and Robert Hartwig take us with them for a day on the water as participants in the Illinois Rivers Project, where students experience a truly interdisciplinary curriculum.

But not every authentic experience requires taking kids out of school. John Duffy writes about how the study of primary documents can become a central feature of teaching history, enabling students to find personal meaning in text while making history classrooms exciting and dynamic places. He believes that primary source literature also helps students to develop their own family stories and to find personal connections to the stories of history.

The next three articles take us Step by Step through some very different authentic experiences. Jim Tebo, a middle school math teacher, asks his students to apply their math skills to the problem of remodeling their bedrooms. When this high-interest problem is placed in their laps, the students are able to see that math can be a very handy problem-solving tool. Shelley Rosenstein-Freeman writes about taking students into the exciting world of the Museum of Contemporary Art in Chicago, where inner-city students became docents, learning about art, personal communication, and work. Finally, Linda Bailey tells how her school used "Me" portfolios as a way of starting the school year, setting some deep patterns of sharing and challenging students and teachers to explore themselves, their families, and their places in history. Linda writes that the "Me" portfolios project was the most successful one she ever developed because it centered the curriculum on the students while it built community in each classroom and across the whole school.

# Further Reading

Bayer, Anne Shea. 1990. *Collaborative-Apprenticeship Learning: Language and Thinking Across the Curriculum K–12.* Mountain View, CA: Mayfield.

Chancer, Joni, and Gina Rester-Zodrow. 1997. *Moon Journals: Writing, Art, and Inquiry Through Focused Nature Study.* Portsmouth, NH: Heinemann.

Horwood, Bert, ed. 1995. *Experience and the Curriculum.* Dubuque, IA: Kendall-Hunt.

Kraft, Richard J., and James Kiesmeier, eds. 1994. *Experiential Learning in Schools and Higher Education.* Boulder, CO: Association for Experiential Education.

London, Peter. 1994. *Step Outside: Community-Based Art Education.* Portsmouth, NH: Heinemann.

McVey, V. 1989. *The Sierra Club Wayfinding Book.* Boston: Little, Brown.

Nabhan, Gary, and Steven Trimble. 1995. *The Geography of Childhood: Why Children Need Wild Places.* Boston: Beacon Press.

Saul, Wendy and Jeanne Reardon, eds. 1996. *Beyond the Science Kit: Inquiry in Action.* Portsmouth, NH: Heinemann.

Shor, Ira. 1987. *Freire for the Classroom: A Sourcebook for Laboratory Teaching.* Portsmouth, NH: Boynton/Cook.

Stephens, Lillian. 1995. *The Complete Guide to Learning Through Community Service: Grades K–9.* Des Moines, IA: Allyn and Bacon.

Wigginton, Eliot. 1985. *Sometimes a Shining Moment: The Foxfire Experience.* Garden City, NY: Anchor Press/Doubleday.

# Variations

## Carver's Woods: Science in a Dump

PETE LEKI

They stood in the morning sun. Twenty fourth-grade students. Binoculars pressing into their eye sockets. Sue Friscia points across the baseball field behind the school where a group of the throaty sea birds squat.

"Uhhh. Ring neck gull," one child shouts. Nineteen others chorus the same answer a second later, "Ring necked gull."

Ms. Friscia is a science resource teacher at Carver Primary School in the Altgeld Gardens on Chicago's far south side. She loves birds and knows them by the merest flash of a tail or faintest call. For her, taking these kids out is a great and apparent pleasure.

"And what's that up on the chimney? What do we often see on the chimney? What's that?"

Binoculars rotate to the pearly western sky.

"What are these things we're standing on?"

"Rocks."

"Rock dove," says one thin voice.

"Rock dove," joins the chorus.

"I can't focus. How you work these things?"

Sue got these binoculars with Carver's discretionary funds. There are enough so that each child can learn to be comfortable with them. One child, Cynthia Barrett, totes Sue's own tripod and telescope, bringing tiny, insignificant species up close so that eye rings, tail stripes, and idiosyncrasies of habit can be seen.

"Look. Over there. Black bird, short tail."

"Crow."

"Crow, crow."

"A crow is a big, big black bird. This one's smaller. Short tail." She waits. "Stars on its chest . . ."

"Starling."

"Starling. Starling."

"European starling. Right."

Shavanna Jackson is the group's secretary. She writes down everything, adding it to the list on the clipboard. Phillip Allen flips through the field guide, finds *starling*, and walks down the line showing the page.

Now, single file, we enter the woods that stand between Carver and the Little Calumet River. In the marshy, wet understory we hear a peculiar cheeping.

"Stop. Hear that? What is that?"

"Frog."

"What kind of frog? What do you call it when people sing together?"

"Fun."

"Music."

"Choir."

"Another word for choir?"

"Chorus."

"Right. Western Chorus frogs are singing to us this morning."

The woodland habitat around us is unique to my experience. Besides the scrub wood growth of box elder, maple, poplars, and a few big cottonwood, there are dozens of scattered garbage mounds. And everywhere are TV sets, picture tubes gutted and broke, circuit boards showing garishly through cracked simulated wood exteriors. There are night stands, tar paper shingles, plastic hoodinkis, and four million tires. This place has the curious quality of seeming to exude tires from the earth. To these things Sue pays no attention. She is all given up to the birds, the kids, the sounds of the day.

"Kirchee."

"Look. Long tail, black bird. Look at the head. See how iridescent it is."

"Grackle."

"Grackle. Grackle."

"Right."

In the distance just across the river is the Dolton dump. A Caterpillar tractor labors up and down the hill pushing dusty clay over the wasteland.

Sue tells me, "They aren't allowed to expand horizontally anymore. But they can keep piling up vertically. So we'll see how high they go before the whole thing topples over."

Much of this land was subdivided years ago but has remained untenanted. What was supposed to be a strip of lovely riverside lots became undesirable in this abused and neglected corner of the realm. Its neighborhood includes two monster landfills, a steel mill, a Metropolitan Water Reclamation District (MWRD) sludge-drying site, and the tiny isolated community called Altgeld Gardens. Abandonment gave rise to dumping of trash and all the other wasteland dangers, including drug dealing and thuggery. Two human bodies were disposed of here last year, doused with gasoline and burned.

I break from the group when I see an overgrown sidewalk appear and disappear into an overgrown patch of blossoming hawthorn. It ends at an abandoned basement and foundation, now filled halfway up with brown water and hundreds of tires. Through the tires, silver maple saplings shoot up and leaf out. Beyond this ruin are acres of open prairie with hawthorn edges. It is really very beautiful.

Some teachers at Carver are hesitant to visit the site. Children are warned not to enter except as a classroom activity. But they hope to reclaim the land as a nature preserve and wildlife sanctuary, connecting Carver and Altgeld Gardens contiguously to the Beaubien Forest Preserve to the southeast.

Passing through the woodland dump section, we arrive at the bank of the Little Calumet, one of Chicago's neat anomalous morainal drainages. Most rivers catch water from the upland and erode downhill in a dendritic pattern, tiny tributaries linking up to make bigger ones, like the veins in a leaf. But the Calumet area drainage follows long, looping courses parallel to the lake boundaries around sand spurs deposited by successive receding stages of Lake Chicago. We pause here in the shade of a huge overhanging cottonwood to look at the catkins hanging down from a young poplar like ornaments.

The muddy waters are being aerated downstream by a series of man-made waterfalls in an attempt by the MWRD to resuscitate life in the waters fouled by effluents from the sewage treatment plant. Toxic ammonium levels caused by heavy industrial loading at the plant are discharged into the river and oxidized to nitrates, depleting oxygen available to living things. These sidestream elevated pool aeration (SEPA) stations apparently work well, adding another oddity to this manhandled river system and geography.

The rutted trail that runs along the river may be where 135th Street was supposed to go had the development plan worked out. Instead, it traces a path through a wet prairie teeming with life, occasional stereo speakers, lost boots, and tires.

"Flicker!" Sue points to a small stand of poplars ahead.

Cynthia sets the scope. The children mutter, "Where? Where?" and search thorough the dappled branches. "I see it. It's a woodpecker."

Sue had hopes a few years back that the City or the State or the Department of Conservation or the United Nations might buy up this piece of land, throw a fence around it, patrol it, stop trucks from dumping. It seemed the landholders were saddled with a loser, a tax liability with no future. Then Mayor Daley started making noises about building an airport near the site and hopes for a cheap sell-off vanished. But with the airport project abandoned, and the woods leafing out, and the migrating birds making every day an adventure, hope begins to spring eternal once again.

Carver School has signed up with the Nature Conservancy's Mighty Acorn project, where school children learn science and ecology through stewardship activities in natural areas. Carver is scheduled to begin work at the Beaubien Forest Preserve.

Diane Reckless, chief Mighty Acorn, agrees with Sue that the abandoned strip has a lot to offer. "Not only as a wonderful habitat for birds and animals and prairie plants, but because it's part of the neighborhood. Part of what we hope to teach is a sense of connection to the land. Part of the Mighty Acorns is about social studies, how and why areas become wastelands, degraded and unavailable to communities. And how they can be reclaimed through stewardship and study."

"Look. Look." Sue points to a bird, whose name I thought my brother had made up for me, "A yellow-bellied sapsucker."

"'tsa woodpecker."

"I don't see no yellow."

I couldn't see yellow either.

We cross over a tiny drainage creek and Ms. Jackson, the homeroom teacher, sinks her foot in the mud. "Worse things have happened," she says. "I'll clean it off later."

Sue says she's seen crayfish in this creek and this makes me glad because decapods are not pollution tolerant. I walk into the tall skeletons of last year's goldenrod and poke around in a riffle hoping to see one. The water is clear, with leaf litter along the edges. An isopod scurries away, aquatic cousin of the terrestrial sowbug. Not a decapod, but not a bad sign. Except for the growl from the dump and the background rumble of I-94, it is very peaceful here. I realize that I'm sitting on the rusting carcass of a spring bed frame, thoroughly comingled with the grasses and weeds.

I find out later that Altgeld Gardens and this strip of land was once the dump for Pullman Standard. This woods sits on garbage. Across the river is garbage. Across the highway is garbage. And to the north is sewage. Sue and Cynthia, Diane, Shavanna, Phillip, and Ms. Jackson are building their hopes on garbage. They are rethinking this place, renaming this garbage dump. Maybe, Carver's Woods and Nature Preserve. The renaming will help envision a different place. Like calling a bird a rock dove where others see only a pigeon.

# Rolling Along with Rivers

KATY SMITH, RALPH FEESE, AND
ROBERT HARTWIG

The Freshmen Studies program at Addison Trail High School is a three-period interdisciplinary block that integrates English, biology, and social studies. Our program was piloted during the 1993–94 school year with sixty students, and we are thrilled that the enrollment has grown steadily ever since.

One of the most exciting activities that we have been involved in is the Illinois Rivers Project. Coordinated by Southern Illinois University at Edwardsville, the Rivers Project involves students and teachers from more than 250 schools in interdisciplinary study of the waterways of Illinois and neighboring states. Students perform scientific water quality tests, study historical and geographical aspects of different river sites, and read and write poetry, stories, and articles about river experiences. The test results can be used locally or can become part of a computer database through the SOILED NET system (the Southern Illinois Education Network), and students are encouraged to submit their work to *Meanderings*, the project's publication of student writing.

Our involvement in the Rivers Project first began with a two-day teacher-training workshop. At this session, we learned water-testing and computer procedures, received packets of instructional materials to use with our classes, and enjoyed the opportunity to network with other teachers from around the state. When we returned to class the day after the workshop, we were very excited about what lay ahead of us. The kids got excited, too, as we shared with them the plans for our first water testing day: Earth Day, April 22.

We chose as our test site a nearby section of Salt Creek where it runs through the Cricket Creek Forest Preserve. This location is close to our school and has safe access to the water. Because it is part of the local forest preserve system, it also has restroom facilities and a covered shelter, important to us in case of emergencies and bad weather. As it turned out, our testing day was beautiful: cool, sunny, and dry. We divided our students into four groups. After spending some time picking up trash at the site, the groups rotated through four stations. In the science station, they collected water samples and performed the water tests, checking for dissolved oxygen, phosphates and nitrates, pH level, and temperature change. In the language arts station, the students wrote observation

**Figure 6.1** Both students and teachers got out on the water in the Rivers Project.

journals and poetry. During their time in the social studies station, they walked the creek bank, looking for evidence of the interrelationship of humans and nature. Our math department chairman joined us for the day and set up a station where the students measured depth and velocity in order to determine the volume of water passing through a given point of the creek (see Figure 6.1). All of us thoroughly enjoyed being in the natural laboratory of the great outdoors.

Not all of our activities took place on Earth Day, however. Long before we went to the creek, the students were learning the lab procedures they would use. They prepared for the geographical surveying by studying river terminology and map interpretation. One of the readings that prepared them to consider the interrelationship of people and the environment was "The Conservation Aesthetic" from Aldo Leopold's *Sand County Almanac.* The students were also interested to learn the history of how their village has been influenced by the presence of Salt Creek. In fact, many of them have had firsthand experience with flooding, since a portion of the town has struggled for generations with flooding problems. Because of this history, they were very interested to see how the flood control basins have been designed to work and how the village has improved this difficult situation.

The activities continued after Earth Day as well. One of the water tests, the Biochemical Oxygen Demand (BOD) test, was done back at school after the water samples had been left to sit for five days. This test, like the Dissolved Oxygen test, was a favorite of the students: it helped them see the effect oxygen has on different types of organisms that can potentially live in the water of Salt Creek. The students analyzed the data from these and the other tests and worked on their lab write-ups. They assembled collages, which included one of their writing pieces from the day. They worked with contour maps to examine the flood plains of the area. One writing assignment that extended the Rivers Project was a children's storybook project. The students wrote and published children's stories that included a river motif; later, we visited a nearby elementary school to read the stories to the children there.

The Rivers Project is a natural for interdisciplinary instruction, and the three of us have tapped into different facets of the project each year. We have enjoyed developing related activities with our colleagues at Addison Trail as our own program has expanded. Our initial experience "on the river" was a positive one; and each year since, the students have really enjoyed being involved in firsthand environmental study. They come away with a feeling of hope for their environment, knowing that their actions can have a positive impact. We feel confident that our future students will share this enthusiasm, and we look forward to continuing our involvement in the Illinois Rivers Project.

# Using Primary Sources: Bringing Literature and Students to Center Stage

JOHN W. DUFFY

When I began teaching American history in 1972, I quickly learned how dreadfully inadequate secondary textbooks were. They were poorly written and uninspiring, but most important they failed to address the issues my students encountered in their daily lives. When my African American students complained that our book "only talked about slavery," they sensed the passivity and acceptance that textbooks encouraged from students. Some asked why great leaders like Fred Hampton were not in their textbooks. He was from their neighborhood, had attended our school, and at the age of fifteen led the youth committee of the NAACP in a protest to integrate a segregated community swimming pool. When he was eighteen, he became chairman of the Illinois Black Panther Party. At nineteen his death at the hands of the FBI and Chicago police led to investigations and trials that would radically change Chicago politics and make possible the multiracial coalition that elected Harold Washington as Chicago's first black mayor.

On another occasion, a local businesswoman who was a Crow Indian told our class of the wonderful relationship between the U. S. government and her tribe going back to the nineteenth century. She challenged my students' impression that the history of U. S. and Indian relations had always been one of broken treaties, and the students wondered why voices like hers or other Indians were not part of our text. When some of my female students pointed out the gross inequities in our boys' and girls' athletic programs and challenged male stereotypes of women's roles, the only hint of the long history of women's struggle for equality in our text-book appeared in a single column on the suffrage movement. Incidents like these, together with the historical and esthetic shortcomings of text-books, helped me realize that only by finding and sharing real voices from the past might my students begin to see any relevance to studying history.

With a similar goal at just about the same time, the Committee on History in the Classroom was founded. Scholars and teachers who formed the Committee on History in the Classroom established the twin goals of incorporating primary documents as an alternative to textbooks and placing greater emphasis on developing the art of teaching history. It is my strong belief that these two goals are not linear, but integrated and interdependent. I believe that the use of primary literature should be a central feature of history teaching. However, the use of primary documents as the fundamental texts will only make a significant qualitative difference in our classrooms if we place the literature and students at center stage. Only when students are allowed a variety of ways to find personal meaning in a text, when reading becomes more than responding to teacher-generated questions, when students are able to interact with, re-create, and move beyond texts in a variety of imaginative and critical ways will the use of primary literature begin to make history classrooms exciting, dynamic places for students to be. In short, using primary documents must also be accompanied by a more central and active role for students and a lessened emphasis on the teacher as dispenser of knowledge.

Primary literature is not just an effective way to enrich lectures or more vividly illustrate mass-marketed textbooks. It is the central ingre-dient in allowing students to construct historical meaning, to begin to understand the meaning of personal agency, to develop their own stories, to re-create the histories of their families, and to uncover the history of their own neighborhoods and communities. Early and frequent use of primary sources becomes the pathway to the time in my course when students become authentic historians—when a Vietnamese student tells for the first time the narrative of his family's sea escape from Vietnam, and another second-generation Vietnamese American, after reading primary literature on the Vietnam war, takes on the persona of a Viet Cong soldier in a student presentation based on selected readings of oral histories; when a child reads the transcript of his interview with his cousin and breaks down before he can relate the trauma of village battle; when a girl interviews her mother who tells the stories of her involvement in the student freedom movement and the terrifying night spent in jail in Mississippi; when a panel of civil rights veterans visit our school and a fellow teacher on the panel relates her family's friendship with Medgar Evers; or when world cultures and U. S. history students, after reading student accounts of the freedom movements in South Africa and America, work together to produce a musical drama connecting nonviolent resistance and divestment for an all-school assembly during Black History Month.

# Primary Sources in U. S. History

Now, let me share some ways I use primary materials in junior American history classes at Hinsdale Central High School, where I have taught for the last several years. One common feature of all these lessons is a basic strategy to guide students before they read, while they read, and after they read. Sometimes the entire class reads the same document; sometimes documents are part of a set that everyone reads in common. At other times, students may have a choice or a range of related documents on a common theme. On other occasions small groups of students might read representative samples of related documents on a common theme and then share what they learned with the whole class.

Through the years I have learned several techniques that make the use of primary literature more successful for my students. A key element of my pedagogy is introducing documents in a variety of ways. Certain literature and themes provide different opportunities for introduction. Before reading Columbus's diary accounts of his encounter with the Arawaks, I ask students to compose hypothetical diaries which we share in class as we explore the concepts of bias and frame of reference. Before studying the struggles of working people during the Industrial Revolution, oral reading from *The Autobiography of Mother Jones,* especially the chapter "The March of the Mill Children," provides students with a feeling for the human impact of the industrial policies of the late nineteenth century.

Prior to reading a set of primary texts on the impact of World War

II on American and Japanese citizens, I read the powerful children's picture book *The Faithful Elephants,* by Yukio Tsuchiya. In an informal writing students record their reactions to this story about how Tokyo zookeepers carried out the planned destruction of zoo animals out of fear that they might escape and threaten citizens during the American bombing. Students first share their reactions with one or two other students and then with the entire class. Finally, as students choose from a variety of individual personal accounts of the war, they are motivated and prepared to encounter the agony, courage, and horror the war brought to both Americans and Japanese.

Films like *In Country, Platoon,* or *Letters Home from Vietnam* are excellent methods for raising long lists of questions about the impact of the Vietnam war on American veterans and heightening student interest and curiosity. Personal narratives, both fiction and nonfiction, may also serve as an introduction to a study of larger set of primary documents. Before reading oral histories of Vietnam, I have read Tim O'Brien's description of a soldier's first encounter with death in *The Things They Carried.* Richard Wright's narrative of growing up in the South in the *Ethics of Living Jim Crow* provides a child's perspective of confronting racist America and helps establish a fuller understanding for reading and discussing authors like Dubois, Washington, and Garvey and exploring which direction the African American freedom movement should have taken in the first decades of this century. All these strategies allow students to mentally and emotionally transport themselves to the historic ground where they will meet authentic actors of history.

I have used primary literature effectively around the American Revolution in several ways. Simulation and role playing around policy conflicts and political decisions vis-à-vis England can be enriched by providing students with documents from Frank Moore's *Diary of the American Revolution.* Sets of selected documents from Moore also provide excellent background reading for narrative fictional writing about an imagined character of the revolutionary era. This year students created a radio documentary about the lives of soldiers after reading sets of documents about battles, prisoners of war, and how the war affected people's lives. Clearly, extended student response is not possible with all primary literature, but providing students with creative options that allow them to work critically with literature in personal and imaginative ways brings a liveliness, challenge, and excitement too often absent from history classrooms.

Before studying Indian issues in the early nineteenth century, students have role-played dialogues between missionaries and Indians, then read Red Jacket's response to missionaries asking to preach to his people. This activity becomes an introduction to exploring the great debate between Tecumseh and Pushmataha. Before this culminating large group activity, students read an excerpt from Chief Black Hawk's autobiography. They are asked to keep a reading log that is guided by a few simple questions like identifying Indian perspectives on land, religion, and culture and treaty relations with the United States. The goal here, as it should be when any manageable, well-written documentary reading is assigned, is to encourage students to find their own meaning in texts. Specific questions to guide students are:

- What did your learn about the Sac way of life from Black Hawk?
- How and why does his attitude toward the U. S. change?
- What did you find most amazing, interesting, or disturbing in the reading?

I also ask students to choose a passage or selection that they think has special literary quality worth reading to the class.

In small groups, they read additional short excerpts from Indian speeches found in Tehschick's *To Touch the Earth* and Nabokov's *Native American Testimony* as well as Tecumseh and Pushmataha's speeches, which are found in a wonderful two-volume anthology called *To Serve the Devil* (Jacobs and Landau). Each student then composes a formal statement to be read at tribal council meetings, where the proponents of resistance and the proponents of conciliation make their cases. One chief reads Andrew Jackson's letter to the Chocktaws at the beginning of the council meeting. At the end of the debate another student provides a dramatic reading of the beautiful and moving speech by Chief Sealth of the Chinook. The best experiences with this activity, which takes at least one full week of school, is a feeling in my class that we have come as close as humanly possible to understanding the agony and anguish Indians went through in deciding whether to fight or accommodate to further white encroachments.

Crucial themes in social history often receive but brief mention in textbooks. In such cases, well-written chapters or excerpts from secondary sources provide excellent ways into primary literature. For example, students studying abolition have read chapters on African Americans in the North and abolition from *Then Was the Future* by Douglas Miller and selected essays on slavery and abolition from Lockwood and Harris' *Reasoning with Democratic Values*. They then read original selections from Frederick Douglass, Solomon Northrup, David Walker, and other abolitionists.

A sure way back into time to the Seneca Falls women's rights convention is a fun reading of Anthony Brown's *Piggybook*, a children's picturebook that deals with domestic division of labor in contemporary families. A follow-up directed reading of the Seneca resolutions leads to a comparison with gender issues today. Students are then given choices of primary readings about nineteenth-century women who vividly described the conditions of their lives. A seminar structure allows two or three students to choose one of the women, discuss the implications of her character, and then share with the entire class.

Until recent years, there had been little sense among students that perhaps Columbus was not the great American hero. For years I have introduced interpretation, evidence, bias, and frame of reference by having students initially create hypothetical diaries or dramatic skits about the first encounters between Europeans and the Arawaks of the Bahamas. Students then read excerpts from Columbus' diary; compared his accounts with the versions presented in their text and read critical perspectives on Columbus like that found in Howard Zinn's *A People's History of the United States*. This year following this exercise, several students looked at the way Columbus is depicted in children's literature. They then created revisionist children's literature that presented a more realistic look at the Arawak Indians and Columbus in a style that was critical yet sensitive to the developmental needs of younger students. Other students examined textbook versions of Columbus and interpretations gleaned from reading Columbus' diary entries. One group of students interviewed people about popular perceptions of Columbus and created a video to share their findings. In addition to responding to primary literature in creative ways, this early look at Columbus helped students become aware of critical concepts relating to historical investigation and also addressed an important political question: In whose interest are textbooks written?

On a regular basis I allow students to respond to primary literature in a varied and personal way. Readings might be guided by a set of general prompts that allow students to personalize their reactions to an author without the constraints long lists of teacher questions place on their enjoyment of reading. Free responses can be kept in individual student journals. I might give students a range of response choices such as:

■ Write a letter to a character.
■ Compare a group of individuals.
■ Predict the future of the individual.
■ Speculate on how that person might react to issues and settings at other times in history.
■ Evaluate the choices a person makes in his life.

Most important, regular response writing to primary document reading provides a vehicle for students to make connections among the past, the present, and their own lives. They learn firsthand the human drama of history, the constant play of ethical decisions in people's lives, and the importance of individual actions in influencing the world. So a study of the Indian debate on resistance raises questions about just war, then and today, in the Persian Gulf or Bosnia. Indian removal and treaty rights become contemporary ethical problems as students examine the Navajo resettlement conflict, Chippewa fishing rights in Wisconsin, and the use of Indian mascots in their own communities. Reading about how women described their lives in the nineteenth century leads to contemporary questions, such as:

- What are the relationships between men and women in our school, community, and homes?
- Are males and females treated differently in school?
- What experiences have you had with sexual harassment?

Reading Indian perspectives on American history, slave narratives, and abolitionist attacks on slavery brings students face-to-face with a racism that textbooks either omit or gloss over. Primary literature provides the opening to explore racism today. The response prompts now become:

- Have you been the victim or witness to similar racist actions in your community?
- Why did this happen?
- What can be done to change this situation?

In these ways, primary documents serve as a rich conduit between the past and the present and provide the opportunity for reflective critical writing, discussion, and—hopefully—actions that will make our communities more democratic and just places to live.

Just as students need options in writing responses to reading assignments, they also need ongoing choices in the selection of reading materials. My students, be they remedial or advanced placement, thrive on opportunities for choice in reading material. Obviously, there is a certain body of primary and secondary literature we want all students to read and understand. But we need not look further than our own lives to be reminded of the motivating power of personal choice. Choice is influenced by curiosity, and the more options we create for students, the more curiosity and desire we will generate in our classrooms. I use a set of oral histories from World War II taken from several anthologies currently available. I start by realizing there are hundreds of fascinating oral histories that my students might read. Why should I make all their final choices? I sometimes provide them with a short excerpt from an account, or at least a description of the person and setting. They choose with great interest and motivation. They now possess the crucial ingredients for learning—curiosity and ownership.

To bring authentic voices into the classroom, to provide time for students to reflect, wonder, imagine, and reconstruct our collective past, their individual pasts, and our collective future, I have made primary literature a major part of teaching and learning in my classroom. Most of all, these strategies seem to be part of that magic combination that says to students, "I can relate to this. It has a personal connection to my life. I am beginning to understand the world better and I am enjoying the process."

# Step by Step
## Home Improvement: Remodeling Mathematically

JIM TEBO

In teaching seventh- and eighth-grade students, one of my goals is to incorporate as much real-life math application as I possibly can. I find that kids like to learn math when they understand the meaning behind their learning. One of the ways I try to accomplish this is by assigning a project called "Home Improvement." The kids are given the job of redecorating any one room in their house the way they would like to have it done. Each student is given a $2,000 budget and is encouraged to spend as much of it as she possibly can.

My agenda is to get the students to use their knowledge in perimeter, area, scale drawings, and budgeting in an actual situation. In order to do this, the students must follow certain criteria, which ensure that they will use each of the key math concepts and calculations this project is reinforcing. They are encouraged to choose any room in the house to decorate, and most kids choose their own bedrooms. They must carpet or tile the floors, wallpaper or panel at least one wall, paint the ceiling and remaining walls, and put up a border or chair rail. After spending the money on these necessary items, they can spend the remaining money on items they would like to buy for themselves to improve their room.

To get started, the kids are given a list with four steps to follow. The first step is to write out a plan sheet. This is generally a one-to-two-page written list of all the possible plans the student has thought up. The ideas range from the color and style of carpeting to the design of the wallpaper

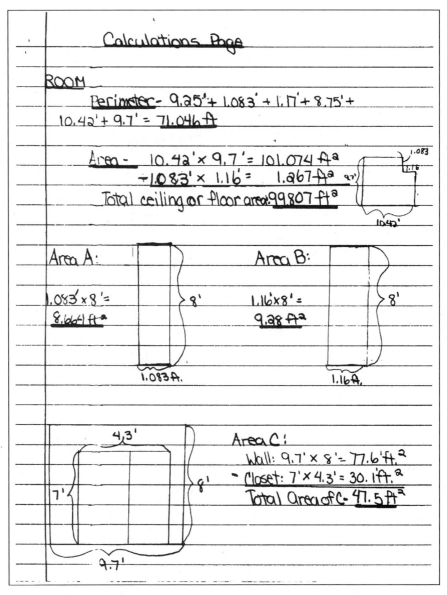

**Figure 6.2a** Calculations used to determine quantities of materials needed.

and even to extra things like a new bed if they have enough money. The purpose of this step is to get the kids to think about what they would like to do and to create a plan that they can follow.

The second step includes a fact sheet and a scale drawing of their room. The fact sheet is a list of the area of every wall including the area of any windows, doors, or closets, the area of the floor, and the perimeter of the room. From this information, the kids are to make a scale drawing of their room on graph paper (see Figures 6.2a and b).

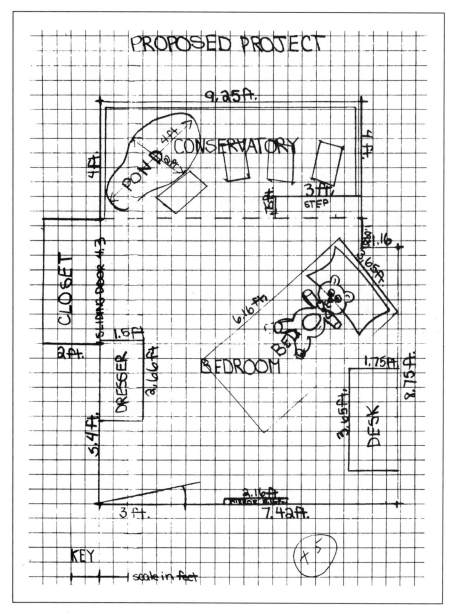

**Figure 6.2b** Diagram of one student's room (teddy bear not to scale!).

The third step, the price guide, is probably the most challenging and eye-opening experience for the kids (see Figure 6.3). For every item the students wish to purchase, they must find a minimum of two prices. This requires looking in sale circulars, calling different stores for prices, or actually going out to the businesses to obtain information. This step is a great learning experience about comparative shopping. During this step the kids must also keep a updated balance of their account. Along with

| SUPPLIES | ESTIMATE 1 | ESTIMATE 2 |
| --- | --- | --- |
| | ACE | HANDY ANDY |
| **Bedroom** | | |
| 1. Paint | ✓$6.79/gal | $18.99/gal. |
| 2. Wallpaper | $40.77/3rolls | $59.98/2rolls |
| 3. Chair Rail | ✓$19.35 | $29.58/5-9ft lengths |
| 4. Varnish | $11.49 | $7.28/per quart |
| 5. Carpeting | $300.00* | $299.09/8.99sq yd. |
| | | |
| **Conservatory** | | |
| 1. Contractor's Estimate | $8,000.00 | — |
| 2. sand → pond | $4.00 | $128.39/plastic liner |
| 3. stepping stones → rocks | $3.16/4 | $1.96/4 |
| 4. hose | 3.77/50ft. | $9.37/50ft. |
| | | |
| **Backyard** | | |
| 1. cement → fence | $47.92/40lbs. 8 bags | $11.96/4 bags 80lbs. |
| 2. Picket fencing | $219.60/10ft | $299.80/14.99 set. |
| 3. posts | $56.49/2.00 per post | $51.24/2.49/post per |
| 4. arbor | $199.98 | $200.00/100 per cubic |
| 5. paint → flat | $26.47 | $65.97/3 gallons |
| 6. sand → pond | $8.00 | $238.00/plastic quart liner |

**Figure 6.3** Shopping list students used to obtain prices from two different suppliers.

this step, I ask the kids to cut out any pictures of items they would want to purchase. By doing this, the kids, their parents, and the teacher can really get a good look at what the kids have in mind.

The last step is called the closing remarks. Here, the kids write about and describe how their project went. Was it easy or difficult? How much was spent? Was $2000 enough money? Since I ask the students to share their final report with their parents, I ask the students to write about their parents' reactions. I have had a number of cases where the parents were so impressed with their child's work and effort that they actually allowed their child to do the redecoration.

I really enjoy this project because the kids get so wrapped up in doing it. They love using their imagination and having total control to do whatever they would like to their room of choice. The students really use the math skills of measuring, scale drawing, and budgeting, and they have a good time in the process. One word of caution: during this period, kids will come to school excited and curious, with an abundance of questions ranging from prices to measurements to budgets. So be prepared for anything and have fun.

# Student Docents Discover Modern Art

SHELLEY ROSENSTEIN-FREEMAN

According to *Webster's Unabridged Dictionary of the English Language,* a *docent* is a teacher or lecturer. If you ask Vincent Robinson, a freshman at DuSable High School in Chicago, what a docent is, he'd give you a shy smile and a much more detailed explanation.

Vincent was a member of the first group of "student docents" or tour guides to be trained and employed by the Museum of Contemporary Art in Chicago (MCA) to lead public tours of museum exhibitions. In a unique program developed by Museum Education Department staff members Roger Dell, Margaret Farr, Erika Varrichio, and me, the art educator at Farren Fine Arts School, twenty Farren students spent a series of fourteen Saturdays sharing and learning about art history, painting, sculpture, public speaking, communication, and art criticism and having a great time doing it.

The Farren School–Museum of Contemporary Art Student Tour Guide Program, funded by Metropolitan Life Foundation, was conceived and implemented in 1994. The partnership was developed with benefits for both the participating students and the MCA. The program would enhance the students' education by giving them greater knowledge of art, showing them the many different jobs performed within a museum, and exposing them to a number of different museums through field trips. Additionally, the student docent training would provide valuable communication skills and a learning environment that would boost student confidence and self-esteem. In return, the student tour guides provide the MCA with a means of educating the public that had not been available, namely, students guiding other students through the exhibitions. With the assistance of student guides, the MCA would also be able to provide greater access to more youth groups.

There were so many details to consider while planning the program. The calendar of meeting dates had to be arranged so it would not conflict with school holidays; fourteen Saturdays were chosen from November, 1994, through June, 1995, and teacher and parent chaperones were selected to accompany the students. Transportation needed to be easy and safe: we rented a school bus to meet the kids at the neighborhood Boys and Girls Club at 12:30 P.M., and they would be dropped back there at 4:00 P.M. The Boys and Girls Club was a safe place where the kids could gather together indoors, out of harm's way in their often treacherous neighborhood.

It had been stipulated in the grant that each student selected for the program would be paid to attend—we wanted the students to learn responsibility for accepting this "job." But we knew that regular attendance could be a problem, so we decided that each student must attend a minimum of eleven of the fourteen sessions to receive their stipend of $75.00. Those students selected to give tours after the training sessions were to be paid $4.75 for each tour completed.

Of course we needed to select students who would be interested and enthusiastic. In addition to posting notices around the school, I handed out invitation letters to many of the sixth-, seventh-, and eighth-grade students. We decided to hold a meeting for all interested students after school in the art room at Farren and required that a parent or guardian accompany each student. The MCA staff brought a slide presentation about the museum and its collection and prepared folders to hand out to each student and parent, including a detailed description of the program. Farren Principal Bill Auksi spoke to the group about his support and interest in the project and the MCA's Roger Dell described the program in detail. I briefly discussed with the students how this project tied in with the art curriculum at Farren.

I was pleased that many of the attending students were talented members of the eighth-grade class. Although I wanted some of the group to be students who would continue with me at Farren, I knew that the eighth graders would have the maturity to be the leaders in this group. It was our hope that the group selected would become close, cooperative, and supportive of one another. Of the thirty or so kids attending, twenty were eventually selected for participation based on attitude in art class, parent involvement, and interest in the program.

After the "graduation" ceremony, the students felt proud and accomplished. After participating in the MCA program, the kids became serious art students and leaders in my classroom. I was delighted with their attitude and perception of themselves. More important, they seemed delighted. Several of the eighth graders proceeded through the summer, calling into the MCA independently to receive their schedules, and showing up (using bus tokens given by the MCA) on public transportation to give their tours and assist Museum Education Department staff with important work.

Recently, I spoke with Vincent Robinson when he stopped by Farren for a visit. He was one of the most involved members of the student group, which had indeed become like a little family. Vincent was devoted to the program and to his own drawing. He had shown tremendous promise when I met him as a sixth grader and grew consistently in the several years we spent together. Now he was returning as a high school freshman, and I asked him to reflect about the MCA student docent experience:

SRF: Why did you want to participate in the MCA student docent program?

VR: I wanted to learn more about art, new ways of doing art, and hoped I could accomplish this through the program.

SRF: What did you feel were the best features of the program?

VR: I enjoyed the social interaction with the kids in the group, but I also liked helping out around the museum and helping the public appreciate the museum.

SRF: Which field trips did you like best and why?

VR: I liked the trips to the Terra Museum, the new MCA site, and the Art Institute. It was interesting to look at new things. They gave us free passes so we could return on our own. I have gone back to see more sculpture and three-dimensional work at the Art Institute.

SRF: Would you participate again if invited, and was the payment important to you?

VR: I would definitely participate again—I hope to work in the new museum when it opens. The payment was important a little bit but I like the art.

SRF: Did you feel that the program was good preparation for other work, and how so?

VR: The program taught us about working habits, like how to carry yourself, how important it is to look a person in the eye when speaking to them, to dress nicely for an interview, how to speak in the right way to be understood.

SRF: Did the program create any particular change or impact on your life?

VR: Yes! I became more interested in helping people. The MCA staff helped us out with transportation, getting us in the program and paying us. I think the program helped to change a couple of people in the [student] group—how they behaved. I feel like an important person by helping other people out. I liked all the people that helped with the program and feel fortunate that I was chosen to participate.

# "Me" Portfolios: The Way to a Classroom's Heart

LINDA BAILEY

Nicky sang. Tony showed his two lucky pennies and photos of his eight brothers and sisters, most of whom still live in another town with his mother. His twin, Tommy, related with his photos the series of places they have lived since they left their grandmother's home in 1990. Leonardo shared a hand-carved keychain that his grandfather made for him in Guatemala. Although he was speaking Spanish, even we monolinguals knew how precious this memento was to him. We also discovered how much scientific knowledge Leonardo had about dinosaurs, as he showed his models and described their diet, habitat, and geological era. Pamela was happy to translate for him this time. Erika demurely displayed a large fan of certificates and awards she earned over the years in school, her first baby bootie, her First Communion book—carefully protected in plastic—which was her only memory of her great-great-grandmother, her foreign money collection, her favorite mystery book, and a poem of which she was especially proud. Rebeca showed her miniature mask collection, two tiny white teddy bears from "someone special," letters that she saves, and photos of her family.

Erika was a stellar student, destined to be the class valedictorian, the kind of student we all love to have in our classes. Rebeca was not. Yet both Erika and Rebeca did a great job of presenting their "Me" portfolios. Erika and Rebeca were equally expert on their topics, had researched them thoroughly, and took genuine pride in their presentations. Each felt good about sharing personal information and artifacts about herself, and each had taken thoughtful care in the selection of each item in her portfolio. Each knew that the teachers and students with whom she shared her "Me" portfolio were learning more about the real and whole person she was. They were willing to expose themselves because everyone in their learning community at Burley School in Chicago, including their teacher, had made a "Me" portfolio.

Paula Saks-Zellhofer, Burley's second-grade teacher, brought photos of her handsome son and her farm in Wisconsin, a stone fragment from the Temple of Jupiter in Athens, and an unidentifiable lump that had melted on her stove (to signify her culinary prowess). Steve Wolk, the seventh-grade teacher, brought photos he had taken and "memory cards," on which he had written special memories. I brought a sample of the jewelry I make, photos of my husband and children, a toy soldier with the international "no" symbol taped to it, and a memoir I had published in the local newspaper.

Students presenting their "Me" portfolios found that classmates and teachers were eager to learn about their personal lives, literacy, and interests. Classmates asked questions at the end of the presentation that delved deeply into one or more aspects of their portfolios and asked to examine some items more closely. They discovered that their teachers and their classmates were genuinely caught up in the story of who they are.

It all started when the Burley faculty sat around tables during the planning days at the end of the school year. We were looking for a really engaging activity to grab the students the following September, pull them out of their summer stupor, get them into the dynamics of school, and begin to build a true community of learners. We wanted something that the whole school could do, that integrated the curriculum, motivated our students, and excited them about returning to school. We decided that a variation of the literacy portfolio idea might just do it. Many of the primary grade teachers already had planned self-exploration as part of their curriculum anyway, and when I raved about the successes my students enjoyed with literacy portfolios the previous year, the whole faculty enthusiastically embraced the idea.

During summer planning sessions, we revised and fine-tuned the project to meet the curricular and assessment needs of different grade levels. We wrote parent letters, prepared student handouts, and gave a completed package to all teachers on the first of the preclass institute days.

During the first week of school, the teachers shared their own "Me" portfolios with their classes. Since I, as writing specialist, did not have my own classroom, I went to almost all the classes and presented mine as an additional model. The students were receptive and respectful. They were amazed that teachers really had children of their own, and asked all kinds of questions about my two sons. They were surprised that I actually watched *Star Trek* on occasion and were curious about my favorite book. They were eager to start their own portfolios.

Student presentations of the "Me" portfolios began the second week of school. Burley was bustling with excited kids bringing in colorful boxes and bags, filled with personal treasures and precious mementos. The children were proud of their portfolios and wanted as much audience as

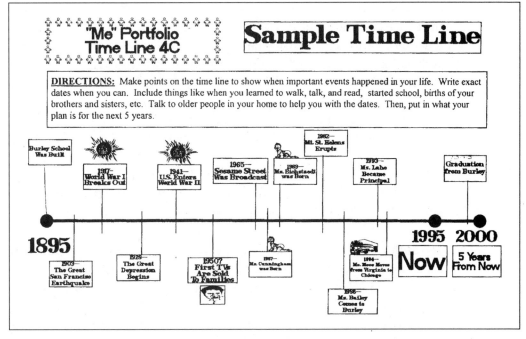

**Figure 6.4** This time line was used to show students how to create their own.

they could get. As I ran into students in the hallway, the lunchroom, or the playground, they would eagerly show me their portfolio container, and invite me to see their presentation. The little ones were impressed that they had the same assignment as their older siblings, and the older sibs were happy to help the younger ones. Parents were engaged in helping their children dig up family and personal history, and many expressed joy in the memories and feelings that resurfaced during this endeavor. A bond between home and school was forged. The whole school was focused on the same purpose at the same time. It was a powerfully moving time to be a teacher.

Older students did "Me in the Universe" graphic organizers to visually place themselves in the greater scheme of things, as well as time lines of their lives (see Figure 6.4). Grade-level clusters or individual teachers modified the "Me" portfolio plans to suit their instructional needs. The fourth-grade group decided that it matched their curriculum better to have their time lines begin in 1895, the year that Burley was built, and extend five years into the future. The second grade and below brought in five to ten items for the collection, while the fourth grade and above were requested to bring in ten to twenty items. Each item had to be accompanied by a 4-inch by 6-inch index card on which the student had written about the object. These were useful in their oral presentations, but also served as short, student-centered writing activities. Some classes mounted their items or photos of their items on poster board, with accompanying descriptor cards. These poster-board displays, placed all around the room and in the hallways, told in no uncertain terms who reigned in these classrooms.

The students understood the value of the project too. Hugo España said, "It was good to do the 'Me' portfolios at the beginning of the year because we didn't know each other and it helped us to feel comfortable in the class." Alberto Estrella added, "I liked them because we learned about our families and how we were as little children." Jose Luis Gonzalez said, "We learned about each other's lives and the things that are important to them." They also knew that who they are was important to their teachers.

Burley teachers had only positive responses to the "Me" portfolio experience. Rusty Burnette, our upper-grade special education teacher said, "During 'Me' portfolio presentations, it was evident the bond between everyone in the classroom strengthened. We each had a spotlight to share what makes us tick." Meghan Cunningham, the intermediate bilingual teacher, added, "I thought it was a wonderful way to build trust, and it served as a wonderful introductory assessment/index of their writing [language arts outcomes]." Nancy Laho, the principal, and Mary Beth Groene, the assistant principal, were ardent advocates of this project and even suspended our "no toys in school" policy for the duration of the "Me" portfolio presentations. Ms. Laho plans to continue to start each year with "Me" portfolios. "We are excited about the thought of observing over a period of years the growth and development of our children as manifested in their 'Me' portfolios," Ms. Laho said.

The original inspiration for this project was an article by Jane Hansen, "Literacy Portfolios: Helping Students Know Themselves" (1992, 66–68). I first tried the idea in September, and I found that the students loved it. Few things have warmed my heart more than seeing a big, burly Burley eighth grader show his cute little bare-bottomed baby picture, or the collection of toy cars with which he still plays. I got a new perspective on the very sophisticated young lady who constantly tries to sneak into school wearing make-up, yet still sleeps with her held-together-by-a-thread teddy bear and collects trolls with neon-colored hair.

Donald Graves (1983) stresses the importance of teachers knowing their children, not only academically but personally as well. He suggests we keep notes about the personal information we learn about our students, so we may relate to them on another level. My one regret with the upper-grade classes I had was that I did not take notes. I thought surely

I'd remember which student loved astronomy and which collected miniature shoes, but after sixty-odd literacy portfolios, it was hard to remember which student just vacationed in Guatemala with her grandparents and which wrote that stunning poem about death. It would have been useful to know whose favorite book was *Charlotte's Web* or who had the collection of Mexican minipottery. I now strongly recommend that teachers take notes during portfolio presentations. Many of our teachers also decided to take photos.

In all my years as an educator, our "Me" portfolio project was the most successful I'd ever undertaken. It integrated the curriculum for the first big project of the year; motivated the students and got them immediately focused on school; centered the curriculum around the students; built community within the classroom and the school; presented real purposes for writing and creating art; and gave teachers, students, and parents a precious opportunity to know each other in an individual and personal way. There is substantial value in inviting the students to see their teachers as real flesh-and-blood human beings with a life beyond the school parking lot. If about half the art of teaching is getting the students' attention, then firsthand knowledge of the teacher-as-true-mortal should help grab and maintain that attention. It's harder to turn off to someone who has let you glimpse her soul.

The "Me" portfolio project also gave teachers a quick response when Maria whines, "But I don't know what to write about today." Her teacher can check her notes and respond, "Why don't you write about that darling blue dress that your grandmother so lovingly crocheted for you when you were a baby?" or to Adam, "Tell about the day that you won that track medal." With a "Me" portfolio, students will probably never run out of real reasons for writing.

# CHAPTER 7
# Reflective Assessment

I N A MINUTE, this chapter will become practical and constructive. Shortly, we will discuss ways to help students become self-monitoring, self-regulating individuals who take charge of their own learning, set ambitious goals, monitor their own progress, keep their own records, adjust their efforts, make good decisions, and become part of a collaborative community that grows by means of healthy and measured mutual feedback. We will introduce six specific methods for monitoring student growth that will help teachers to balance assessment in their classrooms.

But first, we must address the toxic role played by certain kinds of assessment in our educational system. We must make a careful distinction between constructive, classroom-rooted, "Best Practice" forms of student evaluation, and the more prevalent, high-profile standardized tests that are at the center of today's education debates. These standardized measurements are of little use in guiding student learning, they distort our expectations of individual kids, and they frequently lower the standard of teaching as they drag teachers down to their level of gamesmanship and test coaching.

## The History of Standardized Testing

All through human history, including the last few thousand years, which we compliment ourselves by referring to as "civilization," people could only judge each other's intelligence or capabilities by what someone said or did. All that really mattered, as we might put it today, was what a person "knows and is able to do." This all changed in 1908 with the invention of mental measurement. Albert Binet introduced the idea, later institutionalized in America's Army Intelligence Tests, that a paper-and-pencil test of assorted multiple-choice questions could determine what people knew or could be expected to do much more quickly than actually observing or knowing someone.

Among the first uses of mental measurement was the ranking of ethnic groups by intelligence. In 1917, Binet tests administered to American immigrants revealed that 83 percent of Jews were "feebleminded," as were 80 percent of Hungarians, 79 percent of Italians, and 87 percent of Russians. As mental testing became more prevalent, the distribution of intelligence among putative "races" was widely established. At the pinnacle were "Nordic" peoples, followed by "Mediterraneans" (Italians and Spaniards being dimmer than Swedes, apparently), on down through Asians, Indians, and finally, at the very bottom, Africans. Early IQ testers also promulgated a kind of lowerarchy of intelligence for "mental defectives," which ranked "morons" in the top slot, down through "imbeciles" to "idiots."

In short, early mental measurement was mainly the exercise of scientized racism, as has been amply documented by Stephen Jay Gould in *The Mismeasure of Man* (1981) and by Alan Chase in *The Legacy of Malthus* (1977). As these scholars have shown, early standardized mental tests had no more validity than the "sciences" of phrenology and craniology that they replaced. Among the scientifically indefensible assumptions of early mental measurement were two especially crude ideas: that intelligence is a single trait, and that it is permanently fixed. These deterministic fictions remain at the heart of mental measurement seventy-five years later. We still talk about the construct "IQ" as though it were an actual, inherent, internal feature of human beings. We still run our educational system as through intelligence were a unitary trait, in spite of articulate challenges by people like Howard Gardner (1983). To this day, we screen, track, reward, and segregate people—children and adults alike—using tests rooted in bad science and redolent of bigotry.

The main use of standardized tests in America is to justify the distribution of certain goodies to certain people. This kind of misuse has penetrated our educational system as thoroughly as any branch of society. For example, from the 1950s into the 1980s, the National Teachers Examination was used to grant or renew teaching licenses in many states, despite the fact that testmakers had never shown any correlation between scores and teaching performance. The test was eventually removed from the marketplace by its unrepentant makers only after decades of protest by outside scholars who documented its irrelevance. Right into the 1990s, the Preliminary Scholastic Aptitude Test was used to hand out tens of millions of scholarship dollars disproportionately to male applicants, even though the test's discrimination against females had been documented for decades. The ongoing use of IQ tests to place students in special education or gifted programs, entrance exams to admit freshmen to colleges, and placement tests to select candidates for certain programs, continues to be more pseudo than science.

As this book is written, voter referenda in Texas and California, both designed to abolish affirmative action, have recently forced state universities to rely more heavily on standardized test scores in admissions decisions. The immediate result: a catastrophic drop in Hispanic and African American student admissions to medical and law schools. The New York University Law Review projects that minority enrollment will be cut from 26 percent to 3 percent if this increased reliance on standardized admissions tests spreads from California to Texas to professional schools throughout the nation (Bronner 1997, 8). Meanwhile, state universities are scrambling to create new admissions processes to prevent what the *New York Times* article calls "virtually a return of racial segregation" (1). But then the use of standardized tests to block minority access to education would have come as no surprise to Dr. Martin Luther King. In 1950, contemplating graduate school studies at Boston University, he took the Graduate Record Exam, like the SATs, another Educational Testing Service product. The man now considered by many to have been the greatest orator of this century scored in the third quartile on "verbal skills"— below average.

If teachers feel threatened by standardized tests in their own schools or communities—and most American teachers surely do—history warns them to be skeptical but realistic. These tests are clearly here to stay, and very real punishments will be handed out to students and teachers who don't perform well on them. But accommodating the reality of standardized tests doesn't mean being ruled by them, catering to them, or even believing in them. It means giving your students the coaching they need to show their best on the tests—and then returning to the real business of education, which is nurturing the growth of individual students' thinking, over years, across disciplines, and among collaborators.

## Let Them Eat Tests

The people running our country's "official" education reform movement, that is, politicians, state legislators, governors, and blue-ribbon panels of businessmen, don't know or care much about the structures of Best Practice education—workshop, integrative units, or collaborative learning. Indeed, few of them could probably tell a center from a conference. But they do care a lot—a whole lot—about test scores. Indeed, in many states and localities, the only tangible outcomes of a decade's worth of school reform are new layers of standardized tests, with their attendant schedules of penalties for low-scoring kids, teachers, and schools.

As pretense of reform, mass testing is a pretty tempting commodity. Testing is relatively cheap, it sounds tough, and its numerical results are irresistible media fodder. Since most standardized test scores correlate highly with socioeconomic status, any new round of testing will usually reconfirm the unworthiness of the underclasses and comfort the privileged. The predictable test score results invite the blaming, shaming, and stigmatizing of low-scoring schools and communities. After all, why should we spend more money on those people, if they can't even pass the tests?

In Chicago, for example, we currently have over one hundred schools on probation, a status determined solely through standardized test scores. Virtually all the probation schools serve poor children. The result is that these schools, in addition to facing the daily challenges of working with kids who may live in public housing projects, endure tremendous family stresses, speak other languages, or run with gangs—these schools are also publicly humiliated by their test scores, their teaching staffs repudiated, their neighborhoods further disgraced. But in the ultimate zero-sum game that is standardized testing, it has to be this way. Some schools must by definition occupy the bottom half, the lower quartile, the tenth decile in the distribution. And no matter what the test, does anyone seriously expect rich suburban kids, whose "Nordic" neighbors create and sell these tests, to wind up at the bottom?

Amid the hubbub of school reform, teachers are actually receiving a schizophrenic message: teach in creative, innovative, constructive ways, but your students will be tested very differently. Monty Neil and Joe Medinal of FairTest, a testing watchdog organization, argue that the teaching methods that are effective in raising scores on tests of lower-level cognitive skills are nearly the opposite of those strategies that develop complex cognitive learning, problem-solving ability, and creativity. Test scores provide little useful information to improve instruction, and many teachers, in attempting to make sure that their students are prepared for the tests, must abandon the innovative and challenging instruction in which they are engaged in order to "dummy down" the curriculum to conquer the test.

According to school reform expert Roland Barth (1992), teachers need to be encouraged to take chances where a safety net protects those who may risk and stumble. Many principals encourage, and seem to understand, this kind of classroom risk taking. However, standardized test results often place so much pressure on principals that they pass that pressure right along to their teachers. According to Peter Johnston (1992), each year the average elementary student loses four days of instruction to taking standardized tests, an upper elementary student loses six days, and a junior or senior high school student loses approximately ten days. These numbers don't reflect the days spent preparing for the tests, which grow as we continue adding layers of tests. With all that is known about the importance of instructional time, it is unconscionable to devote such large amounts of time to a procedure that is inconsistent with what we know about good instruction.

Of course there are genuinely ineffective schools in Chicago and elsewhere, which should be identified by some means, and promptly improved. Some test scores probably do accurately point toward schools that are doing a lousy job, that are not giving their students "value added," even taking into account the special challenges or difficulties the children there may face. If standardized testing were used mainly to aim massive aid at such failing schools, its negative effects might be counterbalanced with constructive outcomes (although we hardly need more tests to know where to send the massive aid, right now).

But in most of America that's not how testing is used, now that it has become the main ingredient of many "reform" programs. Schools do not receive the resources to raise achievement, only the mandate to measure it more often. There's little or no help for any struggling school or district once the scores are in. Numbers are published in the papers, the line-up of winners and losers is officialized, and life goes on with no reallocation of resources. Perhaps this is because raising achievement would cost real money and might even—who knows—upset the standard scoring patterns and undermine the advantages currently enjoyed by the children of blue-ribbon businesspeople who sit on panels that prescribe more standardized tests for low-scoring schools.

If this all sounds a bit intemperate and suspicious, perhaps that is because in twenty-five years of working with schools we've come to see large-scale, standardized assessments as the force that always messes things up, that derails the best efforts, that keeps genuine reform from taking root, and maintains and perpetuates the status quo. Because of the subskills-based items on the citywide reading test, teachers dare not take time to read aloud to students or to let them discuss their own books in literature circles. Because the statewide science exam covers scores of topics, teachers are afraid to let students linger for a whole month at the nearby riverside, studying the ecosystem in depth. Because of the threat of probation, schools give up most of January, February, and March to test coaching for the spring testing season. Instead of reading real books, kids read and fill out sample standardized tests. The tests literally become the curriculum. And the test obsession strikes most severely, of course, at the schools who score the lowest, which are most in jeopardy from further low scores. The schools that stand to lose the most, and who have the least chance of actually beating the tests, are the ones that are most ruled and distorted by them. The kids who need Best Practice teaching the most—who need authentic, holistic, developmental experiences—are guaranteed not to get it because of standardized tests.

# Constructive Assessment

This is all politics—important politics, but politics nevertheless. No matter how the results of standardized tests are used, they offer little help to classroom teachers, who must guide and document the learning of individual students 180 days a year. And most of this chapter so far has also been pretty negative, focusing on things that don't work and don't help. So, what does work? What kind of assessment is constructive? What models and procedures can teachers employ to steer kids toward growth? After all, teachers need real structures and strategies to assess and support students' growth inside the day-to-day reality of the classroom, within a close coaching relationship with each individual child.

In a moment, we will talk about the six structures of what might be called "Best Practice assessment." But because we still worry about the toxic legacy of assessment in American education, because these six structures can so easily be corrupted back into the same kind of accountability testing that we are trying to mitigate, we want to be very clear about the principles behind these six key strategies. The following twelve ideas can help us make sure that our new assessment methods really do enact the ideals of Best Practice.

**1. Assessment should reflect, encourage, and *become an integral part of good instruction.*** While many traditional measures occur separate from or after teaching, the most powerful assessment activities—such as conferences, analytic scoring scales, and portfolios—are ingredients of good instruction. When assessment overlaps with instruction in this way, it helps teachers to be more effective in the same amount of instructional time. Ideally, assessment activities should unequivocally reinforce state-of-the-art curriculum and teaching methods. At the very least, the evaluation of student work should never distort or obstruct exemplary classroom practice.

**2. Powerful evaluation efforts focus on the major,** *whole outcomes* **valued in the curriculum:** real, complex performances of writing, researching, reading, experimenting, problem solving, creating, speaking, and so on. Traditional assessment has been largely devoted to checking whether students are receiving the proper "inputs," the alleged building blocks, basics, or subskills. In contrast the new assessment paradigm dares to focus on the higher-order outcomes of education, the real payoffs in which kids orchestrate big chunks of learning in realistic applications.

**3. Most school assessment activities should be** *formative.* This means that we assess primarily to ensure that students learn better and teachers teach more effectively. Summative evaluation, which involves translating students' growth to some kind of number, score, or grade that can be reported outside the classroom, is just one small, narrow, and occasional element of a comprehensive assessment program.

**4. Traditional norm-referenced,** *competitive measures that rank students against each other (such as letter grades and numerically scored tests) provide little helpful formative assessment and tend to undermine progressive instruction.* Instead, constructive programs increasingly rely on *self-referenced growth measures,* where the student is compared to herself. This means teachers must have ways of valuing, tracking, and recording individualized factors such as growth, improvement, effort, good faith, insight, risk taking, rate of change, energy, and so on.

**5. A key trait of effective thinkers, writers, problem solvers, readers, researchers,** *and other learners is that they constantly self-monitor and self-evaluate.* Therefore, a solid assessment program must consistently help (and require) students to take increasing responsibility for their own record keeping, metacognitive reflection, and *self-assessment.*

**6. Skillful and experienced evaluators take a** *developmental perspective.* They are familiar with the major growth models, both general cognitive stage theories and the models from specific curriculum fields (stages of reading, mathematical thinking, invented spelling, etc.). Rather than checking students against arbitrary age- or grade-level targets, teachers track the story of each child's individual growth through developmental phases.

**7. Teachers need a rich** *repertoire of assessment strategies* **to draw from in designing sensitive,** *appropriate evaluation activities for particular curriculum areas.* Among these broad strategies are anecdotal/observational records, checklists, interviews, portfolios, performance assessments, and classroom tests.

8. **It is never enough to look at learning events from only one angle;** *rather, we now use multiple measures, examining students' growth from several different perspectives.* By triangulating assessments, we get a "thick" picture of kids' learning, ensuring that unexpected growth, problems, and side effects are not missed.

9. **Teachers need to** *reallocate the considerable time that they already spend on assessment,* **evaluation, record keeping, testing, and grading activities.** They need to spend less time scoring, and more time saving and documenting student work. Instead of creating and justifying long strings of numbers in their grade books, teachers should collect and save samples of kids' original, unscored products. This reallocation of time means that, once they are installed, new assessment procedures don't require any more time of teachers than the old ways—or any less.

10. **Sound evaluation programs provide, where necessary, a data base for deriving** *legitimate, defensible student grades.* However, major national curriculum groups have recommended (and we concur) that competitive, norm-referenced grading should be de-emphasized and replaced by the many richer kinds of assessments that will be outlined further on.

11. *It takes many different people working cooperatively* **to effectively evaluate student growth and learning.** In every classroom, there should be a balance between external assessment (such as district standardized tests, state assessments, etc.), teacher-run evaluation, student self-evaluation, parent involvement in assessment, and collaborative assessments that involve various contributions of these parties.

12. **The currently available state and national standardized tests yield an exceedingly narrow and unreliable picture of student achievement,** *are poor indicators of school performance, and encourage archaic instructional practices.* Therefore, professional teachers *avoid teaching to standardized tests.* Instead, they show colleagues, parents, and administrators the more sophisticated, detailed, accurate, and meaningful assessments that they have developed for their own classrooms.

How can these principles be put into manageable and practical use in classrooms? We can see six basic structures of constructive, formative, reflection-oriented assessment that may be used at any grade level, in any subject, with any students.

- Portfolios
- Conferences
- Anecdotal records
- Checklists

- Performance assessments
- Classroom tests

In order to provide the deepest and widest view of students' growth, these strategies need to be implemented in a balanced, healthful mixture. Below we describe each in a kind of declining order of progressiveness, moving from profoundly formative, student-centered assessment practices like portfolios and conferences, toward more nearly traditional procedures like performance assessment and classroom tests. These structures, especially the first five, have been quite well-documented in recent years. Happily, there has been a long-overdue burst in literature about alternative forms of assessment, including many teacher-written books replete with useful models, samples, and stories. The listing of such resources at the end of this chapter will be particularly helpful for teachers looking to implement and troubleshoot some of the more complex and promising assessment structures.

*Portfolios* represent a diametrical shift from old-style assessments. Where we used to prize strings of numbers and letters in a grade book, symbolizing the outcomes of long-discarded test papers, we now collect and study the raw materials of students' learning. In using portfolios, we invite kids to *collect* samples in working folders—rough and polished; written, drawn, acted, and painted; individual and collaborative. Depending on the subject and grade level, students may include videotapes of class performances, findings from experiments, graphs of research results, audiotapes of reading aloud, photographs of themselves at work, artifacts from projects, comments from partners and parents. From the large collection in their folders, they *select* important pieces to be included in their portfolios. These pieces are chosen for various reasons: their best work, a piece that exhibited growth, a particular genre, a good use of detail, the first foray into a new medium, to name a few. The students are then invited to *reflect* on the work that they chose to include in the portfolio. Students use this reflective work to help them set goals for the future.

As an assessment tool, the portfolio provides an exceptionally deep and thick record of kids' learning. If a student is struggling with math facts or spelling, evidence of these problems will be evident in the work. But larger strengths and weaknesses will be manifest as well: can the student conceive and pursue an inquiry? Can he make connections, draw analogies, support a position, notice contrasts? For reporting to parents or school authorities, a well-made student portfolio provides a body of evidence, a basis for decision making, that surpasses the validity of any

**Figure 7.1** Portfolios are a key mechanism for nurturing student goal setting and self-assessment.

test score number. And as we ask students to create and regularly review their own portfolios, talking and writing about what they see there, we are inculcating the habits of reflection, self-monitoring, responsibility, and planning. Some teachers have student-led conferences for parents where the students take their parents through their portfolios, a productive experience for all involved.

*Conferences* are an elegant example of how assessment activities can actually become one with instruction. In a writing workshop classroom, for example, it is integral to the model that students have regular one-to-one conferences with the teacher to review individual pieces of writing in progress as well as talk about general strengths, weaknesses, trends, and goals in their writing development. In other words, the purpose of the conferences is to help students reflect on their work, from the lowest-level elements, say the impact of one word choice against another, all the way to the most global characteristics, becoming able to step back and think about one's emerging style as an author. Even as conferences teach students to reflect, they also obviously help the teacher to gather much information about what a child knows and needs, and to offer personal, precisely targeted feedback. Providing that the teacher keeps simple notes or records of these meetings, conferences truly can combine instruction and assessment in a single seamless activity.

*Anecdotal records,* sometimes called "kidwatching," involve the teacher in making regular, written notes about each child's learning and growth. Some teachers do this by focusing on three to five children per day, carrying a clipboard with these kids' names on it and jotting down, in the seams and intervals of the schedule, what they notice about each child's learning. The teacher's style of note taking may be quite personal and telegraphic: "10:45—Jim helps Marianne use the protractor." Some teachers try to jot the child's own comments: "I don't get these cross-products, Miss K." These notes become part of the teacher's thinking, planning, and cumulative record keeping for each child. They are particularly useful for tracking a student's growth over long periods of time, and provide a strong basis for conversation with students and parents. "I see here that back in October you were confused about cross-products but now you're doing them right most of the time. What helped you figure it out?"

While anecdotal records are typically open-ended, *checklists* are a more anchored form of observational assessment. Again, teachers devise some kind of schedule during which they pay special attention to individual children—usually one or just a few at a time. Then they observe using a prepared list of competencies or behaviors, noting the degree of each student's progress. For example, in a first-grade classroom, the teacher might be checking whether each kid "Rarely," "Sometimes," or "Always" makes predictions while reading, adjusts her reading rate to the text, or retells a story accurately. One advantage of checklists is that teachers can create them together with their grade-level teammates—or with students themselves ("Let's make a list of the things that good readers do"). Classroom checklists can also be specifically designed to reflect an official district curriculum, so that teachers can use the instrument to see if their instruction is working as planned. In some schools and districts, the classroom checklist becomes an integral part of the report card, telling parents, in more detail than any "A" or "B" ever could, exactly what their child knows and is able to do.

While in traditional classrooms teachers have mostly been concerned with tallying the accumulation of subskills—the alleged building blocks of educated behavior—Best Practice directs our attention to larger, higher-order, more complex performances. That is, we want to assess not just whether a child can tell if words are nouns or verbs, but whether the student can craft an original, logical, well-organized piece of writing out of a whole lot of nouns, verbs, and other parts of speech. But assessing so complex a product as a piece of writing—as opposed to a multiple-choice test—requires a new kind of instrument. *Performance assessment* is just such a tool, and it is simply a means developing a set of specific criteria for successful performance of a given activity, and then weighting the criteria in a scoring guide. Thus, for example, you might determine (as the state of Illinois has) that an effective piece of persuasive writing has four ingredients worth 25 percent each: focus, support, organization, and mechanics. Now, writing teachers across the country might quibble with this formula, but at least it tells students what some of the inarguably necessary ingredients of successful writing are. It invites them—before they write, as they draft, and while they revise—to attend to and balance these features so that the final product will be effective with its audience.

At the very least, performance assessment is a big step ahead of the days when teachers assigned students grades on projects and papers without ever revealing the criteria for assessment. Performance assessment is most meaningful when teachers invite students into the rubric development process, brainstorming together what the formula might be for a well-done lab report, an effectively enacted scene, a well-done geometric proof. Creating this kind of scoring guide thus becomes part of instruction, helping to make curricular goals transparent and explicit. Good performance assessment tools can remind teachers to teach and students to master the elements of successful performance in the field of study at hand. And finally, while performance assessment can genuinely bring students into the process and make the criteria of success more public, it can also be used to generate the kinds of numerical and comparative results so hungrily demanded by many school systems.

*Classroom tests,* of course, are familiar to all teachers and former students. When used formatively to monitor and guide student instruction, teacher-made tests can be one ingredient of a balanced assessment program. There's nothing wrong with the occasional spelling quiz or math test, as long as the items represented and the scoring system used are reasonable measures of what has been studied. In Best Practice classrooms, though, classroom tests tend to look a little different. Since there is much curriculum jigsawing, with student groups studying different chunks of curriculum, it would be a rare occasion when everyone sat for the exact same test, at the same time. Chances are that even the weekly spelling test would be individualized, including some words chosen by each student from their own reading and research, and entered into a personal dictionary for study and mastery. Also, since teachers are most interested in students' higher-order, conceptual understandings, classroom tests would likely try to gauge those learnings and not focus much on disconnected factual recall. Chances are the students would help design any test that was given, would have input on scoring, and would be responsible for fitting their results in with other items in their own self-assessment process.

As we noted at the outset, we've presented structures of classroom assessment in a roughly declining order of student-centeredness—that is, portfolios and conferences seem more harmonious with Best Practice principles of authentic, developmentally minded education than performance assessment or classroom tests. But in the real world, a blend of these different types is undoubtedly realistic and perhaps even healthful for kids. On this matter we tend to be highly pragmatic. If teachers are under the gun to employ some competitive, norm-referenced assessment measures along with the more individualized, student-centered ones, so be it. We think it is fine, as a practical matter, for teachers to average the two together in creating grades and other reports. For example, teachers can assign point values to never-sometimes-always checklists (0, 1, or 2 points) and create tallies that average into grades. Kids can set their own goals in conferences, assess their percentage of attainment (I conquered 80 percent of my spelling demons) and plug that into the report card.

The articles in this chapter show teachers and schools working with evaluation in exactly this way, trying to create balanced assessments that enact Best Practice principles in a complicated, real world. They are feeding the grading monster as necessary, while also trying to give kids meaningful, personal, and constructive feedback on their growth. They are trying to turn more responsibility over to students, to help them become more reflective, self-aware, self-guiding people.

Leading off our Variations, Luanne Kowalke tells how she tracks the development of two very different students and the patterns of their thinking over a year's time. Luanne opens a window on the kinds of anecdotal records that can help teachers document cognitive growth. Next, Pam Hyde shows how assessment and instruction can be seamlessly woven together when both teacher and students focus on the higher-order outcomes of the curriculum. Readers may be surprised to see how complex and sophisticated assessment can actually be in third grade, and they may also notice that this long-term performance assessment is highly applicable to teaching at other levels. Returning to the earlier issues of testing and accountability, Art Hyde and Marilyn Bizar recount how one group effectively coped with standardized tests. By taking control of the testing situation and interposing an intermediate step, they were able to prevent the kind of bad policy decision that might have resulted from an unquestioned, "normal" administration of the instrument.

Looking at assessment Step by Step, Luanne Kowalke returns to show how she helps students to become self-reflective, setting their own goals and monitoring their thinking throughout the school year. Lyle Griegoliet offers examples of how, even in subjects like science, it is possible to replace traditional evaluation instruments with more challenging and worthwhile assessments. Lyle argues that if students can translate scientific concepts, such as the organization of cells, into another language (like poetry or myth), then they have demonstrated deep understanding.

# Further Reading

Azwell, Tara, and Elizabeth Schmar, eds. 1995. *Report Card on Report Cards: Alternatives to Consider.* Portsmouth, NH: Heinemann.

Cambourne, Brian, and Jan Turbill, eds. 1994. *Responsive Evaluation: Making Valid Judgments About Student Literacy.* Portsmouth, NH: Heinemann.

Graves, Donald H., and Bonnie S. Sunstein, eds. 1992. *Portfolio Portraits.* Portsmouth, NH: Heinemann.

Herman, Joan, Pamela Aschbacher, and Lynn Winters. 1992. *A Practical Guide to Alternative Assessment.* Alexandria, VA: Association for Supervision and Curriculum Development.

Hill, Bonnie Campbell, and Cynthia Ruptic. 1994. *Practical Aspects of Authentic Assessment: Putting the Pieces Together.* Norwood, MA: Christopher-Gordon.

Johnston, Peter H. 1997. *Knowing Literacy: Constructive Literacy Assessment.* York, ME: Stenhouse.

Porter, Carol, and Janell Cleland. 1995. *The Portfolio as a Learning Strategy.* Portsmouth, NH: Boynton/Cook.

Rhodes, Lynn K., ed. 1993. *Literacy Assessment: A Handbook of Instruments.* Portsmouth, NH: Heinemann.

Rhodes, Lynn K., and Nancy Shanklin. 1993. *Windows into Literacy: Assessing Learners K–8.* Portsmouth, NH: Heinemann.

Woodward, Helen. 1994. *Negotiated Evaluation: Involving Children and Parents in the Process.* Portsmouth, NH: Heinemann.

# Variations
## A Tale of Two Students

LUANNE KOWALKE

In our fourth-grade class, my students and I do a great deal of reflective assessment. The children develop many of their own performance assessment rubrics, write commentaries on their own learning process, and are constantly encouraged to "think about their thinking." Indeed, one of my main goals as a teacher is to foster students' metacognition—their ability to monitor, evaluate, and guide their own thinking.

But these are deep skills that develop slowly over time, so it is important for me to collect students' work samples and my own observational notes all year long. To show how I assess students' developing metacognition, I have compiled samples of work from two recent students, Jan and Alan. I chose these two students because I had had concerns about both of them in the area of metacognitive development since the beginning of the school year.

Jan is a student who is highly regarded by her past teachers. She writes neatly, displays confidence in her abilities, enjoys artwork, works quietly, and gets the correct answers on assignments. An only child, she is used to getting lots of attention at home, and always likes to be right. In the eyes of a traditional teacher, Jan might be described as "the perfect student."

As part of our thinking curriculum, I regularly ask the students to reflect, predict, infer, evaluate, and transfer. Jan had a hard time doing any of these things. This is evident in her early reflections, including her rubric comments from her verb book, and her research report reflections about working with a partner. At first glance, they look well written; Jan always likes to do a perfect job. On closer inspection, however, one realizes that she isn't saying anything that would be considered profound, soul searching, or reflective.

For example, in her rubric reflections, Jan gives herself the highest mark in "Responses are well thought out," because, "I thought my responses were well thought out." She gives herself a 3 for effort because, "I felt I didn't really do my best on it. All though I did do a good job on it."

In her reflections about working with a partner on a research report, she states that what she learned about working with a partner is that, "you can get more work done. You could split the report in half and you can do a half and your partner can do a half . . . If your partner makes a mistake, you can point it out to them and correct them." So much for teamwork.

Periodically I would talk to Jan about looking for deeper meaning when she was writing her reflections and participating in class and group discussions. I was not seeing metacognitive growth during discussions, and I wondered if perhaps the research was right; that metacognition could not be fostered in some children before the age of twelve. Slowly, very slowly, as I pushed Jan to look deeper, I began to see small improvements in Jan's written reflections. At the end of second quarter, Jan's comments about the areas in which she had shown the most growth emphasized cooperation and following directions.

> I feel that I have improved on working cooperatively with my classmates. I still need to work more on that, but I know I did better than last time. I also feel that I have improved on following directions. I listen carefully, and I give whoever's speaking eye contact.

The goal she sets for herself for third quarter is to put all her papers into folders so her desk won't get so messy. Although not earth-shattering, this was definitely an improvement over first quarter. As third quarter rolled around, I was still not seeing any signs of reflective growth during class and group discussions. When we did some reflecting at the end of third quarter, however, I was quite pleased with her thoughtful responses.

For example, Jan wants to learn "how to be creative, and express you're feelings and imagination . . . I also want to learn more about history, and geografy . . . I suddenly have a sudden interest in those subjects." Jan also talks about our read-aloud lessons being helpful to her. She comments, "Read-aloud has helped me become a better thinker, by using my imagination, and to picture what Ms. Kowalke is saying, it has also helped my sense of humor!—Alot!"

Jan still needs to work on being able to verbalize her reflective thoughts—in that area, she's shown little growth since the beginning of the year. Nevertheless, her improvement in written reflections shows that she is indeed capable of deeper thought. It is my hope that she will continue to stretch herself in this area.

Alan is quite a different story. He is outgoing, slightly eccentric, and quite sloppy in his work. He has an easy smile, is eager to please, and was very unsure of himself when he entered my class in the fall. At the beginning of the year, Alan literally could not complete any task independently. He would approach me seventeen to twenty times daily to ask for clarification (Yes, I really mean seventeen to twenty; I counted!) on any and all tasks. The reasons for these check-ins seemed to be fourfold. The first reason I could surmise was his eagerness to please; he wanted to do everything just right. The second reason was that Alan was unsure of himself, and needed assurance that he was doing things just right. The third and fourth reasons were that Alan was just a bit impulsive, and it was easier to let someone else do the thinking than to take the time and do it himself.

Alan needed reassurance and support, but he also needed to learn to stand on his own two feet. I let him know very quickly what types of questions I would not answer for him—questions he would easily answer for himself with a little effort. Then we began to work on the others. Some questions I would answer for him. For others, I would send him checking with his peers, and still others, we would work through together, with me questioning him instead of him questioning me. An example of this would be:

A:   I don't get it.
LK:  What don't you get?
A:   I don't get the directions.
LK:  What don't you get about them?
A:   I don't know.
LK:  Well, what do they say?
A:   [Reads directions out loud.]
LK:  All right, now what does that mean?
A:   It means I'm supposed to . . . Oh, I get it!
LK:  So, you understand now?
A:   Yeah. Thank you.
LK:  Alan, who really answered your question?
A:   I guess I did [flashes a quick smile].
LK:  Right [smiles back].

As time went by, I began asking Alan to use the strategies he was learning to answer his own questions and to think for himself. Eventually, Alan's requests for help lessened to ten per day, then to five, then to days when he would not request help at all. Once in awhile he would relapse; on about his third trip to me we would flash each other knowing smiles, and he would return to his desk to figure out the problem for himself.

Alan's few lingering requests for help became much more valid than they used to be. One day, Alan approached me with a page from a book he was reading in his spare time. "I can't make this make sense, can you help me?" he asked. Looking at the book, it took me a moment to figure out what was wrong with the page as well. It turned out that four lines of text were completely out of order—no ordinary typographical error, here! It is hard for children to comprehend that books can have mistakes, but he had found a huge one. In the past, Alan might have skipped over the passage; instead he used all the strategies he knew to make sense of the passage. When that didn't work, he knew it was time to get help. That's progress.

Alan started out the year with about as much skill in reflecting as he had in answering his own questions—very little. When asked what he did well on his verb book, he wrote, "The thing I did well on was my pictures. I think I did well on them was that I tryed my best on them." What would he do differently next time? "I would have maken the words neatlyer so that people can tell what I'm say easlier."

In his comments about his verb book rubric, Alan had this to say:

1. I picked number four because I thought that I used all the verbs correctly.
2. I chose three for quality of writing because I think that most of my writing is clear.
3. In mechanics I got one error and I tried my best to write neat [this does not match his comment above about writing "more neatlyer"].
4. My effort is one of my best things I did with this book.
5. My quality of reflection was mostly thought out.

Considering we had already talked several times about careful reflection at this point in the year, I was a little worried about Alan's seeming lack of metacognitive awareness. In his first quarter reflection he stated simply that, "I improved on not getting any more late slips. I need improvement on not doing my spelling on the last minute. I sort of improved on science. Like I like to listen about an atom is made out of $H_2O$."

By second quarter, Alan had made a bit of headway, commenting that he felt he had improved on "getting my homework done. I get my homework done by getting into my room and not wath [watch] TV . . . I think on need improvement on my cursive in the morning." As future goals for third quarter, Alan wanted to improve by using "cursive in the morning. My plan is to write it down in my assignment note book. My second goal is to keep all of my D.O.L. papers. My plan is to put them in the same folder." These comments were more specific and thoughtful than first quarter's, but I still hoped for more from Alan.

As third quarter drew to a close, I again asked students to reflect on a variety of topics. When asked what they had learned about themselves this year, Alan wrote, "I have learned that I can think better than I thought

I could." Alan also commented that what he would like to learn about learning is "how you now [know] exactly know when you are learning about learning. I would lik [like] to know how the brain works." Alan made many metacognitive advancements throughout the year. He began using a variety of strategies to answer his own questions, pondering more thoughtfully to answer reflective questions and reminding himself to stop and think before giving in to impulse.

Alan and Jan began fourth grade with very little "instinctive" metacognitive ability. Through discussion, coaching, and practice, both developed a greater sense of their reflective selves. It is my hope that they will continue this growth, not only in fourth grade, but throughout the rest of their lives. It is a skill that will serve them well.

Facilitating thoughtful, metacognitive learning in the classroom is not especially difficult, but it does take time, understanding, and a vision that goes beyond the traditional classroom values. The end result, however, is an increased awareness for students; not only of what they learn, but how they learn it and what they can do with that knowledge. In the words of Henry A. Taitt, "Teach a child *what* to think, and you make him a slave to your knowledge. Teach a child *how* to think, and you make all knowledge his slave."

# Understanding Mathematical Concepts Through Performance Assessment

PAMELA R. HYDE

It is very important to me that the assessment of my students' mathematical thinking and understanding be authentic and valid. There are many new concepts to learn in math in third grade, and because of the added pressure to have most of them understood by the middle of March in order to do well on the state math assessment tests, I want to make sure my teaching is efficient and complete. I need to know exactly what my students understand, how they conceptualize the content, and if that conceptualization is consistent with the cognitive model I am trying to convey. If there is a breakdown in understanding, I want to know where that breakdown occurs and some indication of what direction I should take in helping my students fully understand the problem before them. I feel, as most teachers do, that I have no time to waste. I want to integrate assessment into the curriculum and have it function as an instructional, as well as an assessment, tool.

As a student, I experienced frustration with instructional methods and especially with the assessments traditionally used in mathematics classrooms. I have been in the situation where the tests I have taken have not demonstrated what I knew, where anxiety has devastated test scores. I feel a strong commitment to my students to enable them to be capable of learning math concepts and to feel confident about themselves in this area. I want to alleviate "test and math anxiety" so that I can accurately view their depth of understanding instead of having to wonder what went wrong on a paper and pencil test. Some of the assessments I used were done independently by the students, and a product was the end result. Sometimes the product was a written explanation, sometimes a picture or a model made with manipulatives. I will quote some of their responses exactly as they were given to me. Some of the assessments were my observations that I wrote down, others were interviews with children. Their oral responses will be verbatim.

In the beginning of the school year I want to find out which students need a quick review of the concepts covered in math in second grade, and which ones need to have more extensive reteaching. This way I know what I can build on conceptually. The first assessment addressed concepts that traditionally have been covered in second grade.

# Colors in a Jar

In this task I was assessing their ability to estimate, adding three two-digit numbers together and using carrying. The usual method of evaluation for this concept is to give students three numbers that don't refer to anything, already set up in the algorithmic form of two columns. There is no counting or thinking involved, they merely manipulate numbers. I wanted to make it a broader task involving objects they were familiar with. I wanted to be able to evaluate the thinking it takes to solve the problem. I filled a jar with cubes of three different colors: 18 white, 14 blue, 13 red. Students were told to look at the jar and first estimate, without counting, how many cubes were in the jar, then determine which color they saw most, and which color they saw least. These questions were used to help them really look at what was in the jar. Then they were asked to pour the objects into a shoe box lid and figure out how many cubes there were of each color. Then they were to find out how many cubes there were all together. Finally, they were asked to show their work on paper, and to write an explanation of how they reached their answer.

While I watched them working on this task, I realized that many of them had no idea how to set the problem up, had a hazy idea of place value, and even less knowledge of base 10 and how to carry one 10 into the tens column. For example, one student counted all the colors individually in such a way that he counted a few cubes twice and got the wrong numbers for each color. He then started all over again, counting one by one to find the total number of cubes. When I asked him if he could think of another way to do it he said he couldn't. I prompted his thinking by asking how many reds he had, how many whites, and how many blues. He had not written those numbers down when he counted the cubes, so he counted again. I asked if those numbers could help him in any way. He said no. When he wrote his explanation on how he found his answer, he simply wrote, "I cownted."

This example was typical for four of my students. It told me that they did not see the problem as a whole but as segmented parts. They did not see the connection of counting the individual colors, and combining those numbers to get the total. They started over again, using a one-to-one correspondence in counting, and some were not even able to do that correctly. They were at a primitive level of cognitive development in number sense.

The majority of my class was in a middle range on this task. For example, one student counted the individual colors and wrote, "There are 18 white one. There are 14 blue ones and 13 red one. I couted them up. There are 45 objects in the jar." Another mid-level response said, "I figured it out by counting by twos. ther are 44 cubes. there are fourteen blues there are thirteen reds there are eighteen whites." Even though they had the right number of the individual colors, they didn't see that adding the three numbers would get them the answer.

Compare these to some typical high responses: "18 + 14 + 13 = 45 I first counted the wite then the blue and then the red. then I added them together." "14 blue 13 red 18 wight 45 all togather 27 + 18 = 45 How I did it. First I counted each color by its self. then I added them togather." These higher responses not only saw right away that the three numbers should be added together to find the total, they added correctly, remembering to carry the ten from the ones column.

# Perimeter

I have come to believe that the different strands of mathematics should be taught and assessed in an integrated fashion. Perimeter is one of those concepts that has been taught as a separate entity when it is probably one of the richer vehicles available to connect to other concepts. After many hands-on activities, lots of discussion among the students, and between the students and me, it was time to check their level of understanding

**Figure 7.2** Assessment can be part of good instruction in mathematics.

for information that would direct my instruction. I wanted to evaluate the students' ability to understand both metric and customary measurement, how they use measurement tools—especially when the measurements were larger than the measurement tools themselves—the concept of perimeter, and a continuation of adding numbers requiring carrying. I also wanted it to be an experience where they were actively "doing mathematics" in a real-world situation.

The students were put in cooperative groups of four to five to encourage them to make sense collaboratively of the mathematics involved and to communicate their mathematical ideas to one another. The instructions were to find the perimeter of the front chalkboard, the front face of the heater, the project table, a handwriting book, and the entire room. They had to label the dimensions of each object and show the math involved in solving each problem. They were each given a sheet of paper with the objects to be measured listed next to small drawings that were the approximate shapes of the objects. They were all rectangles and all but one was a large object. I provided them with various tools including meter sticks and measuring tapes and rulers with metric and customary measurements on them. This part of the assessment was to be done in the metric system, but I purposely had tools with both measurements on them so that students would have to distinguish between them. They would repeat the activity using customary measurements on another day.

They started at different parts of the room so they were not in each other's way. While they measured the objects, I walked around taking notes on what I observed. This activity took more than one class period to complete. I could see that some of the students had a hard time distinguishing centimeters from inches. Since it was a group activity and I encouraged them to discuss their strategies with each other, the ones who had a problem were helped by their group members. Some students had not experienced using measuring tools other than what we had done in the classroom when I had introduced measurement. I noticed that the less experienced students were not careful when lining up the end point of the ruler to the end point of the object they were measuring. The experienced students in their group pointed that out to them by explaining, "put it edge to edge or we'll get the wrong number."

When they had to measure the perimeter of the really large objects, such as the front chalkboard or the room itself, they had various ways of marking off the measurements. One group used five meter sticks laid end to end, picking up the first and placing it at the end of the fifth one, then the second one they used after the sixth one, and so on. Others used only one meter stick, marked the carpet or chalkboard with chalk at the end of the stick, then put it down at their mark, and repeated the process to the end of the room or chalkboard. Some used one meter stick and their fingers to mark where it ended, others used the tape measure and their fingers to mark where it ended to see where the tape should be laid next. That group counted the whole room in centimeters instead of meters. It was very interesting to hear all of the groups reason which was the most efficient way to accomplish the task and note the level of sophistication with which many of them measured.

This assessment was very broad, and I wanted to be open to discovering as much as possible about several areas addressed by this activity. Several issues became apparent to me. The first issue was measurement. I was looking for answers that were reasonable as opposed to being exact. Most of the students were able to come very close to the actual dimensions. Of the few who did not, the reasons varied. For example, one student added 99 many times to calculate his dimensions. He was using a meter stick which is 100 centimeters long but the last number printed on the sticks is 99. That last centimeter ending at the edge of the stick is not labeled. His problem stemmed from improper use of the tool. When I asked him how many centimeters were in a meter, he knew. When he looked closely at the meter stick, he realized his mistake. A few children made the mistake of labeling the longer sides of the rectangle with the measurement of the shorter sides. While they understood the concept of perimeter, they did not understand the situation well enough to use the picture effectively and did not realize that the dimensions did not make sense in the real-world setting.

The second issue I looked at in this assessment was conceptual. There were a couple of cases of incomplete conceptual knowledge of perimeter itself. For example, one student had four dimensions labeled, but had the measurement of only one of the sides as the total perimeter. I saw that he was still not conceiving of perimeter as the complete outside measurement of the object. Another student who had the perimeter of the chalkboard significantly bigger than the perimeter of the entire classroom showed me that she was not really thinking about the situation. She was relying on her knowledge of the procedure for finding perimeter rather than the conceptual model I was trying to elicit.

The third issue addressed by this assessment was computation. I was pleased to find that there were relatively few errors in this area, but due to the fact that many of the students had been introduced to addition with carrying only recently, it was something I wanted to follow carefully. For instance, some students had the numbers set up in the wrong columns and added incorrectly. This showed a problem in understanding place value as well as not knowing addition combinations. One student showed a sophisticated computation strategy for a third grader in finding the perimeter of the classroom. He added one long side of the rectangle to one short side, then added that total twice. This shows a higher level of computational reasoning as well as a more abstract understanding of perimeter. This had never been taught; he inferred it on his own. This assessment allowed me to see this capability.

After I examined these papers, I gave the class a chance to revise their answers. I wanted this to be a valid learning activity as well as an assessment activity. Giving them a second chance to work on a product alleviates anxiety about tests and math in general, which is one of my goals. I have not found that it makes them less careful in their original work because they knew they would have to do the work correctly at some point. I compare it to writing, where your best work has been thought through and revised.

Student writing in mathematics can help teachers obtain more insight into the conceptual models a student has. I asked the class to write a few sentences in response to three questions about perimeter. The first question dealt with the concept of perimeter, the second question dealt with the procedure used to find perimeter, and the third with the application of perimeter in a real-world setting. This activity showed that I had quite a wide range in the classroom. In a high-level response, one student answered:

What is perimeter? "The outside measurement of any object."
How do you find perimeter? "Measure the sides of the object and add them together."
When would you ever need to know the perimeter of a space? "When you're going to fence a yard you need to know how much fence you need."

In dramatic contrast, one of my students wrote:

What is perimeter? "Sq. yard."
How do you find perimeter? "You add all of the numbers and put it down on the paper."
When would you ever need to know the perimeter of a space? "To find out how long the building or house is."

Comparing these two papers, it is easy to see that the high-level response had a good understanding of the concept of perimeter. He explained the procedure used to find the answer and had a good real-life situation in which perimeter would be used, putting a fence around a yard. He even states that it would tell you how much fence you need to buy. In contrast, the lower-level paper shows little grasp of the concept of perimeter. He shows he is confused between perimeter and area when he referred to "Sq. yard." His understanding of the procedure is restricted to knowing that the operation used is addition. His idea of the application of perimeter is rather superficial. From this piece I could see that his learning in this area was minimal, and I would literally have to start from the beginning with my instruction. Luckily there were very few students in the class who were at this level of understanding. Besides being a valuable assessment tool, writing in mathematics also enables students to learn to communicate using mathematical language, which is a goal of the NCTM standards. It was another way of uncovering misconceptions. Knowing what needed to be done for whom, I was able to tailor my instruction to meet the needs of my students.

This unit led into our work with area. The students would learn that there was a different type of measurement that used the same dimensions they were used to working with, but in a new way. I demonstrated how the inside measurement of a space was different from the outside measurement, even though they were using the same numbers. They worked with many hands-on activities where I made the distinction between the measurement on the top and bottom of a rectangle, referring to columns of individual units, and the measurement on the sides of a rectangle, referring to the number of rows of units. These two terms were at the core of my communication with them about the figures they would be investigating and were therefore very important. They used square manipulatives in many different arrangements to create rectangles. The squares were separated into vertical arrays, or columns, and into horizontal arrays, or rows, so the students could see that the area of a rectangle was made up of a series of groups. This is an experiential base for multiplication and some of the students saw that right away. These rows and columns were then pushed together to form a solid rectangle. After a couple of weeks of working with various manipulatives, I wanted to assess their progress and see what I needed to emphasize in my instruction.

## Area

While the students were out of the room, I made rectangles by laying out several square ceramic tiles and tracing the outline onto the carpet with chalk. Some were made out of large tiles, and some out of small tiles. I placed them around the room so there would be ample space to work in groups of four or five. I left the appropriate-sized tiles next to each diagram, in a box with many more tiles than were needed to fill the inside of the rectangle. I put a number in chalk in the middle of each rectangle.

I put the students into groups and told them to make sure that they were all on the same side of the rectangle, and that the number inside the outline on the carpet was right side up. This was critical because if the group was looking at it from a different perspective, the number of rows and columns would be backward. Each person received a paper with the six rectangles, drawn and identified as corresponding with the outline of the rectangles on the carpet. Next to each rectangle on the paper, I had written "rows =" and "columns =" and "area =." The instructions were to use the tiles to cover the area of each rectangle, and to draw on their papers the columns and rows that they saw inside the rectangle on the carpet. Then they had to label the number of columns and rows on their drawings to show the dimensions of the rectangles. Next they were to write in the number of rows and columns next to those words, and calculate the area of the figure. I circulated among the groups, taking notes on my observations of how each child was thinking about this task. Because this assessment is less broad than the perimeter assessment, it was fairly easy for me to see how the children's thinking and understanding fell into categories.

The high-response papers were characterized by correct numbers and accurate drawings, but most notably by the lack of erasures. There was no confusion between rows and columns, their pictorial representations were correctly drawn on their first attempts, and the area computation was correct and labeled using the words "sq. units" or "sq. t's" for square tiles. I was surprised to find that all of this group wrote the multiplication algorithm on paper to find the area. In my observations I noted that these were not memorized facts, but actually done by successive addition, which was very appropriate for this level. About half the class was at this level. I felt confident that they had a complete understanding of the concept assessed.

Another group of students had some confusion between rows and columns when they were writing those values next to the words "columns" and "rows," but labeled the drawing correctly. I infer from this that when looking at the concrete model, they could understand which was which, but when it became a little more abstract, they were still a little confused. Their pictures of the models were drawn correctly and did correspond with the model they had created on the carpet. A few of the children wrote the multiplication algorithm and got the wrong answer. A few students in this group calculated the area by successive addition, but most of them counted the squares one by one. There were very few calculation mistakes in this group.

Students with a lower level of understanding displayed some confusion between columns and rows when they labeled the drawings as well as when it was taken to the abstract step of writing the number next to the words. A few of the pictures were drawn wrong, again confusing columns and rows. I could see that they were having a problem translating the model accurately to the pictorial level of abstraction. They were not able to conceive of the area in the way the other two groups did. They still needed more hands-on experiences to develop their understanding. All of these students calculated the area by counting each tile. There were a few mistakes in the calculations.

The low-level responses were most easily distinguished by the number of erasures and the lack of correspondence between the picture and the model. Not only did they confuse the number of rows with the number of columns, but also used numbers that were not even related to the drawing. I could see from this that there was almost no understanding of area. While observing them building the model I noticed that they were able to cover the space with the tiles, and they knew that they needed to count the tiles. They were very confused about assigning numbers to the dimensions of the figure. It showed me that this group needed more experience and instruction in relating the concrete model to the abstract representation, as well as more practice with seeing the rows and columns. I have found that perception and space relations generally are problems for these children. It takes a much longer time for them to visually perceive things that other children see quickly, so using concrete models and hands-on activities are even more important for them than for other students. As in previous assessments, the students went back and revised their pictures and calculations until they were correct. They were encouraged to find their own mistakes and revise by themselves. I intervened only when instruction was necessary.

All of this work with area, seeing it as a system of columns and rows, using natural language to show how to add a number a certain amount of "times" (successive addition) led seamlessly into multiplication. I purposely do not teach the formula A = L x W because I feel it circumvents all the experiential groundwork that is so important. Then children just start memorizing times tables without connecting them to anything real. Jumping to the abstract so soon undermines understanding. The class formally began multiplication and related it over and over again to the activities we had previously spent time doing, building on the rich framework that had been carefully established.

# Reflections

Not only did I find these assessments relatively easy and natural to do, but my students actually enjoyed them, found them less anxiety producing than traditional tests, and thought they learned more. In sharp contrast to conventional assessments, these activities gave me specific information about the extent of knowledge my students had so that I could determine what direction I should take with each child to build their understanding. It helped me identify—and therefore dispel—any misconceptions they might have had and give them more meaningful feedback. It allowed me to watch the evolution and development of their ideas and strategies, instead of being keyed into the "correct answer" only. Encouraging students to revise their work helped them develop persistence, thereby gaining self-confidence in their math ability when they were able to be successful. It also showed them that their work was valued and something to be proud of, something worth making right or "polishing." Finally, the collaborative and interactive nature of these assessment activities mirrors the regular instructional activities in my classroom, with which students are familiar.

Using multiple representations enabled me to get at different aspects of each mathematical concept. It allowed students to clarify and elaborate on their original conception of the idea. In order to draw a picture of or write an expository paragraph about a concept, students have to think about it differently from the way they do when they maneuver numbers in an algorithm. They have to use metacognitive skills to check their thinking when they have to explain something in writing. Their inadequate conceptualization was obvious to them when they realized they could not explain something they thought they understood. I could see the gradations of conceptualization more clearly through these multiple representations. Using multiple representations also allowed for different modalities of learning, which gave my students with learning disabilities more opportunity to succeed.

Authentic assessment uses broader tasks, so I could assess (and teach) several different concepts from the curriculum at one time. This efficiency makes up for the fact that designing and evaluating this type of assessment takes more time. My assessment activities were also invaluable when conference time rolled around. I shared my findings with parents, showing them exactly where their children's strengths and weaknesses were. This information gave parents a clearer picture of what they could do at home to support learning and to help their children grow as mathematical thinkers.

# Measuring Growth in Reading: Coping with Standardized Assessments

ARTHUR HYDE AND MARILYN BIZAR

Schools all over the country are being judged by their performance on highly flawed standardized measures of achievement. Data from these tests is routinely used to make decisions that affect students, teachers, whole schools, and districts. In Chicago, for example, scores on the Iowa Test of Basic Skills (ITBS) are the sole determinant of whether a school is placed on probation, a step that brands the school a failure and puts its teachers' jobs in jeopardy. This kind of high-stakes use of single test score numbers is a problem in many areas of education—but is not always insurmountable. In some cases, like the one we report below, educators can take more control of standardized testing and the interpretations of scores so that programs are not unjustifiably distorted.

In 1989, we completed a three-year study of a project to create classroom libraries in two Chicago Public Schools located in low-income neighborhoods. A local foundation had purchased a large number of novels, storybooks, and nonfiction trade books for each classroom in grades 3 through 6. The project provided staff development sessions for the teachers receiving the libraries, so that they could use the materials according to state-of-the-art Best Practice reading instruction. As project evaluators, we were asked to determine what effect the classroom libraries had on the reading achievement of the children. Reading achievement in Chicago has traditionally been "measured" by the ITBS. Although we continue to question what is actually assessed with this test, it was the only source of data available at that time. Looking at the grade level ITBS scores for the two schools during the three years of the project, we saw generally low scores for each of the grades, every year. Hundreds of students in both schools appeared not to be learning much about reading.

However, two important factors are missing anytime one looks at test score data that sum up all the students at a grade level. First, when a school reports test data on one hundred third graders, the public has no way of knowing how many of those students were actually enrolled in that school all year long. How many arrived the week before the test? How many were in the school the year before? How can one assess "improvement" in reading scores (or any other subject) from year to year at a school without knowing how long the students tested were enrolled at that school? Student mobility and family transiency tend to be greatest in high-poverty schools. In many Chicago schools, turnover rates of 30 to 40 percent are not uncommon. A similar line of reasoning raises questions about student absence versus attendance. What percentage of the students who were tested were absent most of the time? We also know that many Chicago schools have daily absence rates of 10 percent or more. With these distorting factors in city schools, achievement test data may underestimate how much learning is happening for students who are consistently enrolled and regularly present at a particular school.

Second, in trying to determine how much students are learning, wouldn't it be good to know what is actually happening in their classrooms? In the case of the classroom libraries, did all classes and teachers use the books the same amount of time? In the same way? Which classrooms, teachers, and hence, students, used the books in the most effective ways?

In our study of the project at these two schools, we addressed these two factors separately. First, the school staff compiled student test data on the ITBS for the three years so that we could determine which students were in school from one year to the next. Although we did not look at daily attendance or absence data, we did analyze test data for students who actually were enrolled during the year and had the opportunity to participate in the classroom libraries project. Through this process, we obtained data on about two-thirds of the students in each school.

Second, without any knowledge of the test data, one of us visited classrooms during each year to determine to what extent students were actually using the books. The classrooms were then rated high, medium, or low on implementation. For instance, in high classrooms one could see teachers encouraging recreational reading in school, students taking books home, and frequent classroom discussions of books that had been read. (Note that these ratings applied just to the use of the special classroom library books involved in the project.)

Test data for students in each classroom in each year were then matched with the extent of classroom library use. We were particularly interested in the test score gain of individual students from year to year. There were 430 students with usable data at one school and 422 at the other. How much improvement in reading achievement on the ITBS from one year to the next would there be among those who were in classrooms where the books were used effectively? The results were fascinating.

**Reading Score Gains at Three Levels of Implementation**

| Book Use | Mean Year's Gain | Percent, 1 Year Gain | Percent, No Gain or Loss |
|----------|------------------|----------------------|--------------------------|
| High | 1.00 | 50% | 10% |
| Medium | .80 | 40% | 15% |
| Low | .50 | 30% | 30% |

At both schools we found the same pattern. The students in classrooms rated high in the use of the books had average (mean) improvement scores of one year's growth (or gain) in reading achievement, which is the national norm for these tests. Many of these students had much more than one year's gain, but the average was one year. Each year more than half of these students gained at least one year. Only about 10 percent (two or three students in each class) showed no gain (or loss). Students in classrooms rated medium did slightly less well. They averaged .8 of a year's growth each year. About 40 percent gained at least one year and 15 percent showed no gain. However, students in classrooms rated low fared poorly: they averaged only a half-year's growth each year. Thirty percent showed a year's gain and 30 percent showed no gain. The chart above summarizes this information. The difference among the three groups was statistically significant. It is highly unlikely (less than one chance out of a hundred) that the difference could happen by chance.

Therefore, when one looks at the two-thirds of the students who were actually enrolled, even without considering their attendance/absence rates, students did show improvement from year to year on standardized tests. Furthermore, differences in rates of gain appear to be strongly influenced by what is happening in the classroom. Clearly, students from low-income neighborhoods are capable of learning and improving year to year when provided with appropriate classroom experiences.

It is important to note that we only agreed to look at these quantitative measures after evaluating the project for three years, and then only in response to the needs of the supporting foundation. It is our perception that these gains would not have been measurable if we had not given the program three years to become institutionalized in some classrooms. In the previous two years, our evaluations looked at more qualitative features, which were to us the most solid indicators of both student and teacher engagement with the books. Some of these indexes were: time spent on books, number of books read, time spent sharing books with parents and siblings, accessibility of books in the classroom, and teachers reading aloud to students.

What can be concluded from this study overall? Clearly, students from low-income neighborhoods are capable of learning and improving year to year when provided with appropriate classroom experiences. They must be in school, stay in school, and receive good teaching. Their teachers need staff development to help them learn how to teach using the Best Practices that work for all children.

# Step by Step

## Student Self-Assessment: Thinking About Thinking

LUANNE KOWALKE

To make sure that children become intelligent, insightful, educated human beings, we educators must help them become conscious of their own learning and thought processes. Instead of teaching students *what* to think, we need to teach them *how* to think, and how to think for themselves. In other words, we must teach metacognition. But what does this term mean in everyday classrooms?

Put simply, metacognition is thinking about your thinking and knowing what you know. For many people, this is simply called reflection. When we reflect, mull, muse, weigh, contemplate, meditate, speculate, or form and express carefully considered thoughts about our own thinking, we are involved in metacognition. Metacognition is an important kind of reflective thinking that people use, often unconsciously, to help themselves in the learning process, by recognizing and understanding what they know and don't know, and by making decisions about this knowledge. People are metacognitively involved when they plan, monitor, and evaluate their own actions and thought processes.

Understanding what metacognition is, we can recognize its relevance and importance in the classroom. "Educated people are not merely learned, they think well" (Lipman 1987). Many educators have had similar thoughts when considering students who know their mathematics facts and grammar, but are unable to self-monitor their thought processes in areas such as problem solving and reflective thinking. In the words of Arthur Costa, "Intelligent behavior is knowing what to do when you don't know what to do" (1991). We have all seen students paralyzed by indecision and confusion when faced with a new or challenging situation. Research shows that academic achievers use metacognitive strategies in these instances, whereas at-risk students use only limited strategies (Hildenbrand and Hixon 1991, 121).

We have an obligation to teach metacognition. After all, when students have trouble understanding how to add, we show them how to add. If students have difficulty with a science concept, we explain it to them or involve them in an experiment to clarify their understanding. When students don't understand a particular word they have read, we show them how to extract the meaning of that word from context. Doesn't it make sense if children are unable to metacognitively plan, monitor, and evaluate their learning that we make this method of learning available to them? It is vital that we help all of our students to become intelligent thinkers, a first step in fostering lifelong learners.

We can help our students become intelligent thinkers by addressing their needs in the areas of planning, monitoring, and evaluating. In the planning and monitoring stages, we can encourage students to set and reach for their own goals. In the evaluating stages, we can ask students to self-assess their own learning. To nurture all three, we can provide students with the classroom time they need to plan, monitor, and evaluate their own thought processes when participating in discussions and activities on a daily basis.

# Goal Setting

Goal setting is a cognitive process commonly used by effective adults; it is simply the act of targeting an objective or goal, and formulating a plan to reach that goal. Although most people are able to set and attain goals as they mature, helping young people get an early start can be beneficial educationally, personally, and socially.

Each morning I model goal setting for my fourth graders as we begin our school day. "Today, our most important goal is to finish our writers' workshop revisions. Our other goals include on-line voting for the MayaQuest expedition, finishing our bulletin board, and allowing time for literature circles. If we have time beyond that, we'll tackle some spring cleaning and e-mail our buddies. If not, we'll take care of those things tomorrow." This particular example illustrates short-term goal setting.

Long-term goals are important to students as well. I encourage my students to set goals for themselves, write them down, and check in with them periodically to see how they are doing. Some of the goals set by my students include social, personal, and educational aspirations. One of Chris' goals is "to keep my desk neater. I will put my papers in clearly marked folders so I don't have to search all over tarnation for them." Jenny is "trying to work better in cooperative groups. I know I've improved over last quarter, but I still need to get better." Min-Ho, Mito, and Yoon-Tae, English-as-a-Second-Language students, want, respectively, "to be a better writer and reader," to be "less shy," and to "understand [linking] verbs like have or has."

These are all personal goals chosen by the students themselves. At times, I will also request that they set a goal for a particular assignment. Under these circumstances I usually set a few parameters and ask for a written, formal, binding proposal. An example of this would be:

Tell me:
1. Your topic
2. How you will cover your material
3. How you plan to present the information to the class
4. On what criteria you wish to be evaluated

These parameters can be changed to meet the needs of the situation and of each individual student. The important thing I try to remember is not to become too restrictive. The purpose of goal setting is for the students not to "fill in the blanks" the teacher has left for them, but to truly have an opportunity to set, reach for, and attain goals they have chosen for themselves. It is important to remember that goals should be authentic, student generated, and individualized to meet the needs of each student. Teachers can facilitate goal setting by modeling different types of goals themselves and by using student-made goals in the evaluation process.

The following examples are student goals for group science projects about the topic of light. Each group wrote what their topic would be, how they would cover the material, and how they would like to be evaluated.

Dear Ms. Kowalke,

We will be doing a talk show and Katie will be the host. We want to be graded on organization, drama, and the amount of information. The three visitors will be John, Neal, and Lauren. It will be about how light bounces off different objects.

Lauren, John, Katie, and Neal

Dear Ms. Kowalke,

Our project is going to be a mural. We are going to draw a laboratory of people studying light. The thing we would like you to grade us on is drawing, effort, and information.

Sincerely,
Kristin, Abby, Patrick, and Chris

Dear Ms. Kowalke,

Our project is the oral report. We would like to be graded on how well we work together, and how our report is tied into the chapter, and how creative our project is. The report will be about Isaac Newton and how the prism changes colors.

Sincerely,
Sarah, Alex, and Jenny

In a final example of goal setting, a student's blueprint for a complex machine has been included (see Figure 7.3). In this instance, children were asked to apply what they had learned about the principles of simple machines to create a computer-drawn blueprint for a machine that they would build for a final science project. Students were asked to consider whether their project was feasible, and whether they could construct it on their own. Jenny created a Jello Squisher.

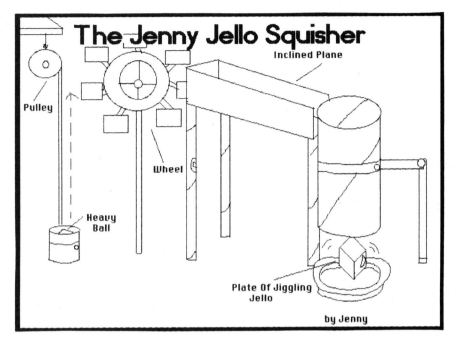

**Figure 7.3** Students used computers to draw blueprints for original machines.

# Self-Assessment

The purpose of assessment should be for students to become self-evaluating. I often ask my students to stop for a moment and assess their accomplishments. This is a difficult yet fulfilling process. In the words of one student, "This is so hard because it makes me really use my brain!" Amazingly, student self-assessments and my own evaluations of them are often mirror images.

When I am going to ask students to self-evaluate, I make sure that I have not made validating remarks about that particular assignment. For example, I would not mark a piece of writing for the grade book and discuss positives and negatives of the piece with the student, then ask them to self-evaluate. Instead, I would ask students to do their evaluation of the piece, then I would complete my evaluation without looking at their evaluation. What I find when I later compare the two evaluations is startling: About 85 percent of the time, our evaluations are extremely close.

Students put so much thought and effort into their self-assessments that I take them quite seriously. They do not tend to rush through a self-assessment when it is meaningful and relevant. In reality, it may take my fourth-grade students forty-five minutes to complete a thorough self-evaluation. In most cases, both my evaluation and the students' carry equal weight in the grade book (unfortunately, report cards are still the reality in our school, so grades are necessary).

At the beginning of the year, I photocopy the "Social and Study Skills" portion of our report card, enough for each student to have his or her own copy. At the end of each quarter, I give each student the checklist and ask them to reflect on his or her progress for the quarter. As we move through the quarters, I give the students their reflections from past quarters to review. Each student completes the checklist thoughtfully, then answers the following questions:

1. What area do you feel showed your greatest improvement this quarter?
2. What area do you feel still needs improvement?
3. What goals would you like to set for next quarter?
4. What would you like me to discuss with your parents during conferences?

I always share report cards with students before they are sent home to parents. At that time, I give each student my copy of the report card, their copy of the checklist, and their reflections. The only thing I request of students is that they find a quiet, private place to look over their report cards. It is wonderful to see what happens next. Students look cursorily for a letter grade in the various subject areas, and then their attention is drawn to the check marks rating their behavior and skills.

Before I began using this self-assessment technique two years ago, students would look at their letter grade in each subject and then hand their report card back to me; it took them about thirty seconds to find out what they wanted to know—their grade. Now, I block out a full thirty minutes for students to look at their report cards, because most take at least fifteen to twenty minutes to look over the check marks, comparing each one with their own assessment. If there is a discrepancy between my evaluation and the student's, we will discuss it. If necessary, changes will be made. This rarely happens, however, because our evaluations are usually so close. I am always sure to ask students if there were "any surprises" on their report card (this would mean that one of us had a very different point of view from the other, and I would want to find out why). In two years, four grading periods each, I have only had two students answer "Yes" to that question, and one of those students received a higher grade than they expected.

Figures 7.4a and b show checklists filled out by Lauren and me. Below

| Social and Study Skills | 1 | | | | 2 | | | |
|---|---|---|---|---|---|---|---|---|
| | Needs More Time to Acquire Skill | Improving | Making Acceptable Progress | Consistently Does Well | Needs More Time to Acquire Skill | Improving | Making Acceptable Progress | Consistently Does Well |
| Assumes responsibility for own actions and words | | | ✓ | | | | | ✓ |
| Relates well to others | | | | ✓ | | | | ✓ |
| Is courteous and respectful toward others | | | | ✓ | | | | ✓ |
| Respects the rights and property of others | | | | ✓ | | | | ✓ |
| Listens while others speak | | | ✓ | | | | | ✓ |
| Accepts correction | | | | ✓ | | | | ✓ |
| Follows school rules | | | | ✓ | | | | ✓ |
| Organizes work and materials | | | ✓ | | | | | ✓ |
| Listens carefully | | | ✓ | | | | | ✓ |
| Follows directions | | | | ✓ | | ✓ | | |
| Works independently | | | ✓ | | | ✓ | | |
| Works quietly | | ✓ | | | ✓ | | | |
| Makes good use of time | | | ✓ | | ✓ | | ✓ | |
| Participates in discussions | | | | ✓ | | | ✓ | ✓ |
| Works cooperatively in group activities | | | | ✓ | | ✓ | ✓ | ✓ |

**Figure 7.4a** Lauren's rubric.

is a sample of her first- and second-quarter reflections. Lauren shows particular growth in her self-perceptiveness from first to second quarter.

## Lauren's First Quarter Reflections

1. I improved on math like I learned how to do multiplacation tricks.
2. I need improvement on science skills. It's a little hard for me.

| Social and Study Skills | 1 | | | | 2 | | | |
|---|---|---|---|---|---|---|---|---|
| | Needs More Time to Acquire Skill | Improving | Making Acceptable Progress | Consistently Does Well | Needs More Time to Acquire Skill | Improving | Making Acceptable Progress | Consistently Does Well |
| Assumes responsibility for own actions and words | | | | ✓ | | | | ✓ |
| Relates well to others | | | | ✓ | | | | ✓ |
| Is courteous and respectful toward others | | | ✓ | | | | ✓ | |
| Respects the rights and property of others | | | | ✓ | | | | ✓ |
| Listens while others speak | | | ✓ | | | | ✓ | |
| Accepts correction | | | ✓ | | | | | ✓ |
| Follows school rules | | | | ✓ | | | | ✓ |
| Organizes work and materials | | | ✓ | | | | | ✓ |
| Listens carefully | | | ✓ | | | | ✓ | |
| Follows directions | | | ✓ | | | | ✓ | |
| Works independently | | | ✓ | | | | ✓ | |
| Works quietly | | | ✓ | | | | | ✓ |
| Makes good use of time | | | | ✓ | | | ✓ | |
| Participates in discussions | | | | ✓ | | | ✓ | |
| Works cooperatively in group activities | | | | ✓ | | | | ✓ |

**Figure 7.4b** Ms. Kowalke's rubric.

3. I think you should talk to my parents about what I'm good at and what I need to improve on. You should also talk to them about how I do in other classes like p.e. or music or something.

## Lauren's Second Quarter Reflections

1. I feel I've improved on a lot of things this quarter. I've improved on math because I used to get late slips pretty much. This quarter I think I only got one. I like having my work in on time. I also

improved on making good use of my time. I work neatly now and go a little faster on my work. I used to write not so good, but now I have fun writing and try to write the best I can.

2. In think I need to improve on listening a little bit more carefully. Sometimes I'm trying to listen but I get all mixed up. I usually understand what the teacher is saying. I also need to organize the things in my desk better. At home I organize things very well.

3. Two or three goals I will try to reach next quarter are to have things I will need in my desk to be ready and right there when I need them. I will try to clean out my desk and put things that belong together like a math page goes in my math folder. Next quarter I will try to remember more things.

In Figure 7.5, I have included an assessment rubric created by the students. The children made decisions about how they should be evaluated after completion of their verb books. They then completed their own rubric, supporting their decisions by making a comment about each rating. I also filled out a rubric form for each student, and both grades were entered in the grade book. Every student's evaluation matched mine to within 5 percent (a student may have rated themselves at a 90 percent while I rated them at a 95 percent, or vice versa). Below is one example of a student's reflections on this rubric.

## Sarah's Reflections

1. I gave myself this mark (#3) because on the vigorous verb page I underlined the wrong verb. (Boom is not the verb, makes is the verb.) But all my defenitions made sense.

2. I chose to give myself a #4 because my writing is clear (very) and my ryming patterns make lots of sense and I used my own in the places that I was supposed to.

3. I think that I deserve to give myself a #4 because I didn't make any spelling errors and my spacing was neat.

4. I gave myself a #4 because I showed my best effort in the whole book. (Aspecially the reflections.)

5. I gave myself a #3 because I thought about my reflections for a long time but they could have been better.

This kind of self-assessment takes time for students to do well. They need time to process their thoughts, but it is well worth the effort. Students become more invested in the work they are doing, and they are truly honest about how hard they worked on a particular assignment. In this way, student and teacher become partners in evaluation, instead of

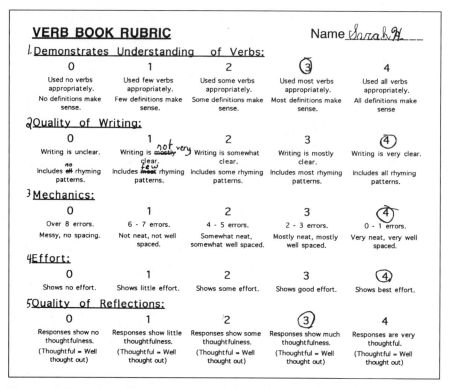

**VERB BOOK RUBRIC**                    Name *Sarah H.*

*1.* Demonstrates Understanding of Verbs:

| 0 | 1 | 2 | ③ | 4 |
|---|---|---|---|---|
| Used no verbs appropriately. | Used few verbs appropriately. | Used some verbs appropriately. | Used most verbs appropriately. | Used all verbs appropriately. |
| No definitions make sense. | Few definitions make sense. | Some definitions make sense. | Most definitions make sense. | All definitions make sense |

*2.* Quality of Writing:

| 0 | 1 | 2 | 3 | ④ |
|---|---|---|---|---|
| Writing is unclear. | Writing is mostly *not very* clear. | Writing is somewhat clear. | Writing is mostly clear. | Writing is very clear. |
| Includes ~~all~~ *no* rhyming patterns. | Includes ~~most~~ *few* rhyming patterns. | Includes some rhyming patterns. | Includes most rhyming patterns. | Includes all rhyming patterns. |

*3* Mechanics:

| 0 | 1 | 2 | 3 | ④ |
|---|---|---|---|---|
| Over 8 errors. | 6 - 7 errors. | 4 - 5 errors. | 2 - 3 errors. | 0 - 1 errors. |
| Messy, no spacing. | Not neat, not well spaced. | Somewhat neat, somewhat well spaced. | Mostly neat, mostly well spaced. | Very neat, very well spaced. |

*4* Effort:

| 0 | 1 | 2 | 3 | ④ |
|---|---|---|---|---|
| Shows no effort. | Shows little effort. | Shows some effort. | Shows good effort. | Shows best effort. |

*5* Quality of Reflections:

| 0 | 1 | 2 | ③ | 4 |
|---|---|---|---|---|
| Responses show no thoughtfulness. | Responses show little thoughtfulness. | Responses show some thoughtfulness. | Responses show much thoughtfulness. | Responses are very thoughtful. |
| (Thoughtful = Well thought out) | (Thoughtful = Well thought out) | (Thoughtful = Well thought out) | (Thoughtful = Well thought out) | (Thoughtful = Well thought out) |

**Figure 7.5** Sarah's self-scoring on a rubric co-designed by students and teachers.

the teacher dictating a grade. Students become self-evaluators—isn't that the ultimate goal of evaluation?

# Assessing Science Through Poetry and Myth

LYLE GRIEGOLIET

When I was teaching freshman biology at Maria High School, my students were also studying Roman and Greek mythology in their English class. The mythology unit happened at the time of year when I normally covered the organelles of the cell. Remembering that the Greeks used myths to explain the various functions of nature in their lives, I decided to make a cross-curriculum assignment that would help my students to see that the pantheon of gods, with their individual functions, parallels the organelles and their specialized functions within the cell.

The assessment rubric was a relatively simple one for this fifty-point assignment. Students would receive thirty points for how well they showed the primary function of the organelle chosen, ten points for the quality of their myth, and ten points for the imaginative way in which this function was shown.

The results of this assignment were quite interesting. Some students went so far as to explain the entire "pantheon" of organelles, while others made simple stories for just one. An example of the whole-pantheon approach is the following myth by Gina Miski.

## King Cell and His Knights of the Oblong Table

Once upon a time, on a faraway planet, there lived a king named Cell. King Cell had a small kingdom, which was in utter chaos. Cytoplasm was leaking into the vacuole, ribosomes were bouncing every which way, and no one was protecting the town.

One day, while watching his town go to ruin, the King had a brilliant idea. He called his faithful knights to his oblong table. "Loyal Friends," King Cell began, "during this time of destruction, you are the only ones who have listened and have done as I asked. Now, I have an even more important task for you. I'm giving you each a special job, which when everyone cooperates, will restore peace and order to our community."

"Cyto," he continued, "I know we have had our differences in the past, but let us put that behind us, shall we? You will play an important role in this, for you will make up most of our kingdom. You are in charge of holding everyone together. Now, how does that sound?"

Cytoplasm thought that sounded very good indeed.

"As for you, Sir Ribosome, you are going to be boss of the protein factories, which will help to build and repair our kingdom. Now, who would like to convert the sunlight into chemical energy?"

Chloro of the Valley of Plasts raised his arm.

"Oh good, but you will have to find someone who will take that energy and change it into valuable compounds for our village," replied King Cell.

"No problem, your Majesty. Mitochondria, the Countess, will be glad to help," answered Chlor-o-Plast.

The King then assigned Duke Golgi Complex III and Comsalpodne Muluciter the Endoplasmic Reticulum to collect, package, and distribute materials throughout the kingdom of Cell. Vakypolus Vacuole beamed with pride when he was told that he was to be the kingdom's keeper of the water.

"Oh, great Nucleus the Wise, will you be the activities director for all the organelles?" asked the King. Nucleus agreed on one condition; his wife, Chromatin, and his son, Nucleolus, could stay with him.

"Last but not least, Cell Wall, Guardian of Cell, protector and supporter of our town." The first thing the Guardian of Cell did was hire Cell Membrane to aid him. Next, Cell Wall called on Nuclear Envelope to surround the home of Nucleus, the Wise.

And everyone was happy for a while, until other nearby rulers began setting up similar, well-organized villages. They named them Cell too after King Cell's brilliant idea. Cell realized he should rename his kingdom when he received a complaint from Cell Wall saying many organelles were getting the kingdoms confused.

It was a tough job; thinking of a name. King Cell thought of his hometown of Greenleaf, and then a light bulb went on in Cell's head. He would call his town Generalized Plant Cell. Everyone loved the name, and there was never any more confusion in Generalized Plant Cell.

Now I am teaching science at the Future Commons High School, a small Chicago public school. Every quarter, I offer another special writing assignment to assess my students' scientific understanding. From my past teaching experience, I know that assigning regular reports only forces me to read bad plagiarism of the encyclopedia, so I decided to design a new activity. Since my major concern is that the students understand the concepts rather than merely memorize facts, I decided that a major scientific concept should be restated or paraphrased, and that the setting or genre of the assignment would be outside the normal domain of science. Also I felt that a cross-curricular approach would be enriching, and I wanted something that would be interesting and amusing to read myself. I eventually decided on poetry.

The instructions given were as follows: "Write a poem that explains one of the following topics. The poem can be in any form as long as it has meter, with the exception of Haiku. The length is up to you; it can be as short as a limerick provided that your topic is explained." Haiku was eliminated because it cannot be used to explain concepts, only to give impressions. Style itself was not a major portion of the consideration of grade. The concept itself was the key. If the student could explain a concept or show a grasp of the concept in this different medium, then it could be assumed that they understood the concept and could communicate it. To avoid repetition, a list of topics covered during the first quarter was developed and only one student per class could choose any one topic.

Sara Kort, a freshman in Biology A, not only listed the parts of the microscope, but also described their purpose and function.

### The Parts of the Microscope

All of the parts play a big role,
From the objective to the stage hole.
The mirror is there to give you some light,
So all that you see is clear and bright.
Now look through the eyepiece to see if it's right.
And make sure that it isn't too dull or too bright.
When your objects appear slightly hidden,
Adjust your diaphragm and some extra light will be given.
Now to your powers and start with the low,
Then move to your high nice and slow.
When changing the power twist the nosepiece.
So what you are viewing its size will increase.
Twist your coarse adjustment to change your view,
If it's out of focus, to the displeasure of you.
After using the coarse move to the fine,
To adjust into focus, to stop on a dime.
Now that the world of the tiny is at hand,
Get ready, get set. Let your mind expand.

Amanda Martinez, another freshman, explained the idea of using the word itself to decipher the definition of scientific terms.

### Bio-Rhyme

The terms in biology
Always seem difficult to me.
Until this poem came into my life
I thought I would be as dumb as can be.
The vocabulary was confusing
Prefixes, suffixes, all in a jumble.
I was upset and agitated
Until I decided to give rhyming a tumble.
*Intra-* and *in-* both mean inside
*Bio-* is life and *hydro* is water.
When thinking 'bout animals
Use *zoo-* is what you oughter.
*Ex-* is out and *proto-* is first

*Auto-* is self, *chloro-* is green
*Photo-* is light and *multi-* is many
*Hetero-* is different. Hey this is a dream.
On to the suffixes
This isn't too bad.
With a little more work
Maybe a good grade could be had.
*-Logy* is study and *-meter* is measure
*-Ation* is process and *-synthesis* is together
*-Scope* is to see and *-gestion* is carry
*-Plast* is living and *-lysis* is to loosen whatever.
*-Phyte* is a plant and *-troph* means food
*-Scope* means see and *-stasis* means still
I was delighted to discover
A leaf who was named *-phyll.*
I was as amazed as I could be
*-Cellular* doesn't mean phone,
It refers to cells;
I felt like such a drone.
My rhyme is almost done
The assignment complete
To have learned all these terms
Is really quite a feat.

The idea of this poetry writing is to get the students to understand that science and English are not hermetically sealed from each other, but can be mutually relevant. The ideal is to get the students to see that school subjects are not just for fifty-five-minute periods, but can be meaningful throughout their lives. This kind of cross-subject integration can be used in many other ways, including "science ornaments" for the Christmas season, mixing science and art, skits or songs performed before the class, bringing drama to science, reading science fiction that illustrates scientific principles, or involving history by studying the effect of a new scientific discovery on society or politics.

# Grade and Subject Index

This chart indicates the grade levels and subject areas in which each of the projects described in this book took place. Most of these, however, can readily be adapted for other ages and subjects.

## Grade and Subject Index

| | Primary | Inter-mediate | Middle | High School | Arts | Language Arts | Math | Science | Social Studies |
|---|---|---|---|---|---|---|---|---|---|
| Centers and Stations: Decentralizing the Classroom | ✓ | ✓ | ✓ | ✓ | ✓ | ✓ | ✓ | ✓ | ✓ |
| **Chapter 4** *Variations:* A River of Miracles by Waters School | | ✓ | ✓ | | | ✓ | | ✓ | |
| Going to Scale: Muralists Use Art and Mathematics to Decry Gang Violence | | | | ✓ | ✓ | | | | ✓ |
| *Step by Step:* Jotting and Sketching: Twenty-Three Ways to Use a Notebook | ✓ | ✓ | ✓ | ✓ | ✓ | ✓ | ✓ | ✓ | ✓ |
| How to Help Your Kids Compose and Publish a Whole Class Big Book | ✓ | | | | ✓ | ✓ | | | |
| **Chapter 5** *Variations:* A Community of Mathematicians | | | ✓ | | | | ✓ | | |
| Poetry Workshop | | | ✓ | | | ✓ | | | |
| *Step by Step:* Conferences: The Core of the Workshop | ✓ | ✓ | ✓ | ✓ | ✓ | ✓ | ✓ | ✓ | ✓ |
| Growing a Reading Workshop | | | | ✓ | | ✓ | | | |
| **Chapter 6** *Variations:* Carver's Woods: Science in a Dump | | ✓ | | | | ✓ | | ✓ | |

## Grade and Subject Index

|  | Primary | Inter-mediate | Middle | High School | Arts | Language Arts | Math | Science | Social Studies |
|---|---|---|---|---|---|---|---|---|---|
| Rolling Along with Rivers |  |  |  | ✓ |  | ✓ |  | ✓ | ✓ |
| Using Primary Sources: Bringing Literature and Students to Center Stage |  |  |  | ✓ |  | ✓ |  |  | ✓ |
| *Step by Step:* Home Improvement: Remodeling Mathematically |  |  | ✓ |  | ✓ |  | ✓ |  |  |
| Student Docents Discover Modern Art |  |  | ✓ |  | ✓ | ✓ |  |  |  |
| "Me" Portfolios: The Way to a Classroom's Heart | ✓ | ✓ | ✓ |  | ✓ | ✓ |  |  | ✓ |
| **Chapter 7** *Variations:* A Tale of Two Students |  | ✓ |  |  |  | ✓ |  |  |  |
| Understanding Mathematical Concepts Through Performance Assessment | ✓ |  |  |  |  |  | ✓ |  |  |
| Measuring Growth in Reading: Coping with Standardized Assessments | ✓ | ✓ | ✓ | ✓ |  | ✓ |  |  |  |
| *Step by Step:* Student Self-Assessment: Thinking About Thinking |  | ✓ |  |  |  | ✓ |  |  | ✓ |
| Assessing Science Through Poetry and Myth |  |  |  | ✓ |  | ✓ |  | ✓ |  |

# References

## Professional References and Further Readings

Allen, J., and K. Gonzalez. 1998. *There's Room for Me Here: Literacy Workshop in the Middle School.* York, ME: Stenhouse.

Anson, C., and R. Beach. 1995. *Journals in the Classroom: Writing to Learn.* Norwood, MA: Christopher-Gordon.

Atwell, N. 1987. *In the Middle: Writing, Reading, and Learning with Adolescents.* Portsmouth, NH: Boynton/Cook.

Avery, C. 1993. *. . . And with a Light Touch: Learning About Reading, Writing, and Teaching with First Graders.* Portsmouth, NH: Heinemann.

Azwell, T., and E. Schmar, eds. 1995. *Report Card on Report Cards: Alternatives to Consider.* Portsmouth, NH: Heinemann.

Barth, R. 1992. *Improving Schools from Within: Teachers, Parents, and Principals Can Make the Difference.* New York: Jossey-Bass.

Bayer, A. S. 1990. *Collaborative-Apprenticeship Learning: Language and Thinking Across the Curriculum K–12.* Mountain View, CA: Mayfield.

Beane, J. A. 1991. The Middle School: The Natural Home of the Integrated Curriculum. *Educational Leadership* (October): 9–13.

———. 1993a. *A Middle School Curriculum: From Rhetoric to Reality.* Columbus, OH: National Middle School Association.

———. 1993b. Problems and Possibilities for an Integrative Curriculum. *Middle School Journal* 25: 18–23.

———. 1995. Curriculum Integration and the Disciplines of Knowledge. *Phi Delta Kappan* (April): 100–106.

———. 1997. *Curriculum Integration: Designing the Core of Democratic Education.* New York: Teachers College Press.

Berger, P. L., and T. Luckman. 1967. *The Social Construction of Reality: A Treatis in the Sociology of Knowledge.* New York: Anchor.

Boomer, G., N. Lester, C. Onore, and J. Cook. 1992. *Negotiating the Curriculum.* London: Falmer Press.

Bowers, C. A. 1984. *The Promise of Theory: Education and the Politics of Cultural Change.* New York: Longman.

Bronner, E. 1997. Colleges Look for Answers to Racial Gaps in Testing. *New York Times,* November 8, 1997, 1, 8.

Brown, C. S. 1994. *Connecting with the Past: History Workshop in Middle and High Schools.* Portsmouth, NH: Heinemann.

Calkins, L. 1986. *The Art of Teaching Writing.* Portsmouth, NH: Heinemann.

———. 1990. *Living Between the Lines.* Portsmouth, NH: Heinemann.

Cambourne, B., and J. Turbill, eds. 1994. *Responsive Evaluation: Making Valid Judgments About Student Literacy.* Portsmouth, NH: Heinemann.

Chancer, J., and G. Rester-Zodrow. 1997. *Moon Journals: Writing, Art, and Inquiry Through Focused Nature Study.* Portsmouth, NH: Heinemann.

Chase, A. 1977. *The Legacy of Malthus.* New York: Knopf.

Claggett, F., and J. Brown. 1992. *Drawing Your*

*Own Conclusions: Graphic Strategies for Reading, Writing, and Thinking.* Portsmouth, NH: Boynton/Cook.

Cohen, E. 1986. *Designing Groupwork: Strategies for the Heterogeneous Classroom.* New York: Teachers College Press.

Costa, A. 1991. *The School as a Home for the Mind.* Palatine, IL: SkyLight.

Countryman, J. 1992. *Writing to Learn Mathematics.* Portsmouth, NH: Heinemann.

Daniels, H. 1994. *Literature Circles: Voice and Choice in the Student-Centered Classroom.* York, ME: Stenhouse.

Davies, A., C. Politano, and C. Cameron. 1993. *Making Themes Work.* Winnipeg: Peguis.

Dewey, J. [1916] 1944. *Democracy and Education: An Introduction to the Philosophy of Education.* New York: Free Press.

———. [1938] 1963. *Experience and Education.* New York: Macmillan.

Edwards, B. 1979. *Drawing on the Right Side of the Brain.* Los Angeles: Tarcher.

Elbow, P. 1973. *Writing Without Teachers.* New York: Oxford University Press.

Ernst, K. 1994. *Picturing Learning: Artists and Writers in the Classroom.* Portsmouth, NH: Heinemann.

———. 1997. *A Teacher's Sketch Journal: Observations on Learning and Teaching.* Portsmouth, NH: Heinemann.

Ferrara, J. 1996. *Peer Mediation: Finding a Way to Care.* York, ME: Stenhouse.

Five, C. L., and M. Dionisio. 1995. *Bridging the Gap: Integrating Curriculum in Upper Elementary and Middle Schools.* Portsmouth, NH: Heinemann.

Fletcher, R. 1993. *What a Writer Needs.* Portsmouth, NH: Heinemann.

———. 1996. *A Writer's Notebook: Unlocking the Writer Within You.* New York: Avon.

Fowler, C. 1996. *Strong Arts, Strong Schools: The Promising Potential and Shortsighted Disregard of the Arts in American Schooling.* New York: Oxford University Press.

Freire, P. [1970] 1993. *Pedagogy of the Oppressed.* New York: Continuum.

Fulwiler, T., ed. 1987. *The Journal Book.* Portsmouth, NH: Boynton/Cook.

Gardner, H. 1983. *Frames of Mind.* New York: Basic Books.

Girard, S., and K. Willing. 1996. *Partnerships for Classroom Learning: From Reading Buddies to Pen Pals to the Community and the World Beyond.* Portsmouth, NH: Heinemann.

Giroux, H. 1983. *Theory and Resistance in Education.* South Hadley, MA: Bergin and Garvey.

Glasser, W. 1986. *Control Theory in the Classroom.* New York: Harper & Row.

Gould, S. J. 1981. *The Mismeasure of Man.* New York: Norton.

Graves, D. 1983. *Writing: Teachers and Children at Work.* Portsmouth, NH: Heinemann.

———. 1991. *Build a Literate Classroom.* Portsmouth, NH: Heinemann.

———. 1994. *A Fresh Look at Writing.* Portsmouth, NH: Heinemann.

Graves, D. H., and B. S. Sunstein, eds. 1992. *Portfolio Portraits.* Portsmouth, NH: Heinemann.

Greene, M. 1988. *The Dialectic of Freedom.* New York: Teachers College Press.

Hansen, J. 1992. Literacy Portfolios: Helping Students Know Themselves. *Educational Leadership* 49, 8: 66–68.

Harwayne, S. 1992. *Lasting Impressions: Weaving Literature into the Writing Workshop.* Portsmouth, NH: Heinemann.

Heller, P. 1996. *Drama as a Way of Knowing.* York, ME: Stenhouse.

Herman, J., P. Aschbacher, and L. Winters. 1992. *A Practical Guide to Alternative Assessment.* Alexandria, VA: Association for Supervision and Curriculum Development.

Hildenbrand, L., and J. Hixon. 1991. Video-Assisted Learning of Study Skills. *Elementary School Guidance and Counseling* 26, 2: 121–129.

Hill, B. C., and N. Johnson. 1995. *Literature Circles and Response.* Norwood, MA: Christopher-Gordon.

Hill, B. C., and C. Ruptic. 1994. *Practical Aspects of Authentic Assessment: Putting the Pieces Together.* Norwood, MA: Christopher-Gordon.

Hill, S., and T. Hill. 1990. *The Collaborative Classroom: A Guide to Cooperative Learning.* Portsmouth, NH: Heinemann.

Hindley, J. 1996. *In the Company of Children.* York, ME: Stenhouse.

Hirsch, E. D., Jr. 1996. *The Schools We Need and Why We Don't Have Them.* New York: Doubleday.

Horwood, B., ed. 1995. *Experience and the Curriculum.* Dubuque, IA: Kendall-Hunt.

Hubbard, R. S. 1996. *A Workshop of the Possible: Nurturing Children's Creative Development.* York, ME: Stenhouse.

Hubbard, R. S., and K. Ernst. 1996. *New Entries: Learning by Writing and Drawing.* Portsmouth, NH: Heinemann.

Hyde, A., and M. Bizar. 1989. *Thinking in Context: Teaching Cognitive Processes Across the Elementary School Curriculum.* New York: Longman.

Hyde, A., and P. Hyde. 1991. *Mathwise.* Portsmouth, NH: Heinemann.

Isaacs, J. A., and J. Brodine. 1994. *Journals in the Classroom: A Complete Guide for the Elementary Teacher.* Winnipeg: Peguis.

Jacobs, P., and S. Landau. 1971. *To Serve the Devil.* New York: Random House.

James, C. 1969. *Young Lives at Stake.* London: Collins.

Johnson, D., R. Johnson, E. Holubec, and P. Roy. 1991. *Cooperation in the Classroom.* Edina, MN: Interaction Book Company.

Johnston, P. H. 1992. *Constructive Evaluation of Literate Activity.* New York: Longman.
———. 1997. *Knowing Literacy: Constructive Literacy Assessment.* York, ME: Stenhouse.

Jones, M. 1969. *The Autobiography of Mother Jones.* New York: Arno.

Jorgensen, K. 1993. *History Workshop: Reconstructing the Past with Elementary Students.* Portsmouth, NH: Heinemann.

Kilpatrick, W. H. 1918. The Project Method. *Teachers College Record* 19: 319–335.

Koch, K. 1974. *Rose, Where Did You Get that Red? Teaching Great Poetry to Children.* New York: Vintage.

Kohn, A. 1995. *Punished by Rewards: The Trouble with Gold Stars, Incentive Plans, A's, Praise, and Other Bribes.* Boston: Houghton Mifflin.

Kraft, R. J., and J. Kiesmeier, eds. 1994. *Experiential Learning in Schools and Higher Education.* Boulder, CO: Association for Experiential Education.

Lappan, G., and P. Schram. 1989. *Communication and Reasoning: Critical Dimensions of Sense-Making in Mathematics.* Yearbook of Mathematics Instruction. Reston, VA: National Council of Teachers of Mathematics.

Leopold, A. 1949. *Sand County Almanac and Sketches Here and There.* New York: Oxford University Press.

Lindquist, T. 1995. *Seeing the Whole Through Social Studies.* Portsmouth, NH: Heinemann.

Lipman, M. 1987. *Teaching Thinking Skills: Theory into Practice.* New York: Freeman.

Lockwood, A., and D. Harris. 1985. *Reasoning with Democratic Values: Ethical Problems in United States History.* New York: Teachers College Press.

London, P. 1994. *Step Outside: Community-Based Art Education.* Portsmouth, NH: Heinemann.

Manning, M., G. Manning, and R. Long. 1994. *Theme Immersion: Inquiry-Based Curriculum in Elementary and Middle Schools.* Portsmouth, NH: Heinemann.

McLaren, P. 1994. *Life in Schools: An Introduction to Critical Pedagogy in the Foundations of Education.* New York: Longman.

McNeil, L. M. 1988. *Contradictions of Control: School Structure and School Knowledge.* New York: Routledge.

McVey, V. 1989. *The Sierra Club Wayfinding Book.* Boston: Little, Brown.

Messick, R., and K. Reynolds. 1992. *Middle Level Curriculum in Action.* White Plains, NY: Longman.

Mett, C. 1989. Writing in Mathematics: Evidence of Learning Through Writing. *The Clearing House* 62, 7: 293–296.

Miller, D. 1973. *Then Was the Future.* New York: Knopf.

Moline, S. 1995. *I See What You Mean: Children at Work with Visual Information.* York, ME: Stenhouse.

Moore, F. 1969. *Diary of the American Revolution: From Newspapers and Original Documents.* New York: Washington Square Press.

Nabhan, G., and S. Trimble. 1995. *The Geography of Childhood: Why Children Need Wild Places.* Boston: Beacon Press.

Nabokov, P. 1978. *Native American Testimony: A Chronicle of Indian–White Relations from Prophecy to the Present, 1492–1992.* New York: Crowell.

National Academy of Science. 1996. *National Science Education Standards.* Washington, DC: National Academy Press.

National Council of Teachers of Mathematics. 1989. *Curriculum and Instruction Standards for School Mathematics.* Reston, VA: NCTM.

National Council for Social Studies. 1994. *Expectations of Excellence: Curriculum Standards for Social Studies.* Washington, DC: NCSS.

O'Brien, T. 1990. *The Things They Carried.* Boston: Houghton Mifflin.

Ogle, D. 1986. The K-W-L: An Interactive Strategy for Reading Nonfiction. *The Reading Teacher* 39: 6.

Olson, J. L. 1992. *Envisioning Writing: Toward an Integration of Drawing and Writing.* Portsmouth, NH: Heinemann.

Page, N. 1996. *Music as a Way of Knowing.* York, ME: Stenhouse.

Paley, V. G. 1992. *You Can't Say You Can't Play.* Cambridge, MA: Harvard University Press.

Parsons, L. 1994. *Expanding Response Journals: In All Subject Areas.* Portsmouth, NH: Heinemann.

Peterson, R. 1992. *Life in a Crowded Place: Making a Learning Community.* Portsmouth, NH: Heinemann.

Porter, C., and J. Cleland. 1995. *The Portfolio as a Learning Strategy.* Portsmouth, NH: Boynton/Cook.

Rhodes, L. K., ed. 1993. *Literacy Assessment: A Handbook of Instruments.* Portsmouth, NH: Heinemann.

Rhodes, L. K., and N. Shanklin. 1993. *Windows into Literacy: Assessing Learners K–8.* Portsmouth, NH: Heinemann.

Richards, L. 1990. Measuring Things in Words: Language for Learning Mathematics. *Language Arts* 67, 1: 14–25.

Rico, G. 1985. *Writing the Natural Way.* Los Angeles: Tarcher.

Rief, L. 1992. *Seeking Diversity: Language Arts with Adolescents.* Portsmouth, NH: Heinemann.

Robinson, G. 1996. *Sketch-Books: Explore and Store.* Portsmouth, NH: Heinemann.

Rodriguez, L. 1993. *Always Running: La Vida Loca: Gang Days in L. A.* East Haven, CT: Curbstone Press.

Rogers, C., and H. J. Freiberg. 1994. *Freedom to Learn.* New York: Macmillan.

Romano, T. 1995. *Writing with Passion: Life Stories, Multiple Genres.* Portsmouth, NH: Boynton/Cook.

Rylant, C. 1984. *Waiting to Waltz: A Childhood.* Scarsdale, NY: Bradbury Press.

Samway, K. D., and G. Whang. 1995. *Literature Study Circles in a Multicultural Classroom.* York, ME: Stenhouse.

Samway, K., G. Whang, and M. Pippitt. 1995. *Buddy Reading: Cross-Age Tutoring in a Multicultural School.* Portsmouth, NH: Heinemann.

Saul, W., and J. Reardon, eds. 1996. *Beyond the Science Kit: Inquiry in Action.* Portsmouth, NH: Heinemann.

Saul, W., J. Rearden, A. Schmidt, C. Pearce, D. Blackwood, and M. D. Bird. 1993. *Science Workshop: A Whole Language Approach.* Portsmouth, NH: Heinemann.

Schulz, E. 1992. Enemy of Innovation. *Teacher* (September):

Serebrin, W. 1998. Empowering Ourselves to Inquire: Preservice Teacher Education as a Collaborative Enterprise. Unpublished manuscript.

Shannon, P. 1995. *Text, Lies, and Videotape.* Portsmouth, NH: Heinemann.

Sharan, Y., and S. Sharan. 1992. *Expanding*

*Cooperative Learning Through Group Investigation.* New York: Teachers College Press.

Shor, I. 1987. *Freire for the Classroom: A Sourcebook for Laboratory Teaching.* Portsmouth, NH: Boynton/Cook.

Short, K. G., and C. Burke. 1991. *Creating Curriculum: Teachers and Students as a Community of Learners.* Portsmouth, NH: Heinemann.

Short, K. G., J. Schroeder, J. Laird, G. Kauffman, M. J. Ferguson, and K. M. Crawford. 1996. *Learning Together Through Inquiry: From Columbus to Integrated Curriculum.* York, ME: Stenhouse.

Smith, K. 1993. Becoming the "Guide on the Side." *Educational Leadership* 51, 2: 35–37.

Spear, K. 1987. *Sharing Writing: Peer Response Groups in the English Class.* Portsmouth, NH: Boynton/Cook.

Springer, M. 1994. *Watershed: A Successful Voyage into Integrative Learning.* Columbus, OH: National Middle School Association.

Steffey, S., and W. J. Hood. 1994. *If This Is Social Studies, Why Isn't It Boring?* York, ME: Stenhouse.

Stephens, L. 1995. *The Complete Guide to Learning Through Community Service: Grades K–9.* Des Moines, IA: Allyn and Bacon.

Stevenson, C., and J. Carr. 1993. *Integrated Studies in the Middle Grades: Dancing Through Walls.* New York: Teachers College Press.

Tchudi, S., and S. Lafer. 1996. *The Interdisciplinary Teacher's Handbook: Integrated Teaching Across the Curriculum.* Portsmouth, NH: Boynton/Cook.

Tehschick, J. 1971. *To Touch the Earth.* New York: Outerbridge & Diensffrey.

Thelan, H. 1967. *Education and the Human Quest.* New York: Wiley.

Vars, G. 1993. *Interdisciplinary Teaching in the Middle Grades: Why and How.* Columbus, OH: National Middle School Association.

Whitin, P. 1996. *Sketching Stories, Stretching Minds: Responding Visually to Literature.* Portsmouth, NH: Heinemann.

Wigginton, E. 1985. *Sometimes a Shining Moment: The Foxfire Experience.* Garden City, NY: Anchor Press/Doubleday.

Wolk, S. 1994. Project-Based Learning: Pursuits with a Purpose. *Educational Leadership* 52, 3: 42–45.

Wood, G. H. 1993. *Schools that Work: America's Most Innovative Public Education Programs.* New York: Plume.

Woodward, H. 1994. *Negotiated Evaluation: Involving Children and Parents in the Process.* Portsmouth, NH: Heinemann.

Worsley, D., and B. Mayer. 1989. *The Art of Science Writing.* New York: Teachers and Writers Collaborative.

Zakkai, J. 1997. *Dance as a Way of Knowing.* York, ME: Stenhouse.

Zemelman, S., and H. Daniels. 1988. *A Community of Writers: Teaching Writing in the Junior and Senior High School.* Portsmouth, NH: Heinemann.

Zemelman, S., H. Daniels, and A. Hyde. 1993. *Best Practice: New Standards for Teaching and Learning in America's Schools.* Portsmouth, NH: Heinemann.

Zinn, H. 1980. *A People's History of the United States.* New York: Harper & Row.

## Children's Literature

Baker, K. 1990. *Who Is the Beast?* San Diego: Harcourt Brace.

Brown, A. 1986. *Piggybook.* New York: Knopf.

Brown, M. W. 1947. *Goodnight Moon.* New York: Harper.

Catling, P. 1979. *The Chocolate Touch.* New York: Morrow.

Cowley, J., and J. Melser. 1980. *Mrs. Wishy-Washy.* Aukland, New Zealand: Shortland.

Fox, M. 1984. *Wilfred Gordon McDonald Partridge.* Brooklyn, NY: Kane/Miller.

Holman, F. 1974. *Slake's Limbo.* New York: Scribner.

Loewen, V. 1990. *The Best Book for Terry Lee.* Hawthorn, Australia: Mimosa Publications.

Paulsen, G. 1993. *Sisters.* New York: Harcourt Brace.

Polacco, P. 1990. *Thundercake.* New York: Philomel.

Speare, E. 1983. *Sign of the Beaver.* Boston: Houghton Mifflin.

Tsuchiya, Y. 1988. *The Faithful Elephants.* Boston: Houghton Mifflin.

White, E. B. 1952. *Charlotte's Web.* New York: Harper.

Wilder, L. I. 1989. *Little House on the Prairie.* Santa Barbara, CA: Cornerstone.

Yolen, J. 1987. *Owl Moon.* New York: Philomel.

# Contributors

*Linda Bailey* has taught in various Chicago Public Schools for twenty-eight years and currently teaches an intermediate and upper-grade language lab at Los Niños Heroes Community Academy. She is the mom of two school-age boys, conducts teacher workshops in language arts, and explores ways to build community in the classroom and school so all children can be successful.

*Dagny D. Bloland* teaches English to eighth graders and high school juniors at Whitney Young High School in Chicago. Married and the mother of a son, Dagny has a Ph.D. in English education and works with National-Louis University's interdisciplinary studies program.

*Steven Cole* teaches art at Farragut Career Academy in Chicago, Illinois. He is also a professional portrait artist and book illustrator.

*Karen Dekker* has taught middle school English and social studies at Carleton W. Washburne School in Winnetka, Illinois, for six years. She recently earned her M.Ed. in curriculum and instruction from National-Louis University in Evanston, Illinois, where she resides with her husband.

*John W. Duffy* teaches student historians and coaches learning styles strategies at Hinsdale Central High School. John lives with his wife, Pat, and their six children in Oak Park, Illinois, where he gardens and cheers on his children's field hockey, soccer, and baseball teams.

*Ralph Feese* has taught social studies at Addison Trail High School for the past twenty-five years and has been involved in interdisciplinary programs for the last ten years. Married, the father of two adult children, and a proud grandparent, he is active in the local teachers' union and the staff development program at Addison Trail.

*Lyle Griegoliet* teaches science, chairs the science department, and is the lead teacher for the Freshman Academy and Teacher Prep Schools within the Future Commons Multiplex in Chicago. Lyle has a Masters in curriculum and instruction and is active in the development of cross-curricular projects and the use of intracurriculum planning.

*Dale Halter* teaches gifted students in grades 2 through 6 in Des Plaines, Illinois, concentrating on developing creativity and problem-solving skills. He has learned a great deal from his wife, Beata, and from his parents, all of whom are teachers.

*Robert Hartwig* has taught high school biology for seven years in Addison, Illinois. A father of two, soon to be three, Robert serves as co-sponsor of his school's science club and is an assistant varsity softball coach.

*Jeanne Heinen* has taught high school English in Chicago for nearly thirty years, twenty-seven of them at Jesse Spalding School where there's a challenging mix of special and regular education students from diverse neighborhoods. Jeanne has also taught creative writing at Columbia College in Chicago, and more recently she has enjoyed an infusion of ideas and energy through the Illinois Writing Project, facilitating writing workshops for teachers.

*Arthur Hyde* is a professor of mathematics education at National-Louis University in Illinois. He juggles his time between courses in methods of teaching mathematics for preservice teachers and staff development programs for veteran teachers in schools in the Chicago metropolitan area.

*Pamela R. Hyde* has taught at various grade levels in Illinois and Pennsylvania elementary schools for twelve years. She is currently an assistant principal at John Mills Elementary School in Elmwood Park, Illinois.

*Judy Johnstone* has taught high school English for twenty-five years and is currently chairperson of the English department at Carl Sandburg High School in Orland Park, Illinois. During her twelve-year affiliation with the Illinois Writing Project, she has led numerous writing and whole language workshops for teachers in the Chicago suburban area.

*Diana Jones* teaches physical education at Illinois State University. Her primary focus is elementary physical education and working with student teachers.

*Luanne Kowalke* has been teaching at Greenbriar School in Northbrook, Illinois, for five years, and holds a Masters in curriculum and instruction. She enjoys incorporating cooperative learning, negotiated curriculum, alternative assessments, student self-evaluation, and technology into the daily routine of her bustling fourth-grade classroom.

*Charles Kuner* teaches social studies/social sciences at Farragut Career Academy in Chicago, Illinois. He has been teaching at Farragut since 1965 and has a Masters in history and sociology.

*Pete Leki,* a water plant operator, chaired the Waters Local School Council for five years. He helped bring land-based ecological studies to the school. He currently is an associate with the Center for City Schools, working with parents in Chicago public schools.

Artistic co-director of Fluid Measure Performance Company, *Donna Mandel* has served as a dance and arts-integration specialist and consultant in Chicago area schools for twenty years. She has conducted workshops and residencies and designed curriculum with teachers under the auspices of the Chicago Arts Partnership in Education, the Illinois Arts Council, the Erikson Institute, Urban Gateways, the School of the Art Institute of Chicago, the Chicago Department of Cultural Affairs, and the Chicago Board of Education.

*Kelly Naperschat* teaches elementary physical education at Eugene Field and Pepper Ridge Elementary Schools. She has a Masters degree in exercise science from Illinois State University.

*Eleanor Nayvelt* has a Masters degree in education and teaches third grade in a Russian bilingual program at DeWitt Clinton Elementary School in Chicago. Her interests include her husband and their three-year-old daughter and translating and editing Russian literature and poetry.

*Shelley Rosenstein-Freeman,* formerly a teacher at Farren Fine Arts School, is currently the student internship coordinator at Best Practice High School. Trained as a visual arts designer and educator, she has taught art, worked in a variety of arts-related areas, and has business and finance experience.

*Suzy Ruder,* a twenty-year veteran French and English teacher, currently supports special needs students and general education faculty as the Inclusion Facilitator at Hinsdale Central High School in Hinsdale, Illinois. With their three children grown, Suzy and her spouse Jim enjoy cooking, entertaining, and traveling.

*Katy Smith* has taught English at Addison Trail High School since 1987 and has been involved in interdisciplinary team teaching there since 1988. Katy received her B.A. from Indiana University and her M.Ed. from National-Louis University, and she is currently working on her Ph.D. in curriculum and instruction at the University of Wisconsin-Madison.

*Jim Tebo* has taught seventh- and eighth-grade math at Lincoln Middle School in Park Ridge, Illinois, for the past nine years. A father of two children, Jim is currently coaching basketball and acting as team leader at his school.

*Linda Voss* teaches fourth and fifth grades at Washington Irving Elementary School in Chicago. She has a Masters concentration in multicultural education and serves as curriculum advisor to the Alonzo Spellman Foundation and the Shedd Aquarium.

*Cynthia Weiss* is professional artist and arts education consultant with Chicago Arts Partnerships in Education. She has worked with teachers for the past ten years to develop integrated curriculum through the arts. Cynthia has a Masters in Fine Arts and has directed numerous large-scale public art projects throughout Chicago.

*Lois Wisniewski* teaches biology at Normal Community High School and biology methods at Illinois State University. She received a Masters degree in biology education and is currently working on an Ed.D. at Illinois State.

*Steven Wolk* teaches third, fourth, and fifth grades at the Foundations School in Chicago. His most recent work is *A Democratic Classroom* (in press).

*Steven Zemelman* is director of the Center for City Schools, National-Louis University, and co-director with Harvey Daniels of the Illinois Writing Project. Steven has co-authored three books with Daniels, including *Best Practice: New Standards for Teaching and Learning in America's Schools*.